Trading Places

The Wonderful World of Vacation Home Exchanging

Trading Places

The Wonderful World of Vacation Home Exchanging

Illustrated by Al Hartley

Bill and Mary Barbour

RUTLEDGE HILL PRESS
Nashville, Tennessee

Published in Nashville, Tennessee, by Rutledge Hill Press,
513 Third Avenue South, Nashville, Tennessee 37210. Distributed in Canada by H. B. Fenn & Company, Ltd., Mississauga, Ontario.

Design by Harriette Bateman
Illustrations by Al Hartley
Typography by Bailey Typography, Nashville, Tennessee

Library of Congress Cataloging-in-Publication Data

Barbour, Bill, 1922-
Trading places : the wonderful world of vacation home exchanging / Bill and Mary Barbour ; illustrated by Al Hartley.
p. cm.
Includes bibliographical references and index.
ISBN 1-55853-127-0
1. Vacation homes. 2. Home exchanging. I. Barbour, Mary, 1924- II. Title.
HD7289.2.B37 1991 91-24375
643′.2—dc20 CIP

Printed in the United States of America
2 3 4 5 6 7 8—96 95 94 93 92

Contents

THIS BOOK IS DEDICATED TO THE 643 EXPERIENCED VACATION HOME EXCHANGERS WHO PARTICIPATED IN THE AUTHORS' INTERNATIONAL VACATION HOME EXCHANGE SURVEY.

THE WEALTH OF INFORMATION AND DATA GLEANED FROM THIS SURVEY REPRESENTS THE FIBER, THE VERY HEART OF EACH CHAPTER.

Preface

HOME EXCHANGE: THE 1990s way to enjoy an inexpensive, fun-filled vacation.

A month of summer sun on the French Riviera . . . a long weekend of winter skiing in Colorado . . . deep-sea fishing in the Gulf of Mexico . . . vacationing in a house, townhouse, condominium, or apartment in London, Palm Springs, Dubrovnik, Hong Kong, Berlin, San Francisco, Acapulco, New York City, or in the Near East, the Far East, Africa, South America, or even in Big Canoe, Georgia! Yes, vacations in such nearby or faraway places are a reality in the home-exchanging community.

The key to your vacation, wherever and whenever you wish to go, is home exchange—simply exchanging the key to your family's home for the key to another family's home.

An invaluable resource for this book has been the data resulting from the recent year-long International Vacation Home Exchange Survey. Through personal and telephone interviews in Europe, the Far East, and here in the U.S., supplemented by a questionnaire keyed to the chapters of this book, more than six hundred experienced vacation home exchangers (with more than 2,500 actual exchanges worldwide), representing forty-three different countries and forty-six U.S. states share with the reader their considerable knowledge of, and experience in, national and international vacation home exchanging over the past three decades.

The authors are grateful for help from these vacation home exchange "experts." The survey provided a vast amount of "hands-on" information dealing with all aspects of vacation home exchanging: the philosophy of a "live-in" vacation; how home exchangers contact each other and make home exchange arrangements; and how aspiring vacation home exchangers can avoid the pitfalls of home exchanging while enjoying their vacations to the utmost.

Featured are the stories of eleven noteworthy home exchangers—some quite typical, others most unique—whose permanent homes are in the U.S., Cyprus, Germany, Australia, France, Holland, and Great Britain. Included, too, are chapters that focus on home exchanging with children and with pets; exchanging cars; exchanging abroad; some humorous (and not so humorous!) home exchange experiences; and much, much more.

Of special note are the twenty-six illustrations drawn by Al Hartley, well-known as illustrator of the "Archie" comics. The comic strips have appeared regularly in one thousand newspapers and the Al Hartley "Archie" comic books have enjoyed sales in excess of fifty million copies.

Finally, included here is a special reference center: suggested letters for making vacation home exchange arrangements and professional services available to the vacation home exchanger.

In their home exchange and business travels, the authors have visited forty-seven U.S. states; have made some thirty trips to Europe; and have traveled in Africa, South America, the Near East, and (extensively) the Far East. Their forty vacation home exchanges have taken them as far west from their Florida home as Hong Kong and as far east as Switzerland, and to many, many destinations in between. From their travel savvy and their vacation home exchange know-how, Bill and Mary Barbour are uniquely qualified to write this book.

Because of the broad range of vacation home exchange information presented and the detailed way in which these chapters are written, we earnestly hope this book will be equally beneficial to the experienced home exchanger, to those new in the vacation home exchange community, and to those desiring to learn more about the home exchange "route" to vacation living and enjoyment.

—The Publisher

Trading Places

The Wonderful World of Vacation Home Exchanging

1 The Vacation Home Exchange Concept

"HOME EXCHANGING MAKES for the best vacations my wife and I have ever had. Living among the 'natives,' local shopping, and meeting people not part of the tourist service industry are the best parts of all," writes a Brooklyn, New York, physician who has exchanged in Italy and France.

Each year fifteen to twenty thousand families in the U.S. and Canada—and thousands of others in Great Britain, continental Europe, Australia and New Zealand, and elsewhere in the world—are actively engaging in vacation home exchanging. Such large numbers seem to confirm the fact that vacation home exchanging (or "house swapping," as the British say) is becoming a here-and-now, worldwide vacation concept worthy of vacationers' earnest consideration.

> In principle, home exchange is simple: two families from different parts of the country—or different corners of the world—schedule their vacations in such a way as to arrange to swap their houses, apartments, or condominiums. The exchange can be as short as a weekend or as long as a few months or more (*AAA World*).

Certainly there is nothing really new about exchanging. Prehistoric man traded crudely made weapons for food, animal skins, firewood, and other basics to living in that age. And down through the centuries, exchanging became a way of life. Although it has to a large extent been replaced by the introduction of currency, exchanging remains a viable means for people everywhere to obtain perceived needs and desired items.

There is little recorded history of the home exchange concept. However, *Signature* magazine (the periodical of Diner's Club, International) claimed that back in the sixteenth century, "Ambassadors to the French court had a housing problem. They couldn't stay in hotels; hotels as we know them today didn't exist. Neither did rented accommodations. So they hit on an ingenious solution. They swapped residences with their ambassadorial counterparts from the French court." The idea has caught on today.

> If you want all the creature comforts and conveniences of home when you're on holiday, then swapping your house, hair-dryer (and even the cat!) with someone, somewhere else in the world can be the perfect solution (*The Woman's Journal*, London, England).

The development of modern-day vacation home exchanging in the U.S., Europe, and elsewhere dates back to the 1950s and '60s, when several organizations—vacation home exchange "clubs"—began to issue annual directories that included complete information, with names and addresses, about those desiring to exchange their homes. Today, each of those club directories lists some six thousand U.S. and international vacation home exchange opportunities.

With these first annual club periodical resources successfully enabling vacation home exchangers to contact one another, a number of other clubs were established during the 1970s and '80s. Some of these organizations limit their listings to specific regions or countries (one directory has listings only in Florida and Great Britain), while others feature listings in the U.S., Great Britain, Germany, France, and elsewhere throughout the world. These various periodicals now provide countless vacation home exchange opportunities worldwide, and exchangers today have at their fingertips resources that can put them in touch with unlimited numbers of other potential exchangers. And these resources have served as the springboard for the quite astonishing growth of the vacation home exchange concept.

> As long as the potential home exchanger is flexible and patient while making the arrangements, vacation home exchanging can prove an enjoyable and an economical alternative to hotels (*Fort Myers* [Florida] *News-Press*).

What is it about vacation home exchanging that attracts large numbers of families who have never previously exchanged homes and motivates even larger numbers of experienced home exchanging families to engage in vacation home exchanges time after time, year after year?

Well, the International Vacation Home Exchange Survey reveals that two basic elements of home exchanging seem to motivate most vacationers: the relatively low cost and living in a *home* away from home. Regarding this matter of cost, a mechanical engineer from Istanbul, Turkey, writes: "If you vacation in hotels, it's so expensive

for sleep and for eat. But when you have home exchange, you pay only the airfare and the regular expenses of living at home." And from a television person in Nunawading, Australia: "Home exchange is a great way for the fixed-income, retired person to travel anywhere in the world."

Three-time exchangers in Europe, a Churchville, Pennsylvania, couple—college professors who travel with their two children—write: "Vacation home exchanging has been a great opportunity for us, one allowing us to enjoy vacations with our whole family that we could not have afforded otherwise." In this same vein, a Manchester, Connecticut, family, having exchanged twice in England, arranged to have their older children (and their spouses) travel with them—inexpensive family reunions enjoyed by all.

A manufacturer's representative and three-time exchanger living in Minneapolis, Minnesota, puts it more succinctly: "In home exchange, you get more bang for your vacation buck!"

Many first-time home exchangers worry about leaving behind their china, silver, and other expensive items, but theft in home exchanging is rarely a problem. Most exchangers feel their possessions are much safer than they would be if their houses weren't occupied (*Modern Maturity*).

Along with the relatively low cost, home exchangers are of one voice in preferring home living over vacationing in hotels, motels, or rented cottages. For example, the deputy headmaster of a school in Scotland (who has exchanged in Spain and the U.S.) writes: "Holiday home exchanging is a wonderful way of truly getting the 'feel' of a country, which, as a two-week tourist, one could never achieve." From a Seattle, Washington, screenwriter, who has exchanged in Hawaii, England, and Scotland: "Vacation home exchanging gives one a chance to stretch out and to truly relax and feel *at home* in the home of one's exchange partner." And, finally, after three exchanges in England and one in Switzerland ("Florida is next on our exchange list"), a civil engineer in Seville, Spain, writes: "I think home exchanging is the best way to visit and to know a country. The best hotel in town is 'nothing' compared to living in a regular home."

All members of a given family may not necessarily be equally enthusiastic about taking that first "giant" vacation home exchange step. A woman in Lima, Peru, writes: "Our two teenagers and I were excited about the possibility of home exchanging; my main problem was getting my husband, a physician, to participate. But we did finally home exchange in a small city, Kempton, Germany. I felt like we were a part of the place. It will always be special. I hate going from hotel to hotel; it may be interesting at the start of a vacation trip, but after 'hotel-ing' for three weeks or so, I just can't take it anymore! Yes, vacation home exchanging is the *only* way to go."

> Thousands of Americans are enthusiastic about exchanging homes while traveling within the United States or abroad. First, it sharply reduces travel expenses, because accommodations are free. Second, instead of having to dine out, you can prepare whatever meals you wish in your own kitchen. Third, exchanges often include use of the family car (*New York Times*).

And talk about unusual, stimulating vacations! How about the family from Big Sky, Montana, whose Caribbean exchange "home" turned out to be a 42-foot sloop, which came fully equipped with a captain and first mate! Or the retired New York City couple who arranged a fifteen-week chain of vacation home exchanges in six different European countries. The retired book publisher and his wife who languished for a week in a million-dollar, twenty-eighth-floor penthouse—a veritable museum of priceless art—overlooking Florida's luxury resort of Turnberry Isle, home port of the yacht *Monkey Business* (of Gary Hart fame). The director of a nursery school in Orleans, Massachusetts, who with her husband and two sons, "used a Florida exchange as the gathering place for my in-laws' fiftieth wedding anniversary (with lovely trays and lace tablecloths courtesy of our exchange hostess!); to be with our son—a student at Tanglewood in Massachusetts; to visit Disneyland in California; and to visit Civil War sites and to do genealogical research in western Maryland." New Jersey exchangers spent six weeks high in the hills of Hong Kong Island, with a panoramic view of that busy harbor and the shopping mecca of Kowloon. This was their first exchange with a pre-paid live-in maid, who not only did the cooking and the house cleaning, but all of the shopping and laundry as well!

Webster's Ninth New Collegiate Dictionary defines *serendipity* as "the faculty of finding valuable or agreeable things not sought after." An English widow of six years experienced a vacation home exchange serendipity some years ago. The listing of her Buckinghamshire home in a 1986 home exchange directory put this woman in touch with exchangers living in New Zealand. Now, there is nothing unusual about home exchangers contacting other exchangers who live halfway around the world. But, as this woman writes: "This story has an especially happy ending: I sold my home in England and moved to New Zealand, where I *married* one of my home exchange partners!"

From Cos Cob, Connecticut, a book manufacturer writes: "Our Hawaiian home exchange a few years ago resulted in a business opportunity for my wife, who is now North American representative for a ladies' fashion house owned by our Hawaiian home exchange partner."

> If you can't live without a sauna and a pool (although some exchange homes have one or both), then vacation home exchanging may not be for you. If you're reasonably flexible and like more than just traveling superficially, a home exchange provides a great deal of satisfaction (*The Denver* [Colorado] *Post*).

From an Oklahoma City registered nurse, on returning from a month of home exchanging in the Dominican Republic: "I was completely spoiled with a maid who had my breakfast ready when I wanted it and was willing to prepare for our guests with only a few hours' notice. But the best part of this exchange was we could swim every morning in our exchange partner's pool. I shall never forget that trip!"

> Thousands of people vacation home exchange every year. They find each other in various of the home exchange directories. They report that their houses are returned to them clean, with laundry done, and the plants watered; that they were much more comfortable than they would have been in a hotel; that they saved a good deal of money; and that they saw much more of local life than they could have as conventional tourists (*The Christian Science Monitor*).

"Wanting to vacation on the other side of the world, we wrote to exchangers in New Zealand, who had actually moved to Australia, where they eventually received our letter. The result: a memorable *Australian* vacation, among the highlights of which was being invited to a New Year's Eve Party, along with ten neighboring couples." So writes a news reporter in Silver Spring, Maryland, who, with his wife and children, have enjoyed fifteen different vacation home exchange experiences.

Having exchanged in four U.S. states, the U.S. Virgin Islands, Mexico, France, and Italy, an East Falmouth, Massachusetts, teacher exclaims: "The vacation home exchange experience heralded a new dimension in my travel life."

And from a London, England, family of five: "We've had eight home exchanges—from Denmark and Norway to Wyoming and Saskatchewan (and other places in between). The most amazing offers drop through the letterbox from February through June. In vacation home exchange, 'the world is your oyster'; you can go anywhere!"

> Exchanging homes lets one enjoy being a tourist while living like a native (*New Choices*).

While many happy endings (and very few *un*happy ones) stem from vacation home exchanging, the facts are that low cost, flexibility in planning, new friendships made while living in a "home away from home," and just the downright fun of it all, are among the more important reasons why with each passing year more and more families and single travelers are becoming a part of the worldwide vacation home exchanging community.

2 People Who Tried It . . . and Liked It

Prior to retiring in 1984, Norman Thompson of Australia had traveled worldwide as a ship's engineer and later was an equipment supervisor for crews servicing long-distance power lines. Dorothy Thompson taught in various Queensland, Australia, schools—initially in a one-teacher "bush" school and later specializing in the six- to seven-year level.

The Thompsons have two sons, Cameron and Mark. In retirement, they find tropical island life relaxing, and travel—vacation home exchanging and otherwise—both enjoyable and stimulating.

Dorothy Thompson writes:

My husband (Norman) and I live in tropical Northern Australia—Picnic Bay, on Magnetic Island, one of the coral islands of the Great Barrier Reef.

Sounds isolated? Well, one certainly might think so, but by fast ferry, we are actually only twenty minutes from the nearest city, Townsville. We island residents thoroughly enjoy a happy blend of peaceful living under the palms and modern city conveniences and services.

Much as we love it here, occasionally Norm and I do get the wanderlust, and this desire to get away once again was our first step into the world of vacation home exchanging.

Already we had enjoyed wonderful (but costly) holidays across the Pacific, but for several years we had set our sights on England—and not just for a few weeks. Retired as we are, we would go by ship, spend three months in England, and return to Australia by air. A dream trip it was; however, with costs of hotels or rentals, a good many meals eaten out, and a car for traveling about, being in England between July and October would surely add up to a packet.

The more we planned and figured, the more discouraged we became—realizing that the trip we had planned was perhaps a bit more than we could manage—until the former owner of our home "prescribed" home exchange as the solution to our vacation dilemma. The possibility of exchanging homes with someone in England appealed to us immensely, but we were naturally cautious. Strangers living in our home? We floated this idea among various trusted islanders whose English relatives just might possibly be interested. No response, so we decided to take the bull by the horns and list our home in a home exchange directory. We were somewhat concerned that if we were successful in making a contact, would these people properly look after our home, our garden, our swimming pool, and our cat? And what about Norm's beloved Triumph car? I must say that we did take some comfort in the large number of successful vacation home exchanges we'd heard about.

Prior to the distribution of the home exchange directory containing our listing, and quite out of the blue, a friend of ours in Australia received a letter from English relatives—also a retired couple—expressing keen interest in the possibility of exchanging homes with us. Their home was in Bexhill-on-Sea on the south coast of England, not too far from London.

Like us, our newfound English friends had no previous home exchange experience. They and we, however, were quite professional, so to speak, in exchanging letters and information about ourselves, our homes, and the communities in which we lived, with some photographs as well. With each communication back and forth between Australia and England, our mutual friendship, confidence, and trust developed to that point where both couples said, "Let's do it!" Finally, there was the matter of cars. Wouldn't it be great if we could also exchange cars? Norm and these folks had a very frank "postal discussion" about car exchange. This was an important aspect of the arrangement for them and for us, so we decided to include our cars as a part of the exchange agreement.

We then threw ourselves into a whirl of preparations as travelers and as vacation home exchange hosts. We installed a garden sprinkling system, and checked and double-checked our home, appliances, car, accounts, and insurance policies. And we prepared pages of directions for the use of our home, our car, and our pool (yes, there was also the matter of taking care of our cat!); recommendations for shopping and other essentials and services; information about our neighbours; and names of persons to be contacted if anything

went wrong. Finally, we arranged with willing friends to add last-minute sparkle to our home, food to the fridge, and fresh flowers for the decor to celebrate the arrival of our exchange partners. Others promised to meet them on their arrival at the Townsville Airport. Our near neighbours couldn't wait to greet the "people from Bexhill-on-Sea," and island bowlers were enthusiastic about the possibility of two new players. Australian good will was overflowing.

In the midst of all these preparations, we received the latest home exchange directory, with our listing included. Immediately thereafter, by letter and by telephone from various parts of England came inquiries from other potential home exchangers—both experienced and first timers, mostly retired—who responded favorably to the possibility of coming to Australia for periods up to three months. From these communications, we had our first clue to the "reality" of home exchanging as a viable and widely accepted approach to vacationing. We were sorry to have to disappoint these people, but, of course, our plans were in place.

Breathlessly, we waved good-byes from the ferry to the well-wishers, and then it was off to Sydney, where our ship was the

Russian liner *Belorussiya*. Through the Suez Canal and the Mediterranean, it was a thirty-seven-day voyage to England—a delightful happy mix of shipboard life and visiting exciting ports of call along the way.

We docked at Southampton under gray skies, too late to catch the through train to Bexhill-on-Sea. Though we were two hours late arriving in Bexhill, like true friends, our England home exchange partners were waiting for us at the station barrier. They recognised us at once, probably because Norm looked so Australian in his broad-brimmed felt hat. After all of our correspondence, what a joy it was to meet these folks in person!

After a lovely picnic-basket lunch on the Downs, our hosts proudly led us up the stairs to Number 16, a delightfully comfortable modern flat (apartment), carpeted throughout, with a balcony "toward the sea." English flowers bloomed in the landscaped garden. At last, this was Bexhill-on-Sea!

Our English hosts had thoughtfully planned to stay over for two days after our arrival. We were particularly appreciative of their doing this for various reasons. First, we had a chance to get to know these (heretofore) strangers who were to occupy our home in Australia. Second, our hosts helped to familiarize us with what was to be our home away from home for the next three months. Also, we had "hands-on" training in the proper use of the flat's appliances (not so different from ours in Australia), met the neighbours who were to become our friends in the weeks ahead, learned about the local services and shopping (including the pick-your-own strawberry farm!), and had our first pub lunch at the old smugglers' pub, The Star. In bidding our hosts a fond farewell on their departure from England, we assured them that an equally warm welcome awaited them on their arrival in Australia.

We had heard that in home exchanging the host's neighbours often helped to turn an otherwise enjoyable holiday into an especially memorable one, and this was certainly the case with our neighbours and new friends in Bexhill. We were guided and pampered by our host's stalwart band of Past Rotarians and their gracious ladies—coffee mornings, luncheons, and a strawberry tea. They opened their hearts, their homes, and their social diaries to us, and we shall always be grateful for the many courtesies they extended to us.

The English weather? Well, the very months we were there turned out to be England's wettest summer in fifty years (we selected the wrong year, because the *next* summer was to be England's sunniest!). Undeterred by the forecasts of more rain, more clouds, more wind, Norm and I set out on our wider travels, first to Stourbridge, where hospitable distant relatives proudly showed us the area in which my father and grandparents had lived. Names of places long familiar in family stories came alive for us! Indeed, we climbed through steep banks of wild flowers in the national park to find my father's favourite picnic spot of decades gone by, Kinver Edge. As Dad had told us, from this very spot one had a patchwork view of five different counties. Without delay, I wrote back to tell my dad in Australia of our thrill in experiencing some of these special places of his boyhood. Sadly, my father died unexpectedly just two weeks before we were to return to Australia, so that visit to Sourbridge and Kinver Edge will forever be special to me.

Using our Bexhill home exchange flat as our base, we also traveled to Wales, Scotland, the Lake District, York, various countries on the continent, and a week in London. One of the many pluses of vacation home exchanging is that one can pick up and leave for a few days or weeks, always knowing that a comfortable home and friendly neighbours await one's return.

With the passing of time, we became quite adept at managing the flat, shopping, handling the appliances and the car, and just generally living as the English do. There was one minor problem for us: There was no clothes dryer or outside clothesline. However, we did survive those months of folding wet sheets around the hot water system in the cupboard—the "airing closet," they called it—and hanging small items from strings in there. On some occasions, under the cover of darkness, we stealthily hung "drip dries" from a string line in our distant garage and then retrieved them from behind its closed door the next evening. (Drying laundry was never visible at that discreet address.)

While at home in the carpeted Bexhill flat, my handyman husband missed his workshop so much that he found odd jobs to do at our neighbour's bungalow: concreting the garden stairway, cleaning the roof, and in other ways serving as perhaps the original "vacation home exchange handyman!"

Never did we dream that three months of our lives could pass so quickly. Yes, October rolled around much sooner than we expected, and it was time for us to bid a sincere fond farewell to our English friends and our lovely flat in Bexhill.

The flight halfway 'round the world was exciting. It was great to be back in our island home and to find things just as we left them. And it was reassuring, too, to learn our home exchange partners from England enjoyed their Australian vacation just as much as we enjoyed those months in England. Chalk up one more successful vacation home exchange!

Reflecting over our first vacation home exchange, we have a few suggestions to others contemplating this sort of "live-in" holiday experience:

1. If you plan on listing your home and holiday aspirations in a home exchange directory, do so at least one year before your planned holiday date. We learned that vacation home exchangers often plan many months ahead.
2. Do not be too "fixed" in your destination plans, nor too exact in your holiday dates (if you are retired). Keep your options open

for that "surprise" holiday that might just turn out to be the best you've ever had!

3. Be sure to provide plenty of cupboard, fridge, freezer, and clothing space for your home exchange guests.
4. Make advance arrangements for forwarding or holding personal mail and make advance payments against telephone, council rates, tax, and other regular bills which will come to the house while your home exchange guests are there.

While the holiday home exchange concept is praised worldwide, we are its unofficial ambassadors here on Magnetic Island in Northern Australia!

Halbo and Eve Algra, residents of Holland, have a claim, so to speak, on a prime position in the Vacation Home Exchange "Hall of Fame"; their first exchange took place in the summer of 1959.

Reflecting over thirty-plus years of holiday home exchanging, Halbo Algra writes:

Having had a lifetime profession in teaching and education administration, always with several months of summer holidays, holiday home exchanging presented my wife, Eve, our two daughters, and me with marvelous opportunities to enjoy many summer weeks home exchanging in England, Scotland, Switzerland, Denmark, Germany, the U.S.A., and also right here in Holland.

During our first years of exchanging, we offered our exchange partners a fourth-floor apartment on the edge of the beautiful old city of Haarlem. In later years, we offered larger apartments and, more recently, our home exchange partners have lived in our semi-detached house here in Heiloo, a small village just fifteen miles from Haarlem.

We home exchangers in the 1990s have a wide range of national and international exchange listings, all excellent resources for making holiday home exchange contacts. But there were few such listings—and few home exchangers, as well—thirty years ago. In those days, most of our exchange arrangements resulted from advertisements placed in a schoolmasters' periodical, and for this reason most of the families with whom we exchanged were also in the teaching profession. Young and middle-aged couples they were, and many had children about the same ages as ours.

At this point, I must say that children seem to respond very well to holiday home exchanging. There are new friends to be made, new toys to play with, new neighborhoods to be explored.

During our longer stays (four to five weeks), we always endeavor to organize a holiday within a holiday. For example, using our exchange home as a base, we often enjoyed ten- to seventeen-day automobile trips in England, Scotland, Denmark, and elsewhere, making use of small hotels, bed-and-breakfast facilities, and youth hostels. Such side trips gave our family holiday more dimension—sightseeing, experiencing different foods, and visiting new cities and towns.

While living in the home of your exchange partner, you become involved in the daily life of the people around you. You meet people like that fine old man who took our family in his boat out to sea off the southern coast of England; that author in Denmark who spoke with the voice of the revolutionary sixties (especially on the new and free approach to sex). There was a designer of Cumbermault, then a brand-new town in Scotland in which the traffic and commercial areas had been separated from the living areas so that children could play and people could sit in their gardens without being disturbed by the fast pace of the traffic and the business community. We met a professor who had developed a new method of teaching mathematics and was delivering lectures in various parts of the world; senior citizens from Massachusetts with whom we dined had the unique opportunities to share stories about our beloved Holland. A reporter we met appeared to have a program on local television, and we found ourselves in front of cameras having a home exchange-related interview. We talked with students in a high school class, and met neighbors who were such a great support following an automobile accident we had in the U.S.A. These are just a few of the countless number of people we met and who we shall always remember.

Also memorable was the contrast in nature: the silent lakes amid millions-of-years-old hills in the north of Scotland and roaring Niagara Falls. There was contrast in the towns and cities: the grandeur of Vienna and the turmoil of New York City. There was contrast in the parks: the quietness of Hyde Park in London and the hilarity of Tivoli Gardens in Copenhagen and the Prater in Vienna.

One can go on and on; the list of all these impressions and experiences is endless. But when you travel in the ordinary way, you can visit the same places and have the same impressions, can't you? The only answer I can give is that in the past we did travel through Europe in the "ordinary" way, but by far the *best* recollections we have are from the places we visited during our holiday home exchanging years. Now, why is this? The reason, I think, is twofold: (1) we truly *lived* in our exchange homes, so there was no need to be rushing here and there, and (2) we talked about our experiences with our new friends, so the impressions grew more profoundly. So, you see, I am very enthusiastic about exchanging homes, and Eve shares this enthusiasm.

Our very first exchange was with the Oldham family of Haslemere, England. This was a simultaneous exchange; that is, the Oldhams were at our house in Holland during the same weeks we were in theirs in England. We had not met these people—only knew them, so to speak, through our exchanges of correspondence. Realizing that our ferryboats en route to England and Holland would pass each other at some point in the English Channel, the Oldhams and we thought there was a very slim possibility of us having an opportunity to have eye contact with each other, and each of us promised to wave a large white handkerchief as the ships passed each other. Of course, a great distance between ships, bad weather conditions, or crowds of people on either ship could easily spoil our splendid intention!

As it turned out, the weather was perfect, and the passing ships were close enough so that each ship's passengers could see the others quite clearly. And, yes, "meeting" each other, each family seeing the tiny white "flags" of the other family, was the beginning of a thirty-year correspondence relationship between the Oldhams and the Algras! Indeed, on June 19, 1989, exactly thirty years after that channel crossing, we finally—for the first time—met the Oldhams in England.

Now this is an unusual story for two reasons. First, there was the coincidence of the shipboard "meeting." Secondly, rarely do holiday home exchangers actually meet each other, since most of the time each partner is at the other partner's home during the exchange period. But both parties oftentimes do get to know each other's neighbors, and with the exchange of letters and greeting cards, these "neighbor" friendships are not only long-lasting, but sometimes even result in additional holiday home exchange arrangements.

While we have nearly always enjoyed every aspect of the holiday exchange houses in which we have lived, once we did get off to a bad start in Copenhagen. Unlike our then light, airy, top-floor apartment in Holland, our Copenhagen partner's home was dark and gloomy; opening its front door was like entering a cave. Further, on our arrival day, the rooms were cold and damp. It was apparent Eve was very disappointed. After viewing the bedroom situation, Eve suddenly burst into tears—visions of pitiful, exhausted children who had to survive a six-week stay in a gloomy, chilly house in a dark street in a country where once Hamlet died! But "all's well that ends well." With some adjustments in the sleeping situation and brighter, more enjoyable weather, our stay in Copenhagen turned out to be a marvelous, educational, relaxing, and enjoyable one.

We have three suggestions we make to all who are interested in the possibility of attempting a holiday home exchange:

1. As home exchangers rarely have repeat exchanges, it is impor-

tant to learn as much as possible in advance about the area in which you will be exchanging. More than likely your exchange partner will provide you with some information about his town or city. In addition, go to your local book store or library and learn more about the history of your exchange destination and the sights to be seen (and possibly not to be seen!).

2. The local customs change from one community to the other and (especially) from one country to another. Your holiday home exchange will be much more enjoyable if you don't try to "fight" the local customs. So, yes, remember: When in Rome, do as the Romans do.

3. Never forget you are living in someone else's home, and thus you have a responsibility to the home's owner, your exchange partner. Realizing this fact, you will want to take the best possible care of your holiday home.

Finally, it is quite understandable that most potential holiday home exchangers will be concerned about the care of their homes ("These people may wreck our home!"). After our thirty-plus years of actual holiday home exchange experience, on a scale of one to ten, we would rate all of our exchange partners a resounding number ten in the care (and often *loving* care!) they have given our homes.

Try holiday home exchanging; you'll like it!

3 Meet Mr. and Mrs. Homer Exchanger

EARLY ON IN THIS BOOK IT would seem appropriate to focus on the vacation home exchanger.

Who *are* these home exchange people? Are they young people, middle-agers, or older folks? Where do they live? How many are retirees? What about their occupations and professions? And what is their vacation home exchange experience? When did they start exchanging? How many times have they exchanged?

The data developed from the survey, in which more than six hundred experienced vacation home exchangers participated, provide a definitive answer to each of these questions and serve as

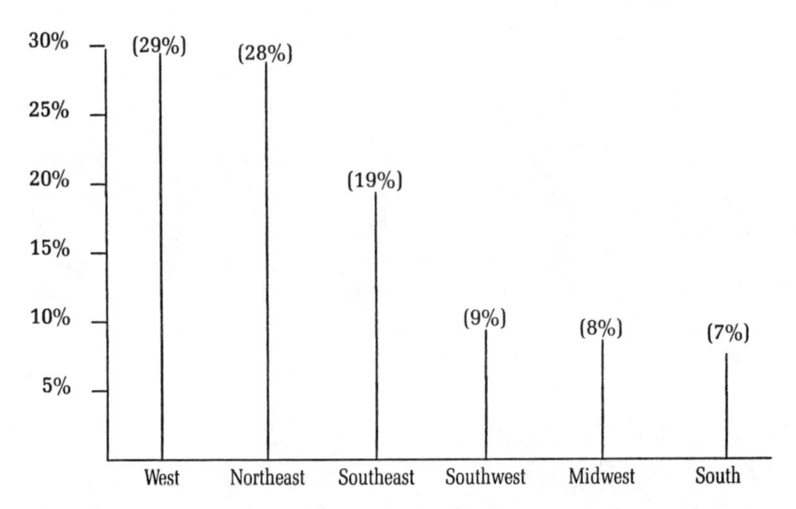

Chart A–1—Where U.S. vacation home exchangers reside.

an authoritative resource for exploring other aspects of the vacation home exchange experience.

Rather than combining the profile data covering U.S. exchangers and their counterparts elsewhere in the world, the survey makes a distinction between these two groups. Not only are the facts and figures derived from the survey of keen interest, but especially interesting are the differences between the U.S. and non-U.S. vacation home exchangers.

Where do these exchangers live? Specifically, in what sections of the U.S. do they live and where outside of the U.S.?

While there are home exchangers in all fifty U.S. states, Chart A–1 underscores the fact that three-quarters of the U.S. exchangers reside in the western, southeastern, and northeastern parts of the country. The Big Three states are California, Florida, and New York.

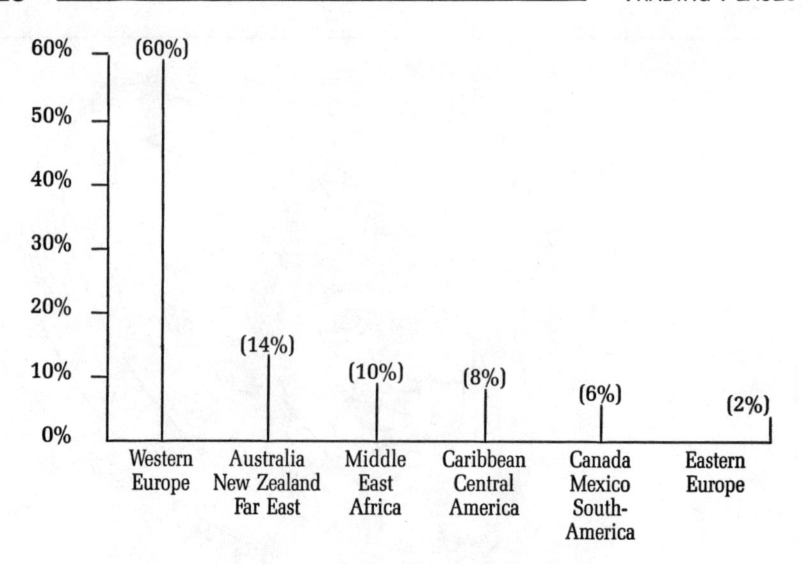

Chart A–2—Where non-U.S. vacation home exchangers reside.

And where do the non-U.S. exchangers live? Chart A–2 shows, perhaps not surprisingly, that well over half of the exchangers outside of the U.S. live in western Europe. The largest number of western European exchangers live in Great Britain, Germany, and France.

Some have said that the vast majority of vacation home exchangers are retired, that the "golden oldies" have lots of time on their hands, and, because of their fixed incomes, this group seeks out "bargain" vacations. This is not necessarily so. Indeed, Chart B–1 shows that nearly three-quarters of the U.S. home exchangers are in

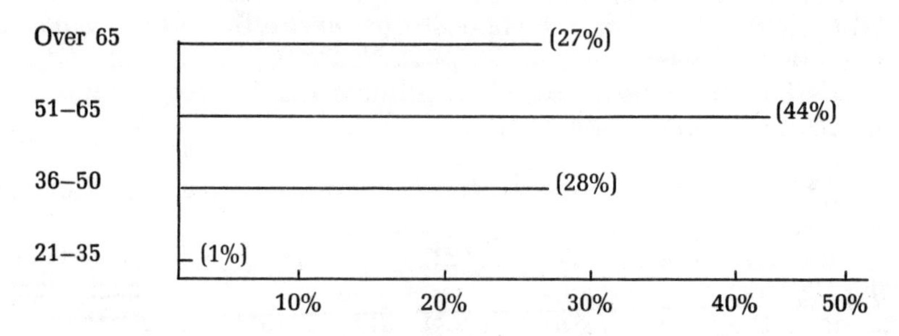

Chart B–1—Ages of U.S. vacation home exchangers.

the 36-65 age group, while slightly more than three-fourths of the non-U.S. exchangers are between the ages of 36 and 65 (Chart B–2). Further, it is clear that non-U.S. exchangers start their vacation home exchanging at an earlier age than those in the U.S.; 8 percent in the 21-35 age group versus only 1 percent of the U.S. exchangers start that young. Note, too, the percentage comparisons between the U.S. and non-U.S. exchangers in the 51-65 and over 65 age groups, showing considerably higher percentages of U.S. exchangers in the latter category.

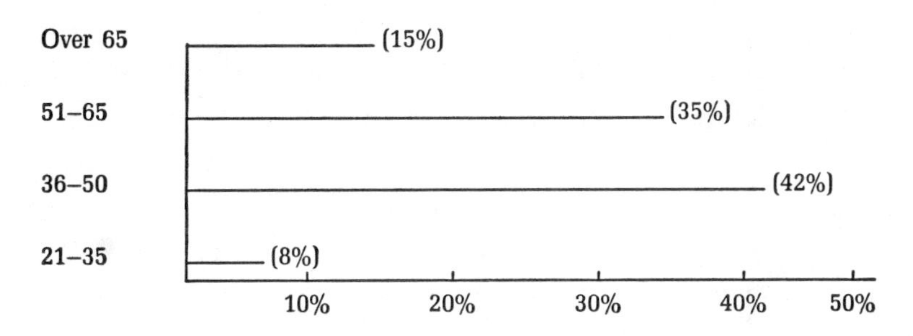

Chart B–2—Ages of non-U.S. vacation home exchangers.

While some single persons do vacation home exchange with friends—widowed women who had home exchange experience prior to their husbands' passing and others traveling alone—85 percent of home exchangers, worldwide, are married.

What about the occupations and professions of these vacation home exchangers? The forerunners of modern-day exchangers were teachers. Yes, teachers topped the charts in the 1960s. Why? Well, teachers have always had ten to twelve weeks of summer vacation and week-long vacations at other times during the school year. A particularly economical way to travel, home exchanging has afforded teachers the opportunity to extend their vacations over longer periods of time, especially during the summer months. Finally, with more available vacation time, teachers also have more flexibility in their vacation planning. (Later chapters will underscore the key role flexibility plays in home exchanging.)

Increasingly, during the 1970s and the 1980s, couples and families in occupations and professions other than teaching latched onto the vacation home exchange concept. Currently, business executives and middle-management business persons top the worldwide list of exchangers' occupations and professions. Charts C-1 and C-2 project other interesting insights into the occupations of U.S. and non-U.S. exchangers.

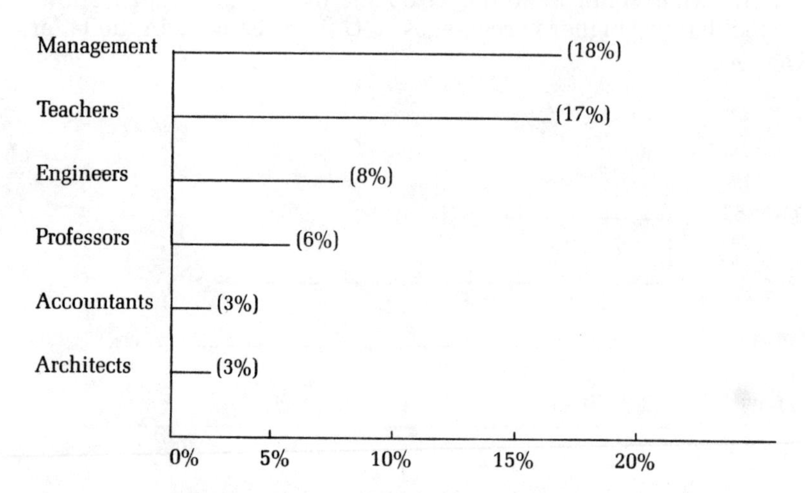

Chart C–1—Top six occupations/professions of U.S. vacation home exchangers.

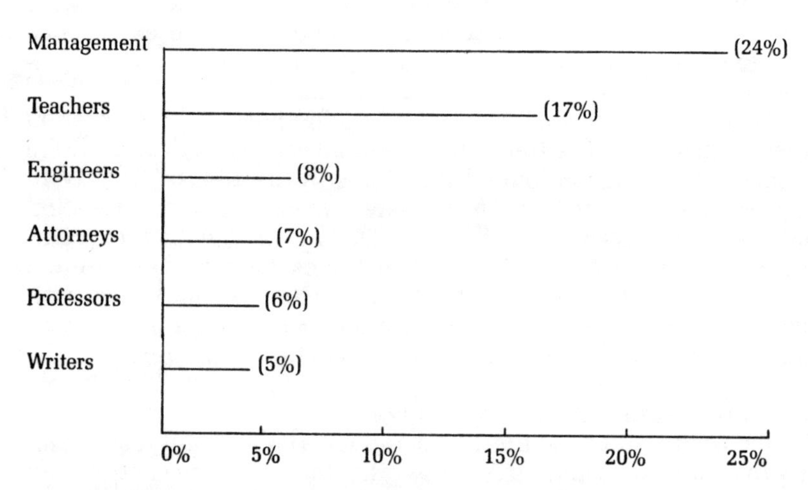

Chart C–2—Top six occupations/professions of non-U.S. vacation home exchangers.

Not included in these charts are many other occupations and professions in which national and international home exchangers are engaged, including

railroad workers	veterinarians
insurance agents	fashion consultants
nurses	funeral directors
police officers	artists
dentists	airline stewardesses
auto mechanics	optometrists
secretaries	civil servants
farmers	ministers
social workers	lumbermen

From this data, one can be reasonably sure that the vacation home exchange community includes men and women in nearly every conceivable occupation and profession, including owners of a fruit farm (apples, pears, and plums) in Staplehurst, an hour from London, England, who exchanged in Florida, and the Vacation Home Exchanging International Three "U's": an *U*ndertaker in Whakatane, New Zealand; an *U*nemployed person in New York City; and an *U*nderground miner in Green River, Wyoming!

Some say that bed and breakfast travel first became popular in Great Britain long before the advent of the London Hilton and motel row near Heathrow Airport. Now this may well be true.

	U.S.	Non U.S.
Before 1980	22%	11%
1980 – '85	50%	34%
1986 – '90	28%	55%

Chart D—Dates of first vacation home exchanges.

But Chart D clearly shows that today's Americans were into vacation home exchanging prior to non-U.S. exchangers. Indeed, before 1985, nearly three-quarters of today's U.S. exchangers had already started vacationing home exchange style, as compared with only 45 percent of those exchangers living elsewhere in the world. But the latter group has certainly taken vacation home exchanging to its heart since the mid eighties.

The final element in profiling the experienced vacation home exchanger is the number of actual "swaps" these exchangers have had. In other words, just how experienced *is* the "experienced" vacation home exchanger? Chart E shows that approximately one-third of U.S. exchangers have had either one or two exchanges, compared with approximately one-half of their non-U.S. counterparts. No doubt most of those one- or two-exchange exchangers began exchanging in the mid to late 1980s. Note, too, that one in every ten exchangers, worldwide, has had ten or more home exchange vacations.

	U.S.	Non U.S.
1 or 2 exchanges	37%	51%
3 thru 6 exchanges	40%	34%
7 thru 9 exchanges	13%	4%
10 plus exchanges	10%	11%

Chart E—Number of vacation home exchanges completed.

The most home exchanging nation in the world? Belgium holds this honor, as this small nation (population ten million) has the world's greatest number of home exchangers in proportion to its population.

This overview of vacation home exchangers projects a very clear picture of Mr., Mrs., and Ms. Vacation Home Exchanger, worldwide: (1) most U.S. exchangers live in California, Florida, and New York, while most of those living outside of the U.S. reside in Great Britain, Germany, and France; (2) the greatest number are middle-aged (36-65 years old); (3) their occupational and professional range is as wide as the world itself; (4) twenty to twenty-five percent are retired persons. (5) With an average of four exchanges each, most have been vacation home exchanging for about ten years.

Of the over six hundred people participating in the survey, many have second homes. Most of these prefer to exchange their second homes, while others exchange both their main and second homes.

How do home exchangers "profile" each other? A ten-time exchanger (who moved to Sanibel Island, Florida, after a home exchange there) puts it this way: "We have always felt that vacation home exchangers are found only in a selected segment of society; that is, they are relatively affluent, educated, stable, and interested in expanding their horizons."

The assumption can safely be made that home exchangers throughout the world have enjoyed participating in the vacation home exchange concept and are looking forward to home exchange as an important part of their and their families' future vacation plans.

4 Setting Goals

OVER THE YEARS, THE VACAtion "habits" of people have changed. A decade ago, for example, most vacations were two or three weeks in length and nearly always took place during the summer months.

In these "think leisure" 1990s, most working people are blessed with an increasing number of vacation weeks (three or four, or more) during any given year. Some people spread their vacation time over long weekends—short-notice family visits, ski trips, or just "getting stuff done around the house." Others—individuals, couples, family groups—enjoy getting away for longer periods of time.

Families with school-age children and teachers still stick to vacationing in the summertime and/or enjoying shorter trips keyed to other school holidays. But retired persons, some professional men and women, and others are fortunate in being able to set their own vacation dates—winter, spring, fall, holiday periods—or whenever they and their home exchange partners choose.

Regardless of how and when you plan your vacation, and whether you travel as a family, as a couple, or as an individual, the home exchange concept may well be just the "ticket" for your vacation enjoyment.

More than likely, spending your vacation living in someone else's home will be a new vacation experience for you and your family. But this is still a *vacation*, and for *any* vacation (home exchange or otherwise), a certain amount of advanced planning is necessary.

Remember, if you home exchange, your vacation plans have to be dovetailed into those of your home exchange partners—those who may be living in your home while you are in theirs. For this reason, the earlier you begin your vacation planning, the better. Experienced home exchangers feel the amount of enjoyment received from a vacation is in direct proportion to the amount of *advance* planning that goes into home exchange vacation arrangements.

Before you actually start contacting potential home exchange partners, it is important to give a lot of thought to what you would consider your "Dream Vacation." Do not waste time and energy initially on *with whom* you will be exchanging homes until you have put together—in detail and in writing, for your own reference—when you would like to go, where you would like to go, how long you would like to stay, and so on. You do this realizing that in all likelihood you will be able to retain, through a proper home exchange arrangement, many (if not nearly all) of the elements you consider important for your best ever vacation.

Among the different aspects of vacationing home exchange style is that, as has been previously emphasized, you will be paying nothing for that roof over your head. This cash saving can either be put in the bank, go toward a new jet ski, be spent on a twenty-fifth anniversary diamond, or be used to *upgrade* your dream vacation—from Boca Raton to Bermuda or Barbados, or perhaps even to Barcelona!

So what are the most important elements of your dream vacation? Many of these are obvious—the same kinds of things you would have considered in planning vacations you have enjoyed in the past:

- When to go and how long to stay
- Where to go
- Facilities required
- Destination transportation
- Cost

When to Go and How Long to Stay

Summer . . . Christmas . . . Easter . . . the High Holidays . . . winter; a week . . . two weeks . . . a month or more. Perhaps you will wish to think in terms of spending, say, a week or two at the shore and then another week sightseeing in Washington, D.C., or in southern California, or two weeks each in London and Paris, for instance, splitting your time into two (or more) different vacation destinations.

Nearly half of American home exchangers vacation for three to four weeks at a time; 24 percent vacation for two weeks; 14 percent for one week; and another 14 percent for more than four weeks. (This latter category includes a large number of home exchangers in the teaching profession and those who are retired.) Fifty-eight percent of non-U.S. exchangers vacation for three to four weeks; 16 percent for more than four weeks; 21 percent for two weeks; and only 4 percent for one week.

A Honolulu newspaper publisher with ten vacation home exchanges in Europe and the U.S. often coordinates his exchange dates with events he and his wife look forward to attending: Paris at the time of the 200th anniversary of Bastille Day and London during the championships at Wimbledon—staying, by the way, at the home of a banker directly across the road from the tennis club.

"I scheduled my vacation with home exchangers to coincide with a get-together with my daughter who was attending boarding school," writes a Chevy Chase, Maryland, professor.

Where to Go

Now where you go, of course, depends on what you want to get out of this dream vacation—your vacation concept: the mountains, the seashore, a quiet lakeside, nearness to family and/or children's activities, skiing, fishing, golf, tennis, or just plain relaxing—*anyplace.*

A botanist from Stockholm, Sweden, his wife, and their young child had an August home exchange in Greece. He writes: "The weather was catastrophically hot in Athens (107°F). My wife got sick—so sick that we went back to Stockholm after one week of a planned month-long vacation. Fortunately, we were able to stay with my parents-in-law, so our Greek exchange partners spent the full four weeks at our home." Do not let this happen to you! Before firming up vacation arrangements, check out the weather with your exchange partners, the local chamber of commerce, or the national tourist bureau serving your proposed destination city or country.

People whose work involves travel have opportunities to tie a vacation home exchange week or two in with their business trips. New Yorkers, after attending a business convention in Minneapolis, might spend ten days or so fishing for walleyed pike in the northern Minnesota lake district. A business trip to London or Paris or Frankfurt affords an opportunity to vacation for a couple of weeks (or more) elsewhere in Europe.

Back to your dream vacation plans. Perhaps you are thinking of spending time in New Orleans . . . or western Canada . . . or Rome . . . or San Francisco . . . or Hong Kong . . . or Acapulco . . . or visiting relatives in Peoria or even in Brooklyn. In your dream vacation planning, if you name a place, the chances are that someone living at that very place (or near there) would consider *your* home and *your* locality in *their* dream vacation planning.

If your sights are set on a known vacation resort area, i.e., spring skiing at Vail, Colorado, or basking in the winter sunshine at Boynton Beach, Florida, or visiting New England in the fall when the leaves are changing color, you may well find yourself confronted with a rental situation. Home exchanging condo owners often rent their condos during a given resort's high season. This is quite understandable from the owner's point of view, but disappointing to vacation home exchanging "purists."

Facilities Required

This is easy. How many adults and how many children are in your vacation party? Two adults and two teenagers? Okay, you will require three bedrooms and will hope to get two full bathrooms. On this matter of bedrooms, a printer from Kingsport, Tennessee, writes: "My wife and I prefer to sleep in separate bedrooms. When traveling on business, we of course cannot always afford a two-bedroom hotel or motel *suite*. But while vacation home exchanging, we always endeavor to get at least two bedrooms—and have yet to be disappointed."

Other basic elements may (or may not) be important to you: an elevator (if someone in your family has a bad knee), clothes washer/dryer, a wet bar, television/radio, VCR, air conditioning (a *must* in certain locations), facilities for the handicapped, microwave oven, dishwasher, garage, nearby shopping and public transportation.

"If it comes to flipping a coin," suggests a book salesman in Hillsdale, New Jersey, "between a home or condo exchange, if one is talking about a two-week vacation, take the home. A home always comes fully equipped with all the basics: more living space, ample bedding, and all of the kitchen supplies, plus 'built-in' neighbors.

Such is not always the case with a seldom-used condo."

Before you entered the wonderful world of vacation home exchanging, for your $1,000 (or more) a week at the shore you got a bare-bones, cramped cottage (no screens attached), very tired beds, a small refrigerator (freezer not working), a television (for an extra two bucks a day), and electricity, featuring an outdoor meter ticking away your precious vacation dollars! A home exchange vacation puts you in a lovely home or condominium with all the conveniences of *your own* home, and it is all yours to enjoy—for free!

Destination Transportation

If your vacation destination is, say, 800 to 1000 miles from your own home, you probably will want to take your own car. If, on the other hand, your sights are set on Hawaii, South America, or the Swiss Alps, there is a very good chance that car swapping with your home exchange partner could be a part of your exchange arrangement. Why pay hundreds of dollars a week for a rental car when you can drive your exchange partner's Volvo station wagon throughout your three-week home exchange vacation in Stockholm? (see chapter 15).

Cost

Exchangers from Jacksonville, Florida, enjoyed their vacation at Whitby Island, in Washington. Later, their "host couple went into the bed and breakfast business. The house we stayed in for three weeks at no cost is now $125 per night!" As vacation home exchangers, you need not budget for hotels, motels, or cottages by the sea. If you drive, you will have gas and tolls to consider, and if you fly or go by train or bus, these fares must also be figured in.

Along with that of transportation, the cost of food is a major element in your vacation budget. Home exchangers always have breakfast and nearly always have lunch "at home." And dinners? Well, this depends entirely on your vacation lifestyle. Part of the fun of vacationing is dining out, and those who usually prepare the meals will be the first to vote for trying out the local restaurants at least a couple of times a week. After all, this *is* a *vacation*! And a vacation indeed it was for a Washington, D.C., journalist and his wife. During a recent fourteen-day London, England, home exchange, these folks attended eleven different performances in West End theaters and dined out every night! This is not typical, however. In a given week, more than half U.S. vacation home exchangers have three to four meals in restaurants. For non-U.S. exchangers, this percentage is slightly lower—about 40 percent.

You can come up with an estimate of the costs of your meals out. Figure that the costs of supermarket purchases for meals in and for necessary household supplies will be about the same as these items would cost at home. Incidentally, these food and household supplies are not really vacation expenses, since you would be spending approximately the same amount of money on food and supplies if you were living at home.

And then there is the cost of golf-related fees, if you are golfers; chartering fishing boats, if you fish; the use of courts, if you are tennis players; boat rental, if you are boaters; and other sports- or hobby-related expenses.

A Cologne, Germany, family of four writes: "We always try to exchange with Americans who offer an apartment in a condominium community. Then we have most outdoor facilities at our doorstep—tennis, swimming pool, barbeque, and sometimes golf, too."

No matter how much time and effort you spend in advance estimating the costs of vacations, after returning home—sun-tanned and rested (?)—when all the bills are in, you inevitably will have exceeded the expected costs. So, in estimating vacation costs, it is always a good idea to add 5 to 10 percent for those inevitable vacation contingencies.

Remember, in vacation home exchanging, there are *two* parties involved: you and your home exchange partner. For this reason a home exchange vacation (unlike a weekend with friends in the country) calls for a considerable amount of advance planning.

At this point, it would be appropriate to make a comparison between the costs of home exchange vacations and regular (or "conventional") vacations.

This first cost comparison is between a two-week home-exchange vacation and a conventional vacation of the same length. It is based on the budget for summer 1992 travel prepared by the Beckers, a retired couple who own a townhouse in Falls Church, Virginia, and their eleven-year-old granddaughter. The Beckers' home exchange partners are a working couple who own a large condominium in Pasadena, California.

While in California, the Beckers will be using their exchange partner's car, and they will be driving around Greater Los Angeles and also to San Diego, Santa Barbara, Lake Arrowhead, and elsewhere. They will be doing a lot of sightseeing and expect to drive about 1,500 miles during the two weeks.

And now the Beckers' budget for this home exchange vacation:

Airfare	$1,247
Meals out (3 persons) (6 evening meals; 6 noon meals)	396
Meals at home and household supplies	190
Sightseeing and sporting events	350
Personal items, gifts, and souvenirs	225
Gasoline	110
	$2,518
plus contingencies (10%)	252
total	$2,770

As vacation home exchangers, the Beckers estimate the cost of their two-week, southern California vacation (with their eleven-year-old granddaughter along) will be $2,770.

If the Beckers were to make this same two-week trip to southern California as "conventional" vacationers in summer 1992, their budget would look like this:

Airfare	$1,247
Hotels/motels (14 nights @ $100)	1,400
Meals for three persons in hotel/motel dining rooms or in restaurants (13 days)	1,050
Automobile rental, compact model	145
Sightseeing and sporting events	350
Personal items, gifts, and souvenirs	225
Gasoline	110
	$4,527
plus contingencies (10%)	453
total	$4,980

As home exchangers, this 1992 southern California vacation for three persons will cost $2,770, $2,210 *less* than the cost of these people taking the same vacation as *non*-home exchangers.

The second cost comparison is also between a two-week home exchange vacation and a conventional vacation of the same length. It is based on the budget for summer 1992 travel (two weeks) for the Foxells, a working couple who own a home (with a swimming pool) in Sarasota, Florida. The Foxells have chosen the Kensington section of London, England, for their exchange vacation—a large home located on Brunswick Gardens (a stone's throw from Kensington Palace, home of the young princes, William and Harry, and their royal parents). The Foxells' home exchange partners and their sixteen-year-old son will be staying at the Foxells' home in Sarasota. Car exchange is to be a part of this arrangement.

During their first week in London, the Foxells will not need their exchange car; public transportation and taxis do the trick there. But during the second week, they will be using the car for sightseeing purposes outside of London.

The Foxells' budget for their first home exchange vacation abroad looks like this:

Airfare	$1,685
Meals out (2 persons) (6 evening meals; 6 noon meals)	450
Meals at home and household supplies	150
Sightseeing and theatre	250

Personal items, gifts, and souvenirs	250
Gasoline (in England it's "petrol")	160
Public transportation and taxis	75
	$3,020
plus contingencies (10%)	302
total	$3,322

The Foxells estimate the cost of their two-week, home-exchange vacation in England will be $3,322.

As a comparison, if the Foxells were to spend two weeks in England on a conventional vacation, here is what their budget would look like:

Airfare	$1,685
Hotels (13 nights @ $200)	2,600
Meals (13 days)	1,050
Automobile rental, compact model*	239
Sightseeing and theatre	250
Personal items, gifts, and souvenirs	250
Gasoline	100
Public transportation and taxis	75
	$6,249
plus contingencies (10%)	625
total	$6,874

*a rented car will not be needed in London—only during the week of sightseeing outside of London

The cost of a two-week "conventional" vacation in England during summer 1992 would be $6,874. That is $3,552 more than a home-exchange style vacation! Why the *big* difference? Home/car exchangers do not pay hotel bills; they have most of their meals at home; and they do not rent cars.

5 Different Strokes for Different Folks

MOST VACATION HOME EXchanges are direct, or simultaneous, exchanges, arrangements under which each party in the exchange occupies the other's home during the same period of time.

It is interesting—yet perhaps not surprising—to observe that experienced vacation home exchangers (and sometimes first-time exchangers, as well) are adding creative new twists to the overall vacation home exchange arrangement. Some of these different types of exchanges take place between persons who own second homes. Most often, however, this new approach to home exchanging takes place between one-home couples and/or families with children.

Among these "new-look" home exchange arrangements are the following:

1. *"Alternate date" exchange.* Two couples are involved. Couple A stays at the home of B, while B perhaps vacations elsewhere. Then, at a later date, couple B stays at the home of A, while A vacations elsewhere. This arrangement is ideal for teachers, retired persons, and others who are in a position to take two or more annual vacations.

2. *"Substitute" exchange.* Two or three couples are involved. Couple A stays at the home of B. Couple B vacations elsewhere, while a member of couple B's family or a friend of couple B stays at A's home, thus substituting for B. This type of exchange can be a part of the arrangements from the start, or it can be used if one of the couples has to abort the original arrangement, thus sidestepping, so to speak, the type of "ultimate disaster" discussed in chapter 22.

3. *"Three-way" exchange.* Three couples are involved. Couple A stays at the home of B; B at the home of C; and C at the home of A. Because all three of these exchanges take place during the same time

frame, the vacation schedule of all couples involved must coincide. If *two* couples have a difficult time fixing on the exchange dates, one additional couple compounds the exchange date problem! But if the three couples making this type of exchange are family members or close friends and if each is willing to be flexible about dates, a three-way exchange can often be successfully arranged.

From experienced exchangers in Maryville, Tennessee: "Our three-way exchange was both interesting and fun. We were offered the exchange by a Maryland couple, whose second home is in the Caribbean. [Not wishing to be so far away at that point], we arranged with a friend who has a place at Kiawah Island, South Carolina, to go to the Caribbean, we went to Kiawah, and the folks from Maryland stayed at our place."

4. *"Time-share" exchange.* Two couples are involved. When a couple owns a condominium for one particular week (or more weeks) in a given year, this is known as time-share, or "interval," ownership. Those who own time-share properties sometimes prefer not to return to the same vacation location year after year. Exchanging their time-share properties enables them to enjoy a variety of vacation destinations, either within, or outside of, their timeshare plan.

5. *"Hospitality" or "Friendship" exchange.* Either two couples, two single persons, or a single person and a couple are involved. Partners A and B stay together at the home of A. At a later date, both partners stay together at the home of B. This arrangement is becoming increasingly popular—especially among single persons and/or retired persons who enjoy making new friends and seeing new places and who have the inclination and the time to get up and go for a weekend or a week or more—anytime, anyplace.

Houston, Texas, vacationers who have hospitality exchanged in France, Monaco, and Italy, write, "Staying with a family is the *only* way to really get to know a country!"

A variation of the hospitality exchange is the "learn-a-language" exchange. A retired French physician and his wife, who have a lovely near-the-seashore second home in Capbreton, France, are interested in exchanging with a U.S. couple—perhaps a month in France and a month in the U.S. Object: vacations during which each couple would endeavor to learn the other's language. Each year, many home exchangers use language learning as a common denominator for vacation home exchanges.

Having done regular exchanges in New York City and in St. Croix, U.S. Virgin Islands, a couple retired to a small farm in Pembroke, Maine, and are looking forward to a "farm hospitality exchange that would afford each couple the opportunity to learn something about farming in another area or another country. There would be lots of time for the farm equivalent of shop talk, and each couple also would have an enjoyable vacation experience.

Not to be outdone in hospitality exchange circles are the Baltimore, Maryland, exchangers, (he an environmental engineer; she a university administrator) who originated the "over-the-bounding-main" hospitality exchange. "Thus far we have hospitality exchanged with people who, like ourselves, have an interest in yachting and own boats. In this way we are able to experience sailing (or motor yachting) in a new area. Because of the complexities of yachting, it is almost mandatory that the owner be available to acquaint the guests with the boat. This is an important reason for this type of hospitality exchange. To date we have enjoyed three 'bounding-main' exchanges: two in Great Britain; one in San Francisco."

Many couples or families, of course, do not own their homes; they rent them; others rent second homes. The terms of some lease arrangements prohibit those who lease from subletting or exchanging their rented properties. No problem . . . a hospitality exchange can come to the rescue!

More than once, a hospitality exchange *has* come to the rescue. A businessman in Apopka, Florida, returned from a home exchange elsewhere in the U.S. to find his "vacation home exchange partner's wife in a local hospital, so we had the husband as our guest for an additional two weeks." Incidentally, vacation home exchanging introduced these Apopka-ites to another travel opportunity: "For the past eight years, my wife and I have been 'escorts' for a travel club working through a travel agency. Four times annually, we serve as tour leaders for groups of up to twenty-five vacationers traveling to various different countries overseas."

6. "Car-for-house" exchange. A husband/wife real estate team in Evansville, Indiana, writes: "We exchanged our second home for the use of a car for three weeks in England. We then drove to our exchange home, the owner of which was at our main home. So we actually had two different exchanges during the same period." Not a bad idea!

7. "Motor home/camper" exchange. Rather than exchanging regular homes, an increasing number of people are enjoying "wheels-down" vacation exchanges in each others' motor homes or campers. A couple (both teachers) in Florida, exchanged homes *and* motorhomes with a couple in Germany. "A great time," they write.

Having had a succesful home exchange in the U.S., an English airline captain and his wife are readying their six-berth camper for an exchange. They have offered to exchange "all of the United Kingdom and perhaps some of the continent, as well" in return for a similar vacation in the U.S.

8. "Pulpit" exchange. Summer (a month or two) is the time some churches actually exchange pastors with churches elsewhere in the U.S. or in Europe—England, mostly. Their respective churches pay the transportation charges, and the pastors each enjoy some vacation time, as they generally are not expected to assume all pastoral responsibilities—just the sermon on Sunday mornings. Of course, while on this type of exchange, the pastors live in each others' homes

and may, or may not, exchange cars, as well. For example, a pastor in Bournemouth, England, had just such a pulpit exchange in Georgia; then he, his wife, and their three children enjoyed a five-week, regular home exchange vacation in Florida.

9. (Strictly) *"Business" exchange.* Over the past thirteen years, a Billings, Montana, couple has exchanged homes in California, New Mexico, and Mexico. Also, these folks have exchanged in New York City more than *twenty* times! They like New York *that* much? Could be . . . But, in actual fact, business meetings take this husband to New York twice annually. Rather than staying in a Manhattan hotel ($200 and up per night), he and his wife swap their second home every six months for ten- to fourteen-day home exchanges in New York. How often do they dine out? *Seven* nights per week! And what aspirations do they have for future home exchanges? Paris, France, and—yes—New York City!

10. "Student" exchange. When one hears about international student exchanges, one thinks of high school or college young people spending, say, a school term with a family in a different country and attending school or college in that country. Generally the families hosting these exchanges have their own young people who are approximately the same age as their student guests. The following term, the guest student becomes a host student in his country. There is a great deal of student exchanging in Europe, where distances from one country to the other are short. Since World War II, various international organizations have been very successful in promoting and sponsoring overseas student exchanges, mostly between the U.S. and England, and the U.S. and France. Among the advantages of student exchanges: these fortunate young people have the advantages of "living" a different culture, learning a language, and often making life-long friendships, not only between the students but between their parents as well.

Perhaps because of the growth and success of international student exchanging, vacation home exchange directories increasingly list young people who are seeking host families. Their families, in turn, will become the host families during either the next vacation or school session. Indeed, the two directories with the largest numbers of vacation home exchange listings and others, as well, now have special youth exchange sections. A fourteen-year-old English student seeks an August exchange in France or Switzerland: "I want to improve my French." A German student says: "I am looking for a family with a girl of my own age (fourteen) for exchange next summer in America." A listing from Brazil reads: "Fifteen-year-old boy wants to holiday-exchange in Europe or U.S.A."

In some instances, home exchange families are exchanging their young people during school vacations; others are hosting them during the school or college terms. For example, a Valparaiso, Indiana, registered nurse hosted a student from France, during a five-week school vacation. "He was fun," she writes, "and interesting, and I enjoyed his stay and corresponding with his parents."

The next year she consented to host a youth for the entire school year, a student from Cologne, Germany. "First I hesitated, but then, since I live alone and he sounded like a nice boy, I agreed. Then I thought, 'What if he's a problem? Why am I doing this crazy thing, when my own sons are now grown and gone? Extra washing, PTA, homework, adolescence, ugh!'"

But this student exchange arrangement worked out wonderfully well, and later this R.N. host visited the families of these young men in France and in Germany. Indeed, recently this student exchange hostess enjoyed six weeks in Germany and later on the French Riviera as a guest of the German student's parents. "You can see," she writes, "how exchanging has expanded and enriched my life—far beyond my wildest dreams!"

Two "distant cousins" of vacation home exchange are the "service" exchange and the "employment" exchange.

In the "service" exchange, the guest provides the host with a service of some kind in return for occupying the home. Oftentimes, the service offered is simply "house sitting" while the host and his family are off on vacation and prefer not to leave their home unoccupied.

A New York City school guidance counselor—a seven-time exchanger—occupied the Saint Croix, U.S. Virgin Islands, home of a person who was hospitalized after surgery. "We enjoyed our midwinter vacation," she writes, "in a home surrounded by a wonderful, blooming garden, with the most beautiful views I've ever seen of land, ocean, and islands."

Two teachers, a husband and wife living in Universal City, Texas, have traveled afar as vacation home exchangers: Paris, London, Germany, and Hawaii. In more recent years, however, they have enjoyed house sitting for others. "I take better care," this woman writes, "of other people's homes than I would of my own. I'm very careful, considerate, particular, neat, tidy and clean. I do not smoke, drink, or (heaven forbid!) take drugs . . . and when we leave a home, it's the same, or better than when we arrived!"

An exchanger who owns a hotel in Aspen, Colorado, offers his vacation exchange partners one of his lodge's two- or three-bedroom apartments. Of course, this hotelier receives no rent for his exchange apartments, but he, his wife, and their young child "have had exchange vacations in Florida, Hawaii, Jamaica, and Spain. On our first exchange in Florida, we bought the condo next door (which we still own), and in Jamaica our 'cottage' came with a private pool and beach, a cook and a butler (who would not let us lift a finger), a gardener, and a car!"

With the cost of commercial dog and cat kennels skyrocketing, vacationers often are on the lookout for pet sitters. On short notice a London home exchanger decided to spend two weeks around Christmas in the U.S. But what to do with her two German shepherds? The kennel route was ruled out, because these particular animals like to "have loving people around." Why not, she thought, try a "pet-sitting" exchange? From a home exchange directory, this lady selected thirty-five potential last-minute pet sitters. Out went the letters. In no time, responses were in from eighteen couples—eight were not interested; the remaining *ten* were. A few letters and a few phone calls later, the dogs' owner had a worry-free vacation in the U.S. The pet sitter (who was "a lovely, independent, and utterly reliable woman from Montreal") enjoyed Christmas in London, and the dogs had a loving person around!

Then there is the "employment" exchange—a natural for families who own second homes in desirable resort areas. Their place needs painting, wallpapering, electrical work, plumbing, or whatever. Arrangements can be made with skilled men and women to move into the home, do the necessary work, and then stay on for a week or two of vacation. The cost? Sometimes no money is involved because the worker—on completion of the work—has enjoyed a free vacation. Other times, the homeowners pay modest fees, but certainly a lot less than if they were to commission local workers to do the jobs involved.

From Massachusetts, one who has had nine exchanges (all in the U.S.) writes: "We have become good friends with two of our exchange families and have been in their homes often. It's not unusual for them to phone and say they'll be away during a certain period and we'd be welcome to use their home if we wish."

A retired salesman with a second home in Florida writes: "After six years of vacation home exchanging in New England, New Jersey, Florida, and various cities in England, Germany, Spain, and Switzerland—with repeat exchanges in nearly every instance—my wife and I have reached what we believe is a unique position in home exchanging, and one which can be attained by other multi-time exchangers. Over the years we have developed close friendships with half-a-dozen exchangers in the U.S. and in Europe. These people know our latchstring's out to them; they can spend a couple or three weeks at our condo anytime it's not occupied, and we also feel quite comfortable picking up the phone and saying, 'We'd love to come to Cape Cod (or London, Nuremberg, Cannes, or wherever) in the spring (or whenever) for three weeks. How does your exchange schedule stack up for May 1 through 21?' We don't always connect on Choice #1, but at least we're a sure bet for Choice #2 (my wife calls this 'armchair' exchanging). There are, however, two catches to this system: 1. you have to like repeat exchanges, and 2. you have to plan at least a year ahead. But, listen, I'm retired. And one thing I've got lots of is time!"

This type of exchange arrangement could rightly be called a "red carpet" exchange, because the exchangers concerned truly do roll out their red carpets to each other by endeavoring to accommodate each other in their respective vacation home exchange scheduling.

Indeed, there are many, many ways—through exchanges or otherwise—in which one's home (or second home) can play an important role in a homeowner's vacation plans and in those of others, as well.

6 Making Arrangements for Your Dream Vacation: Part 1

THERE ARE TWO WAYS TO get into the vacation home exchange "game." One way is for *you* to take the initiative by seeking out home-exchange-minded people who are offering for exchange homes that you feel would meet your vacation needs. The other way is for *others* to take the initiative in seeking you out because they feel the home you are offering for exchange would meet their vacation needs. Either way, both parties stand to win.

Okay . . . But where can you find these potential home exchange partners? What *resources* are available to put potential home exchange partners in touch with each other? The directories, newsletters, and other types of listings prepared and released by various regional, national, and international vacation home exchange clubs constitute, by far, the best available resources for home exchangers' reference and use. Most are not clubs in the true sense of the word, for they have no initiation fees, no annual dues, and no membership, as such. They simply charge for a home exchange listing in their respective directories or newsletters. Complete information about these home exchange resources appears in this book's Reference Center (pages 197–201).

For experienced home exchangers, and those new to this vacation concept, perhaps the best resources are the clubs offering the largest numbers of listings. These larger clubs regularly list vacation exchange homes in the largest and smallest cities and towns throughout the U.S., including Alaska and Hawaii. Some also list international resources, featuring vacation home exchange listings in as many as forty different countries.

If you have not yet arranged for your home to be included in the listing of a vacation home exchange organization (and we will deal with this procedure in chapter 7), *taking the initiative* will be your first step.

But when does one take the initiative? The survey shows that 60 percent of exchangers start their home exchange arrangements four to six months in advance of their vacation dates. Another 25 percent make their initial contacts seven to twelve months ahead. Now and then successful home exchange arrangements are firmed up at the drop of a hat (or a coin in the phone box), but these cases are few and far between. It is an axiom that the more home exchange experience people have had, the more time they allow for their exchange arrangements. Conversely, those aspiring exchangers who endeavor to put together a successful exchange in a few weeks or a month or two are generally disappointed. A New Jersey businessman writes: "We now always allow a year or more to plan our European exchanges, and it's getting to a point where we have to allow more than six months planning time right here in the States. The early [home exchange] bird gets the [home exchange] worm!"

First you will need to secure *current* listing directories from several (or more) of the vacation home exchange listing organizations. (see Reference Center, pages 197–201). Usually there is a modest charge for these directories. With these resources in hand, you will be amazed at the in-depth nature of the listings included. With a few appropriate identification changes, here is the information given in a typical listing appearing in one of the recent home exchange directories:

ORLANDO, FLORIDA, U.S.A.

> Mr. and Mrs. Homer Exchanger are offering for exchange their one-floor home, located in a suburban community eight miles north of Orlando, Florida; with three bedrooms and two baths, five persons can be accommodated; young/older children okay; Walt Disney World nearby.
>
> Six years old, this centrally air-conditioned home features a fully equipped kitchen (including microwave oven and dishwasher), clothes washer-dryer, television/VCR/radio, sauna, large sundeck with barbeque, and a pool with a flagstone patio; weekly pool and yard care provided.
>
> The house is in a secluded neighborhood with a large yard. No pets please; shopping, tennis, golf nearby; car exchange preferred.
>
> In his mid-sixties, Mr. Exchanger is a retired business executive and an experienced home exchanger. Non-smokers, he and Mrs. Exchanger desire a one-floor exchange home (or condominium) in/near Williamsburg, Virginia, or in/near Boston, Massachusetts. Exchange dates desired: two or three weeks between June 1 and August 31, or in October; might consider other dates. Write/phone: Homer Exchanger, 18 Wilburn Place, Orlando, Florida 33855; (555-123-4567).

The above is the information this home exchange listing gives you. The organizations compiling and producing these listings often use classified-ad type abbreviations, and some listings codes (ac-air conditioning; sk-skiing nearby; fn-friendly neighbors; and so on). This coding of vacation home exchange listings certainly makes the directories more manageable, though some users feel that deciphering the codes takes an inordinate amount of effort and time. Thus abbreviated and coded, twenty to thirty different listings can appear on an 8½-by-11-inch page. Some listing organizations carry photos of homes with some of the listings; for photo use, there is generally a modest additional fee. The other advantage of coding is that a coded listing lends itself to use in foreign-language listings; that is, while the coding remains unchanged, the keys to the code can be in French, Spanish, German, and many other foreign languages.

Now back to your dream vacation. If your family has its sights set on a three-week Florida vacation in July and you own a home south of Boston, say, in Duxbury, Massachusetts, you might well find that your family and the exchangers listed above could become home exchange partners. You could enjoy staying in their home, seeing Walt

Disney World and other wonders of Orlando, Florida, and using "your" centrally located Orlando home as a base for automobile day trips to many points in Florida. The exchangers, in turn, would find your Duxbury home perfect for sightseeing in and around Boston, visiting relatives on Cape Cod, or just plain relaxing in "their" New England home!

While the exchangers' listing indicates their interest in a car exchange, your family of four would probably be driving your own car to Florida, so the exchangers would either have to take their own car north or make other transportation arrangements.

Finally, note that the exchangers are retired and are experienced home exchangers. The former is important because retired persons usually can be more flexible in the important date-setting aspect of the home exchange arrangement. The latter is important because experience in home exchanging can be as helpful as it can be in butchering, baking, and candlestick making! In perusing the home exchange listings, also watch for those that carry *two* addresses, a clue that the listing exchanger owns *two* homes. Why watch for such listings? Most second homes are in or near resort areas (ski resorts; oceanside or lake resorts; or condominium communities featuring tennis, golf, private swimming pools, and/or a variety of social activities). Perhaps one of these vacation-centered areas will be just right for you and your family. Those fortunate enough to own two homes can be quite flexible in their home exchange scheduling, and this could be important to you as you make your vacation home exchange arrangements.

In this case, it is the exchangers' home (not yours) that is listed for home exchange, so you must take the initiative and contact them, provided (1) you feel your home would meet *their* needs, as detailed in their listing; and (2) your and their dates (as given in their listing) are compatible.

The exchangers have given quite specific information as to where they would like to vacation: in or near Williamsburg, Virginia, or in/near Boston, Massachusetts. In many cases, however, those listing their homes for exchange are not specific as to where they would like to vacation, so you will frequently see "northeastern U.S." or "any seashore" or even "anywhere." As you review the various listings, watch for these more general destination indications, because, here again, very likely these exchangers will be more flexible in their home exchange arrangements.

Also on this matter of flexibility in planning, another lawyer (from West Palm Beach, Florida), who has exchanged in London and in Ireland, writes: "We have had our home listed in two different directories each year, and we have lost vacation home exchange opportunities, because we have decided *exactly* where and when we want to go. We have just not been flexible enough in our planning."

Do not—repeat—*do not* give in to what is perhaps a natural temptation to make your initial contact by telephone.

Why not phone? First, realize that there is a good chance other potential home exchangers may well be contacting the same people you are contacting, so you want those you contact to *remember you* and the home you are offering. More than likely, they will not remember the details of your telephone call. They will not recall whether you said June or July, and you will not recall whether they said two or three weeks, and they will not recall . . . and so on.

There is another reason for not telephoning initially. Remember, you have seen these people's listing in the home exchange directory, so you know something about them and a lot about the home *they* are offering to exchange. They, on the other hand, know nothing about you and nothing about the home you are offering to exchange. This information you simply cannot communicate in a brief telephone conversation—possibly a call that catches them during meal-time or happy hour or while the baby is being changed!

The exception proving the no-telephoning-initially rule: If for some reason—a developing exchange correspondence has gone wrong, illness, or a plain and simple slow start—your time is short, a phone call to a potential exchanger might just save the day and put you on a fast track to firming up a last-minute vacation home exchange arrangement.

With facsimile (FAX) machines being widely used in business communications by many individuals, an increasing number of home exchangers are faxing some of their vacation home exchange communications. It is fast, produces a written document (and photographs), and is relatively inexpensive.

Unlike conventional vacation planning with travel agents, elaborate tour brochures, advance deposits, and so on, vacation home exchanging is decidedly *personal* in nature. After all, your eventual exchange partners are going to be *living* in your home, sleeping in your beds, and you in theirs, so home exchange communication must be on a personal, friendly basis.

The initial contact should definitely be made in a personal (or faxed) letter, typewritten if at all possible. The suggested Initial Contact Letter (see Reference Center, page 204) need not be lengthy but should include the following:

1. The name of the directory in which you saw their listing;
2. An indication of your possible interest in home exchanging with them;
3. Any questions you still have about their home;
4. Any suggestions you wish to make about exchange dates, in the light of the exchange-date information given in their listing;
5. An interior and an exterior photograph of your home and possibly a photograph of those in your exchange group;
6. Reference should be made to the "Fact Sheet" attached to your covering letter.

Objectivity and honesty are of prime importance, not only in the preparation of your Fact Sheet, but in *all* areas of your vacation home exchange communications.

A retired U.S. Air Force officer living in Hampton, New Hampshire, writes: "When we arrived at our exchange home in England, we learned that along with the house and car, we also had—news to us—'Anna,' the cat! Now, neither my wife nor I are particularly fond of cats, but we did agree Anna could stay. On the third morning of our vacation, next to the milk bottle on the front step—neatly arranged and licked quite clean—was a dead mouse! At least, Anna had accepted *us*!" Exchangers from Eugene, Oregon, had been assured by their California host that the home had a swimming pool. "Right," they wrote, "but the pool was only half full, and the water was covered with moss and slime—unusable."

Five-time exchangers from the island of Barbados write: "It is important one knows how many people the exchange entails. We had stayed in our English host's second home in Marbella, Spain. Later, before he was due at our Barbados home, our exchange partner asked us to arrange a cradle for his one-year-old son; then he arrived also with a twelve-year-old daughter!" Teachers from Pacific Palisades, California, were "misled into believing we were getting a single family home in Great Britain, when actually it was a duplex."

Now, back to the Fact Sheet: on pages 202–03 of the Reference Center is a suggested Fact Sheet, one in which you give some information about yourself and those who will be traveling with you and information about your home and the community in which it is located.

Now this Fact Sheet is a very important document, important because a potential home exchanger will read it to decide whether your home meets his family's vacation needs and whether his family would feel comfortable having your family occupy their home. If this potential home exchange partner has a positive response to your Fact Sheet and he has good "vibes" about the possibility of exchanging with you, he will answer your letter. If he has a negative reaction to your Fact Sheet or he does not wish to exchange with you for other reasons, then either you will get back a "putting-aside-your-communication-for-future-reference" letter or no response at all.

View your Fact Sheet as a *sales* tool—the vehicle that encourages and motivates a potential home exchanger to be in further communication with you. Your Fact Sheet should be objective and must project an honest overview of your home and your family. At the same time, you need not mention that occasionally in humid weather your back door sticks or that your pool man sometimes overimbibes, missing a pool cleaning date!

This Fact Sheet can easily run to a couple of pages and should *definitely* be typed, as you will be using photocopies of it in your contacts with other potential home exchangers. But remember: *always* send a personally typed or handwritten *cover* letter with your Fact Sheet and photographs. Along this same vein, Geneva,

Switzerland, home exchangers received eighty-seven home exchange inquiries during a forty-five day period from their first listing in a vacation home exchange directory. Of these, only *six* were personally written. Since these exchangers—a busy working couple—could not possibly answer the eighty-one *form* letters, all of these were dumped into the wastebasket. Responses were mailed to the six persons who had taken the time to write personal letters. Following a series of letters back and forth—and several international phone conversations—this Geneva couple enjoyed a successful four-week exchange in Florida, and their Florida friends visited them the next year.

To how many different persons should you write? This depends entirely on the number of home exchangers who list homes where you would like to vacation and whose home exchange directory listings lead you to believe they might also be interested in vacationing at your home. If you carefully examine the listings, chances are you will want to write half a dozen, perhaps as many as ten or twelve or more, initial letters, each of which will be accompanied by your Fact Sheet and your photographs.

"Using a vacation home directory, I had written only three families who listed exchange homes in ski areas," writes the wife of an attorney whose main home is in New London, Connecticut. "One of these contacts telephoned and said they had never seen New England in the fall and wanted to use our Sherburne, Vermont, vacation home the next October, which they did. The following March we occupied their ski lodge in Breckenridge, Colorado, and this was a dream vacation come true: our family of nine having a skiing vacation together!"

In making a determination as to whom to write, of course your dream vacation guidelines are most helpful. But perhaps you hoped to go to Virginia Beach in early September, mostly because you like the ocean and your family wants to vacation in the Southeast. More than likely, Myrtle Beach or Hilton Head in South Carolina would suit you and your family members just as well as Virginia Beach. If so, write to those listed in all three of these southeastern Atlantic coastline resort areas, if you feel from their listing information that these people might be interested in exchanging with you. Maybe someone in Virginia Beach is offering just the right place for your family . . . but there is no way you are going to get these Virginia Beach home exchangers to vacation in your Cleveland, Ohio, home when their listing clearly states that their vacation sights are set on, say, Berlin!

The point is that within the general framework of their vacation aspirations, home exchangers should be as *flexible* as is possible, especially in *where* they go and in *when* they go.

Never underestimate the importance of first impressions. If you were going for a job interview, you would be wearing appropriate attire. If you were selling your home, you would have it spic-and-span clean, looking its very best. If you were going to meet your future mother- or father-in-law, you certainly would not take along an old girl (or boy) friend!

There is a story going around New York that one of the top women's fashion magazines had advertised widely for a particular type of model to be used on the cover of an upcoming issue: 5′7″ in height, slim, age 21 to 24, blonde hair, blue eyes. At the appropriate hour, a dozen models gathered for the all-important interview. Yes, they all looked alike, including one who brought along a *monkey* on a green leash. Any one of those women would have been perfect for this assignment, but the job went to the model with the monkey on the green leash! The interviewer just could not forget that monkey on the green leash!

Whether this is a true story is not the point. What *is* the point is that the potential home exchanger to whom you write will undoubtedly be receiving communications from others—perhaps many others. While mailing a monkey on a green leash would be a bit difficult, you do want your initial communication to stand out from the others, and you can do this. Yes, put your best foot forward with a well-written personal letter, the Fact Sheet, and your photographs.

To strengthen the positive first impression you want to make on this potential home exchanger, you might want to send a map of your area on which you indicate the location of your home (an architect in Tel Aviv, Israel, provides potential exchangers with three-color plans—interior/exterior—of the home he offers for exchange), the names, addresses, and telephone numbers of several persons with whom you have exchanged, or a "fan" letter from one or more of these persons, information about places of historical significance in your area (the survey underscored the fact that American home exchangers, by a large margin, rate places of historic significance over seashore, lakes/mountains, ski resorts, and other vacation destinations), or some other enclosures which will influence your potential home exchangers positively and will make them exclaim, "Hey, *this* is *one* exchange opportunity we should follow up on *right now*!"

7 Making Arrangements for Your Dream Vacation: Part 2

HAVING DEALT IN DEPTH IN chapter 6 with steps leading up to the initial vacation home exchange contact, the elements in the initial contact itself, and the ingredients that make up that all-important Fact Sheet, this chapter will focus on:

Trials, tragedies, and triumphs in the correspondence following up the initial vacation home exchange contact;
"Marketing" your home and community as a viable vacation home exchange destination;
The actual vacation home exchange arrangement.

If you get some positive responses from your initial contacts, you should then promptly acknowledge these responses with appropriate follow-up communications. As you move along through this "getting-to-know-each-other-and-our-homes" stage of the correspondence, there are a few matters related to home exchanging correspondence that you will want to bear in mind.

First, to maintain continuity in these correspondence exchanges, one person in your family (or vacation group) should handle all correspondence and, second, copies of all correspondence (photocopies or, carbon copies) should be kept in chronological order for future reference. Very likely, one person will handle all communications at the other end. As you move toward firming up a home exchange arrangement, you and your potential exchange partner will find yourselves becoming friends, writing and answering letters on a first-name basis.

Depending on how extensive their home exchange correspondence becomes, exchangers generally develop quick-reference filing systems tailored to their particular needs. It is surprising how often personal letters are undated. Be sure to date your letters and memos. If you file chronologically, it is maddening to have an undated letter pop up in your file; if you do receive such a letter, simply mark it with the date it was received and file it accordingly.

Before you go from the vacation planning stage to the correspondence stage, it is important that everyone in your vacation home exchange group is familiar with your vacation planning and plays an active role in putting together the vacation plan. After all, it is their vacation, too.

Further, as mentioned in chapter 6, you and your potential home exchange partner must be totally honest and open with each other each step of the way as the planning unfolds.

Finally, all matters related to the exchange must be in writing. Even the details of telephone calls should be noted in writing and dated.

By having one person at each end handling the correspondence; by having each correspondent involve his or her family in the developing arrangements; by having both sides of the exchange correspondence honest and open in their correspondence; and by putting into writing all matters related to the exchange, you will be taking a giant step toward avoiding possible serious misunderstandings as the exchange unfolds.

"An elderly handicapped woman exchanging with us," writes a retired Corpus Christi, Texas, engineer, "didn't tell us until a week before the departure that she would not be able to drive while here. Our nearest shopping center is two miles away. A last-minute scramble to find neighbors and friends who would take her shopping saved the day! Now, we include 'car necessary' in our exchange directory listings."

One serious misunderstanding just waiting to rear its ugly head in the world of home exchanging concerns smoking. "No smoking" is now a recognized fact of life in air, rail, bus, and taxi travel; in public buildings and in offices; in restaurants and in hotels; and now even in car rental. Today, some home exchangers include "no smokers, please" in their exchange directory listings. An increasing number of people do not permit smoking—especially cigar and pipe smoking—in their homes or cars. Also, many nonsmokers are uncomfortable when in the homes and cars of smokers. So this subject must be dealt with during the early stages of vacation home exchange correspondence.

When the preliminary correspondence reaches the point of a very good possibility of a home exchange materializing, you will find the remaining big obstacle is in the selection of mutually convenient vacation dates. The time frame of the actual exchange can be a very large fly in the ointment. Perhaps you and your home exchange partner both want to exchange during the first three weeks in August. No problem; you have a deal. More often than not, however, the date you want will not be the very same date your home exchange partner has in mind. If both parties to a potential exchange are firmly locked into the different dates, obviously you have no deal (though there is always a possibility of an exchange with this potential partner at some point in the future).

This matter of date selection may well challenge the understanding, patience, and flexibility of both parties to a potential exchange. However, if both parties are *genuinely* interested in vacationing in each other's homes, chances are this particular home exchange will eventually materialize. Home exchangers from Florida had three years of communication with a family in the Far East before they agreed upon a firm date. But all this effort finally developed into these people spending a month in Hong Kong and their Hong Kong partners and their two children spending a month in the U.S.

Another way around a date conflict: some experienced exchangers, particularly those with second homes, have developed a system of "banking" exchange time. Reports a nurse in Kansas City, Missouri: "We have two homes. When we find exchange partners who are just 'right' for us, but we can't seem to get together on the exchange dates, we arrange for them to use our second home (most of our exchange partners stay there anyway) for the length of the exchange—two or three weeks. But we don't go to their place at that same time. So, in effect, we have a 'credit' with them for two or three weeks at their place at some future date convenient to them and to us. This year we will pick up this credit and spend two weeks at their ski lodge in Aspen, Colorado, and they were at our home last summer." Some exchangers will thus build up credit (or banked exchange time) with two or three different partners for future vacations.

Understanding, patience, and *flexibility* are key elements in playing the vacation home exchange game and in the handling of the follow-up and follow-through correspondence. A retired accountant living in Jackson, Tennessee, writes: "I sent nearly a hundred initial letters requesting exchanges; ninety percent of my letters were ignored," but she persevered and was successful in arranging several exchanges, including one in Tucson, Arizona—house sitting.

"In my exchange directory listing, I gave 'California' as my destination choice," writes a London exchanger, "and I got a flood of letters—from lovely homes in San Francisco with pools (and one with a Mercedes!) to a man living in the desert in a car trailer! I should have stated in my listing that I wanted to go to Los Angeles!"

A "professional volunteer" from Nanuet, New York, felt she had been misinformed when told her initial home exchange letters should be photocopies: "I hand wrote my fifty-one letters. When I asked my eventual exchangers why they chose me, they said it was because my letters were handwritten." Aspiring vacation home exchangers, take heed: if you send your initial letters *handwritten*, you will turn heads at the other end of the correspondence exchange!

From her first listing in an exchange directory, a home exchanger in Majorca, Spain, received "more than fifty replies."

From Bracebridge, Ontario, Canada, a medical doctor says this: "I don't answer form letters. I find I must write ten letters to get one which may lead to an exchange." A lot of writing, yes. But by following this formula, this doctor and his wife have enjoyed twenty-two vacation home exchanges in ten years—four homes in France, three in Australia, and the others in Germany, the U.S., Italy, Portugal, Holland, and elsewhere.

A husband and wife (accountant and teacher) in Moss Point, Mississippi, write: "Our biggest complaint is that so many people simply do not respond at all. We always answer every inquiry we get, but when we send out fifty to seventy-five letters, we only get responses from fifteen to twenty." Nevertheless, this couple has had five successful home exchanges in Illinois, Louisiana, Pennsylvania, New Hampshire, and Colorado.

"Vacation home exchanging is becoming very popular *and* competitive. Therefore, it's important for the exchange correspondent to move fast and intelligently in the initial contact and in all follow-up communications," says a retired marketing executive now living at Hilton Head Island, South Carolina.

From a husband-wife team (apartment owners/managers) in Santa Barbara, California, who have had seven home exchanges in the U.S. and in Europe: "When we were arranging an exchange in Germany, we had twenty replies to our initial letters. Of these, three families were very anxious to come to our home. [During the correspondence that followed] we had to keep three families 'on the string' [until our decision was made]; then the other two were really disappointed."

From a working mother (caterer for corporate directors' luncheons) living within a stone's throw of London's Hyde Park: "Last year I got fifty-six replies and could not cope, so I went to stay with a friend in Providence, Rhode Island! Now I'm corresponding with a couple in California for an exchange next summer."

"The vacation home exchange correspondence is basically satisfactory," writes a civil servant from Gasteiz, Spain, "but obstacles must be overcome, for example, some offers must be excluded because of the size of family, others due to date conflicts, and still others due to the types and qualities of accommodations offered. So the number of real 'possibilities' may turn out to be very limited. It *does* work, though, as long as you and your corresponding partners are realistic about what you are offering and what you can reasonably expect to get."

The preceding potpourri of comments from experienced vacation home exchangers in the Far East, the U.S., Europe, and Canada make clear that vacation home exchange correspondence is no Sunday school picnic. On the contrary, it is a veritable obstacle course, with exchangers endeavoring to put together the best possible vacations for their vacation groups. Once again, success depends on all parties to the potential exchange having full measures of understanding, patience, and flexibility.

It is more than likely that you and your home exchange correspondence partners will be in communication with other potential home exchangers. You each may have two or three lines of communication going on at the same time. Within the U.S., this is not much of a problem, as first-class letters from one state to another usually will be delivered in two or three days. Nevertheless, all parties to the correspondence should answer letters *promptly*. This is especially true when you go international in your vacation home exchange aspirations. When *you* can fly from anywhere in the U.S. to London in less than twelve hours, why it takes an airmail letter seven to ten days to make the same trip has to be one of the great mysteries of the 1990s! Nevertheless, there you are—seven to ten days over, a few days for the letter to be answered, and seven to ten days back. You wind up waiting two to three weeks to get a simple question answered, such as "How about us deciding on the last two weeks in July for our vacation home exchange?"

Up to now in the negotiations, using the telephone has been a no-no. But when a quick decision is necessary, that is the time to use the telephone (or a FAX machine, if you and your home exchange partner have access to FAX machines) to get last-minute details squared away for the home exchange arrangement.

With the passing of several months, exchanges of letters and photographs, plus a phone call or two and much discussion and difference of opinion among your family members ("This is the place to stay, it's got a pool"; "No, this one's right on a golf course!"; "Wow! A week in Copenhagen"; "Hey, look here, a half-mile from Disneyland"; "Ooohhh, Barbados—let's go there"), you will finally make a decision as to *where* to go, *when* to go, and *with whom* you will exchange homes. At this point you are well along the way to your vacation home exchange.

Heretofore, emphasis has been placed on the home exchange efforts that have come about because *you* took the initiative, because you sought out appropriate partners through the use of the available home exchange directories, newsletters, and listings. Why did people not seek you out? Very simple: your home has not yet been listed in any of the vacation home exchange resources. You have been playing "vacation home exchange" with only one foot in the game. Get *both* feet in by arranging for your home to be listed in several of the existing resources. Then, as new resources with your home listed are released, *others* will take the initiative by contacting you.

If your home is in an "in-demand" vacation area—and there are far too many of these to attempt to list at this point—do not be surprised if you receive fifty, seventy-five, or more exchange communications within two or three months of your initial listings in two or three of the major club directories. If your home is in an area not known as a vacation destination, you will receive fewer communications. But remember, vacation home exchanging is like real estate: it just takes one right person to make a deal.

To get your home into the home exchange marketplace, select two or three (or more) of the vacation home exchange clubs. See pages 197–201 and write each for a listing application form and complete information, including insertion fees, deadline dates for completed listing applications, listing publication dates, and whether or not home photographs accompanying listings are acceptable. Again, do not telephone. If you telephone, the odds are you will not get all of the material you request.

When you receive a listing application, have a couple of photocopies made (ten cents each at Sir Speedy), then carefully read all the listing instructions. If the instructions are not clear to you, this is the time to telephone the club for clarification. We believe you will find that the data on the Fact Sheet descriptive of your home will provide you with all the information you will need for the application. Use a photocopy of the application as your worksheet; then you will not mess up the original, the one to be returned to the club. Type or print this application form carefully, following the club's instructions (if a form calls for a 25-word description of your home, give them 25 words, not 35 or 40). If you decide to incorporate a photo with your listing, be sure you select a photo with high color contrast (dark and light). Otherwise, when your photo is reproduced with your listing, it will lack clear definition. It will look something like a black "smudge," and no one wants to vacation in a black smudge!

When you have finished filling out the application, photocopy the completed original (back to Sir Speedy) for your files and send the original to the club—with or without a photograph—and with a check covering the listing fee. Generally these fees are minimal, when you realize that one listing brings your home to the attention of hundreds—more likely, thousands—of persons, nearly all of whom are interested in the vacation home exchange concept. Along New York's Madison Avenue, this is a textbook case of "targeting the market."

But there are other resources, as a London medical doctor home exchanger found. While enjoying an August vacation at a rented home in a Florida resort area, this doctor and his wife thought it would be great to return there for the Christmas holidays. So off the good doctor went to the classified advertising desk of the weekly newspaper serving the resort area. He was putting together the ad: "English family desires to exchange home in London's fashionable Kensington district for private home with pool during upcoming Christmas holidays." Suddenly the woman at the desk said, "Okay, you can stop right here. My husband and I have just the right home here, with a large pool, for you and your family. And we would *love* to have a Christmas holiday in London!" There were three nice things about this experience—four, actually. First, it is a bonus to a home exchange arrangement when both parties can meet before the exchange date. Second, there was clearly no date-selection problem. Third, all concerned enjoyed their Christmas holidays and are now totally sold on home exchange as a viable vacation concept. And the fourth? Well, this London doctor got away without having to pay the newspaper's classified ad fee!

To attain maximum exposure for their home exchange aspirations, some exchangers run classified ads in newspapers serving the areas in which they would like to locate a home exchange partner, plus similar ads in their high-school or college alumni bulletins or newsletters. These are certainly worth a try. Such ads should include some information about the individuals in your exchange group and should emphasize details about the home you offer for exchange, the number of persons in your group, your date preferences, and the area (or areas) in which you would like to vacation. One sure way to increase the number of responses for these ads is not to use a box number for responses, as many classified advertisers do. Rather, include in the ad your name and address in full (no telephone number). By including your name and address, you may attract a few "kook" letters, but by so doing you will also stand a good chance of doubling the number of responses to the ads.

Important, too, is not being shy about mentioning your vacation home exchange plans: tell your relatives, friends, pastor, fellow church members, doctors, Rotary, and other service club friends. Tell anyone who will listen that you are offering your home in exchange for a vacation home in Richmond, Virginia; Richmond, Indiana; Richmond (Surrey), England; Richmond, California; Richmond, wherever. By so doing, some home exchangers have had vacation home exchange opportunities come right out of the woodwork! Initially, you will find some of those with whom you speak are just a bit nervous about the idea of actually *living* in someone else's home. They will have questions, which you will easily answer, and very likely they will become interested in hearing about your vacation home exchange experiences.

"In Norway we were interviewed by the local newspaper. We invited the young reporter to 'our' home for lunch. He, in turn, wrote a delightful article about vacation home exchanging, which ran with our picture in the paper." So writes a Falls Church, Virginia, retired officer for the U.S. Defense Intelligence Agency and his retired teacher wife. And a teacher in North Andover, Massachusetts, writes: "The kids and I appeared on Boston TV to be interviewed about vacation home exchanging." Media exposure helps promote the exchanger's own home and, in general, showcases home exchange as a viable vacation concept to many others.

A young couple in England wrote to their friend in Tasmania and told her they were toying with the idea of arranging for a hospitality home exchange in Toronto, Canada. Back from Tasmania came, "Oh, you should write to my friend living in Toronto." A few exchanges of correspondence ensued, and some months later this young couple's hopes for a hospitality home exchange in Canada became a happening. A New Hampshire realtor makes this suggestion: "We mail videotapes of various homes to potential buyers not living in our area. Home exchangers also could easily videotape their homes inside and out, mailing the tapes to potential home exchange partners."

Eleven-time (from Hawaii to Denmark) San Francisco exchangers "network" their way in home exchanging: "For instance, we traded with a couple living in a New York City apartment. While there, we talked to others in the same building and now have exchanged with some of them as well. At home and on the road we establish our home exchanging 'reputation' and thus have had many home exchange doors opened to us."

A Hilton Head, South Carolina, multitime exchanger met with home exchange friends, a young couple in Kent, England. In the discussion, these young people mentioned they would love to spend a couple of weeks skiing in France the following winter. The South Carolinian has an exchange friend in the south of France who has a ski lodge in the French Pyrenees. He wrote his French friend asking if he would like to arrange a three-way exchange: The English couple to the ski lodge in France, the French family to Hilton Head, and the family from South Carolina to Kent. By return mail came the letter from France: "Exchange folks are a great, happy family. Yes, of course, I will write your English friends. We can accommodate them, and we will enjoy the sun and fun next summer at Hilton Head." A few letters between France and England, and Hilton Head and England, set this three-way international exchange plan in motion.

If your home is in a home exchange "in-demand" area—and if

you list it in one or more of the vacation home exchange directories—you may find yourself at the receiving end of the initial home exchange correspondence. A retired educator living in Denver, Colorado, a seven-time exchanger, writes: "We have never initiated a request for a home exchange, because our second home is in the middle of six Colorado ski areas; as a result, we get vacation home exchange requests from all over the world." Retired after thirty-one years with General Motors, a six-time national and international home exchanger now living near Los Angeles, California, writes: "Though we still list our home in a home exchange directory, and we do send out some letters, our most successful exchanges are those with people who have contacted us."

There is another side to making contact. What if your home is in an area (or country) not frequented by large numbers of vacationers?

From Middleton, Wisconsin: "Despite the fact that I listed our home in a home exchange directory a year ago, we have thus far had no requests for an exchange."

From Brown's Bay, New Zealand: "I hope you have more success with your book than I have had with home exchanging!"

From Turun, Poland: "I did give my announcement in a home exchange book . . . but till now I have only four inquiries and one exchange—in Germany. Maybe Poland or my city is not attractive."

If you happen to live off the beaten track, it behooves you to take aggressive action. Do not simply list your home in a directory or two; list it in six or eight directories. And then do not sit back and wait for the mail each day. Decide where you would like to go and when you would like to go, and prepare a good "selling" Fact Sheet. Pick out of the directories a hundred or *two* hundred listings in places where you would like to vacation. Then get photocopies of your Fact Sheets, and make a massive mailing. To personalize your mailing, put a brief handwritten memo on each Fact Sheet. Make a commitment to yourself: I *will* vacation home exchange *someplace* next summer! Accept this commitment as a *challenge* and work hard toward attaining your goal: a vacation home exchange next summer!

Alpharetta, Georgia; Fontana, Wisconsin; Port Ludlow, Washington; Manchester, Connecticut; Johnson City, Tennessee; Kenilworth, Illinois; Yadkinville, North Carolina . . . to say nothing of Norway, Turkey, Yugoslavia, Zimbabwe, Liechtenstein, the Dominican Republic. In hundreds—indeed, thousands—of cities and towns in the U.S. and throughout the world, there is vacation home exchange activity. To make successful contacts, however, some aspiring exchangers simply have to work harder—a lot harder—than others. Contacting interested vacationers is like fishing. The men, women, and young people who are out there fishing frequently—really working at it—are the ones who are catching the fish!

Now, the home exchange arrangement: "Arrangement" may sound a bit forbidding. It need not be. In fact, as the home exchange letters go back and forth, many elements of the arrangement will have been agreed upon by you and your home exchange partners (the dates, facilities available, acceptability of young children, pets and no pets, car exchange, and so on).

Here are a few additional elements of the home exchange arrangement to be considered:

1. *Use of telephone*—see pages 103-104.
2. *Use of utilities*—water, gas, electric bills (the host partner covers these charges);
3. *Liability insurance*—check this out with your insurance agent, but chances are your policies will cover your partner and his family, just as they would cover any guest in your home;
4. *Overnight guests*—home exchange partners should share with each other if and when they are to have overnight guests. After all, it is your home, and you want to know who is staying in it;
5. *Pets*—dogs, cats. Acceptable or not? For obvious reasons, many home exchangers do not wish pets to be a part of the arrangements, but there are exceptions, and these exceptions should, of course, be acceptable to both parties to the exchange;
6. *House problems*—plumbing, roof leaks, electric, appliances, etc. The host partner covers the cost of necessary repairs;
7. *House cleaning*—the host partner makes the home available thoroughly cleaned. It is the guest partner's responsibility to keep the home clean and neat during the exchange period and to clean it thoroughly on departure, unless other arrangements have been agreed upon by the two partners;
8. *Damage*—to appliances, to items provided by the host partner, and to the home itself. Generally the guest partner accepts responsibility for such damage;
9. *Cooking utensils, dishes/flatwater, linens*—all are supplied by the host partner.

In preparing for a home exchange, some exchangers feel more "comfortable" if they develop a document that summarizes the more important elements of the home exchange arrangement. This could be put together in a form of a "contract" or a less formal letter-agreement, the terms of which would be acceptable to both partners. A document like this can easily be prepared (see Reference Center). At the same time, many (if not most) exchangers do not feel it is necessary to enter into a "formal" arrangement with their home exchange partners. After all, even if you have not yet met them, your home exchange partners are "friends," welcome guests in your home, just as you are welcome guests in their homes.

Nevertheless, items such as those listed above—and others which may occur to you or your partner—should be dealt with in the various exchanges of correspondence before the exchange date. Remember: a contract is only as good as those whose signatures it bears.

Many, if not most, exchangers go without formal contracts because they feel reasonable people can solve reasonable problems. And certainly the vast majority of home exchanges are reasonable in every sense of the word.

8 More People Who Tried It . . . and Liked It

Gay Burch is her name, and Scrabble is her game. Yes, now retired, Gay has been a professional poker player, a Las Vegas, Nevada, casino dealer, a singer, an executive on Wall Street, and a private detective. Among her primary interests now are her daughter (who serves in the Los Angeles County sheriff's department), directing several Scrabble clubs and tournaments in Las Vegas, and home exchanging. Gay has exchanged in twenty-eight different countries; her goal now is to exchange in all fifty U.S. states—fifteen down, thirty-five to go. What does she like best about vacation home exchanging? "Oh, the people, the people; home exchangers are the most wonderful people in the world!"

Gay Burch writes . . .

Like Hawaii, London, Orlando, Florida (Walt Disney World), and Paris, Las Vegas is a natural for home exchanging. From my listings in a vacation home directory, each year, I receive scores of letters and phone calls from potential home exchangers in all parts of the world—people who want to vacation [or hospitality] home exchange here in Las Vegas. I answer every single communication I receive, and from this correspondence I have more exchange opportunities than any *six* home exchangers could ever arrange! And I manage to line up home or hospitality exchanges everywhere, always just wishing I could find *more time* to enjoy the wonderful world of vacation home exchanging!

Let me tell you about one of the most memorable home exchange vacations I have ever taken.

It all started with a letter from a family in Roquemaure, near Avignon, in the South of France. These folks (with their two teenagers) wanted to arrange a five- to six-week exchange with me—a simultaneous exchange, their home in France for mine in Las Vegas. We exchanged photographs of our homes and ourselves. There was no "convincing" necessary on either side. Shortly, they and we were packed, ready to enjoy each other's homes, cars, and countries. I had decided to make this trip with my friend Jeanie, a particularly appropriate traveling companion, since Jeanie's condo in Florida was also available to our exchange partners. Roquemaure would be our home base, and we would travel out from there to explore France, Monaco, and Italy.

My friends at AAA provided us with invaluable maps of southern Europe and stacks of travel brochures. I laid these out on a table, side by side with the latest V.E.C. directory, and in no time had a sunburst of lines in every direction from Roquemaure, endeavoring to find a home exchange family at the end of each line.

In June, I airmailed letters describing ourselves, our homes, our cities, and our travel aspirations to forty-five potential exchangers. Remarkably, within a month's time I had received positive responses from twenty-four different home exchange families. There was also a phone call from "Georges" in Monaco. (Awaiting me on my return to Las Vegas weeks later were four *more* acceptance letters, and one arrived several *years* later with, would you believe, an apology for not responding sooner!)

Because time was very short, I quickly sent postcards to them all, advising them that we would telephone them on our arrival in Europe to square away the actual exchange arrangements.

Our first exchanger sent a car to meet us at Paris' Orly Airport. Not speaking English, the driver gave us a letter (in English) stating he would take us to lunch and then to the station for our train trip to Avignon. As neither the driver nor we were bilingual, it was one strange lunch, but we muddled through with big smiles and good intentions.

On the train's arrival, we were met by our Roquemaure exchange partners, who gave us a quick tour of their house and its nuances prior to their leaving the next morning for the States.

Before leaving home, we had decided that on this particular trip Jeanie would do the cooking and the cleaning and I would be the chief driver, telephoner, and trip planner. So I called Georges. The next day we left for Monaco, where we were to meet Georges at a predetermined point on the freeway. Following Georges on his motor-

cycle, we were guided to his "extra" apartment overlooking Monaco Bay. It was just beautiful. Bachelor Georges was an English-speaking disc jockey.

Most tourists head for Monaco's casino, but Georges showed us all the things and places tourists never see. Then Georges left for Las Vegas where—with a phone call and some quick planning—he and his friend were house guests of my sister, Elizabeth. Elizabeth is an invaluable aid in my home exchange arrangements. She lives just across the street from my home and helps with the house and car keys, the sightseeing, and the questions—oh, so many questions in oh, so many languages! My exchange partners are well cared for in Las Vegas. Every home exchanger should be so lucky as to have a sister like Elizabeth!

Our next [too] hastily planned home exchange point was in Reggio Emilia, Italy. When we arrived there in our trusty exchange car, because of a misunderstanding we were not able to connect with our exchange partner; he had other guests. So we drove on to Florence, where our exchange partner and his wife had left for the weekend with no apparent arrangements made for us. We phoned Sara, who lives quite near Venice. Could we come a few days earlier than planned? Sara was a darling—and a "no problem" (in English) person. Not only was she our hospitality hostess, but she spent a weekend showing us around Venice (the fabulous "Floating City"), and she also got together a number of her English-speaking friends to honor Jeanie and me at a special party! During the next week we did a lot of sightseeing and followed up on other home exchange contacts. On our last day in Florence, we arranged for Sara to visit Las Vegas and Florida, which indeed she did the following winter.

Wherever we went, our gifts to our hosts were bottles of wine we had purchased in France (some for as little as twenty-seven cents a litre). For the children we had bubble gum, John F. Kennedy fifty-cent pieces, and other small souvenirs.

After Italy, we returned to our "hub" city of Roquemaure and enjoyed a week of day trips in the south of France. Our French hosts, of course, were still in the States, but their neighbors and various home exchangers in the area rolled out their red carpets for us. Avignon was having its annual music festival, and we also attended a performance of *Carmen* in the magnificently acousticized outdoor theater in Orange, France. Much to see, much to do—many more kilometers to go in our little exchange car!

Now, do not think the home exchange life is always a bowl of cherries. Oh, no! During the week we had a kitchen sink problem; it was hopelessly stopped up. With our trusty English-French dictionary in hand, we endeavored to seek the help of our neighbors. We got nowhere. In fact, one lady came over to look at our house, which she understood to be "sinking!" Not "sinking," but "kitchen sink." We did finally get the message across, however, because a man soon appeared with a plunger. Problem solved! Would he accept a few francs for his effort? No, but he did invite us to join his family for dinner!

And our host's garden, with its marvelous pear-shaped tomatoes, peppers, potatoes, onions, strawberries! We really did a number on that garden, which was carefully tended by the gardener each morning. Toward the end of our stay, we learned that our *host's* garden was on the other side of the property. All this time we had been enjoying the neighbor's garden!

Yet *another* of our host's friends invited us to his home for dinner—fifty miles from Roquemaure. They asked us to spend the night so the following day we could visit the gorges of Ardeche. What a sight—truly a Grand Canyon in miniature. These newfound friends (Gerard and Danielle) also absolutely insisted that Jeanie and I spend a long weekend at their lovely condominium near Nice. Grand Motte was the name of the town, which had a commanding view of the Mediterranean and the beach and the boardwalk below.

The next week Alain and Lydie (home exchangers who had been in Las Vegas a few years before) were sweet enough to invite us to Privas for a few days. Their home is a reconstructed thirteenth-century castle, put together stone by stone. While some of the original interior has been preserved, today the home is thoroughly modern. Our "few days" were extended to a full week of sightseeing and fellowship with Alain and Lydie's daughters, Helène and Delphine. Who could forget the freshly picked wild raspberries for breakfast, blackberries for lunch, and Alain's marvelous soufflé for dinner, with a special brandied dessert!

The final European leg of our trip was returning to Paris, where we were house guests of Christian and Janine. As their sons were away, there was ample room for us in their apartment, which was located just a few blocks from the Seine, near Notre Dame. The last days of our trip were also memorable: strolling the bookstall-lined streets while pinching ourselves that we were actually in Paris, seeing Versailles, the Eiffel Tower, Montmartre, the Champs Élysées, and many more of the Parisian places and things we had read and heard about for so many years.

We cried a lot during this trip at the beauty of the countries and (especially) at the beauty of the people and all of their kindnesses toward us. Happily, we still correspond with these friends in France, Monaco, and Italy, and notes at Christmas keep us in touch. Some have visited Jeanie's home in Florida. Others have come to Las Vegas, and we have been fortunate in being able to assist still others in staying at the homes of friends and family members in Las Vegas and elsewhere in the States.

Never in a million years could we possibly have duplicated this trip to Europe for less than thousands of dollars. However, traveling as we did as home and hospitality exchangers, the cost to each of us for this five-week vacation exchange trip, excluding airfare, was a bargain in any currency: just $200!

Mary and Derek Evans live in London, England, where they have their own business management consultancy; their second home is a completely modernized eighteenth-century cottage in Oxfordshire. Active radicals in the 1960s and early '70s, they now refer to themselves (slightly tongue in cheek) as armchair politicos. Mary loves shopping, writes a personal problem page for a local newspaper, and is training to be a psychotherapist. Derek loathes shopping and is hooked on spelunking (exploring caves). Derek's seventy-year-old mother, Clarissa, has come out of retirement to become their bookkeeper. She accompanied Mary and Derek on their first vacation home exchange to the U.S., but unfortunately failed to find the sugar daddy and/or toy boy that has become her latter life's ambition!

Mary and Derek Evans write:

There's no denying it, we felt very apprehensive. We took one last look at the layout of the kitchen and, particularly, our little "presentation." It would be the first thing our home exchangers saw when they entered our Oxfordshire cottage. A gift-wrapped bottle of champagne on the centre of the table, tied with a pretty red bow and welcome card, the neat pile of guide books and maps, and the information pack containing those all-important instructions for operating the cottage's appliances.

Overkill? We had no way of knowing. Was our cleanup thorough enough? We suspected Americans were keen on an unusually high standard of cleanliness and hygiene. We think we got this idea from watching "Dynasty." We gazed at the sparkling kitchen surface, the perfectly transparent windows offering sharply focused vistas of the neat English countryside, and there was not one speck of dust visible to the human eye—we swear it. We stood proud after a weekend of sucking up dirt like it had never been sucked up before. Ants, spiders, and other small insects were sent scurrying for their lives as the vacuum hose flailed in a frenzied sword dance, jabbing into corners, ruffling up the carpet pile, glancing across ceilings, and thrusting under the furniture. There was enough activity that weekend to provide sufficient material for a thousand TV commercials. We dusted, sponged, and polished, using every conceivable product known to man or woman. We couldn't muster that aren't-we-the-clever-ones, self-satisfied smiles that these model housewives have. We just sweated, cursed, and squabbled with each other!

Pleased with the results of our efforts, we hoped our exchangers would like the place . . . but had some nagging doubts. We were still a little uptight as we closed the front door and drove back to London—off to the Gulf Coast of Florida.

All of this came out of a chance meeting the summer before. Our favourite pub, The Churchill Arms, in Kensington Church Street (named after the great British statesman) was, in retrospect, perfectly symbolic, since the walls of its oak-paneled interior displayed pictures and photographs, past and present, of all the British prime ministers and all the American presidents, side by side. Although a popular tourist area of Central London, with many antique shops and the Portobello Road street market close by, this pub is a local haunt of residents, and not that many tourists find their way in there. But then, our newfound friends were not strictly tourists anyway. They were living as "residents" in an exchange home just around the corner.

So they knew the pub and already had an idea of the sorts of characters who frequented the place. Some were in recognizable groups, occupying their favoured territory around the large, three-sided bar area. The all-male, manual worker team, who between them sit on the same bar stools and occupy the same six feet of counter space every evening. The oldtimers—the actors, actresses, and artists who have been in the area a very long time, long before it really got trendy. Their longevity and fading fortunes give a kind of sad aura about them, although they still maintain a certain elegance and style. And what a contrast they are to the young, eager real estate agents who go in there; the visible face of the New Britain, flaunting their "successes" in designer casual wear and brash, confident chatter, for The Churchill, certainly in the evenings, is a young persons' pub, a seething mass of middle-class optimism with apparently money to burn.

So George and Betty from the Gulf Coast of Florida stood out a bit, but there's such a diversity of clientele, it doesn't really matter. It's all held together by the quality of the beer and the personal style of the Irish landlord. Fuller's beer is one of the strongest in Britain and what we call "Real Ale." It's brewed entirely from natural ingredients a few miles away at a small independent brewery; it continues fermenting in the beer cask, and is dispensed or "pulled" by hand-pump without resorting to pressurised carbon dioxide. For the serious beer drinker it can't be any other way. Now that typical Irish charm of the landlord is a matter of taste, or in our case depending on how we are feeling at the time. He's a butterfly enthusiast, and adorning the walls are dozens of displays of framed, pinned, stuffed (do they stuff butterflies?) and breeding, yes, breeding butterflies. The landlord flits like a butterfly from customer to customer, only settling long enough to exchange the most cursory of social niceties. He always has a smile, makes a lot of effort to remember customers' names, and looks after the beer really well, but is rather short on eye contact.

Anyway, this is all to set the scene for what happened next. We spotted this middle-aged American couple in the back of the pub and spontaneously opened up a conversation with them. It was small talk about typical British summers (it was raining at the time), but this led on to things much more interesting. Our newfound friends were no strangers to Britain and were hooked on it, in a way we, after our third American home exchange, have become hooked on the States. This first meeting, in a very peculiarly British cultural setting, was the key, thanks to George and Betty, to a series of marvelous experiences through international vacation home exchanging.

One big plus for both of us was that we were swapping vacation homes. Our small, cozy 250-year-old cottage made of local stone with three-foot thick walls and leaded glass windows, set in the gently rolling hills of rural England, swapped with a modern, spacious, fourth-floor condominium with swimming pool, tennis courts, and expansive views of the Gulf of Mexico. What a contrast! What was more significant for us was the culture swap. We had made an effort to set up contacts for our exchangers to enable them to get a quick induction into village life and culture. Our eighty-two-year-old gardener was a real hit. His life experiences are so varied and interesting, and he tells his stories with such humor and enthusiasm that you can't help but just sit there and lap it all up. Stories about World War II in the Middle East, stories about country life in which he still plays an active part: fishing, fox hunting, eventing (horse jumping), and working dogs. The stories he tells with most relish are those involving the "landed gentry" or the aristocracy. Scandals involving the private lives and business activities of lords and ladies are classic. And not the least, his experience of living thirty-five years in our little village and all the social changes he had seen.

Some home exchangers make a conscious decision not to mix with their opposite numbers, but for us it's the thing that turns a holiday into something quite special. We met up with our first American exchangers on a number of occasions and also spent a fascinating evening with close friends of theirs from Macon, Georgia, now retired to Florida. The hospitality we received was something new to us, and giving thanks for the food and fellowship while holding hands around the table was something we never do in England . . . and something we found very touching.

One thing we've overcome is getting drawn into the comparisons of the relative "values" of properties. We realize that home exchanging is as much about experiencing and enjoying differences in environment and culture as it is about the specific properties. However, we've had some surprises, and one comment made to us—"How do you manage to keep your place so clean?"—only became significant when we first entered one exchange apartment and felt we really had to do a thorough vacuuming before we felt able to unpack our suitcases!

We have become much more confident and pro-active about approaching people, setting up contacts, making offers, doing home exchange "deals," and expanding our international network of vacation home exchangers. Sounds grand, doesn't it? Again, on our first home exchange in Florida, we got to talking to a couple from New Jersey, who told us to look them up next time we were in Manhattan. We took them up on their offer, had a great time, and a few months later they put their son in contact with us back in London. He was in Europe on a journalistic assignment; another enjoyable evening, another new friend. We learnt that we British are very different from Americans; we just happen to speak the same language—well, mostly. We sophisticates from London experienced some difficulty getting out of Miami—having set foot on American soil for the first time. And that's another thing: you don't actually have to set foot anywhere, you just drive there, or through there. It's drive-in everything. We think the drive-in facial scrub and manicure is taking things a bit too far. We mean people will get stuck to their car seats forever!! Anyway, our problem driving out of Miami was to do with our difficulty in trying to find, then read, directional signals amongst all that billboard stuff. Those huge signs advertising peanuts and car exhausts, where the billboards are larger than the buildings underneath them, are both mesmerising and awe-inspiring.

And that trip driving across the Everglades without any air conditioning was hell. It made no difference having the car windows open; we really sweated. In fact, the car did have an air conditioner, but we didn't know about it; we don't have it back home. Having now spent time in Florida and South Carolina, with temperatures in the nineties and humidity at 95 percent, it all falls into place; you just cannot survive in the southeastern part of the States without air conditioning! So once we got it sorted out, we really had a cool time, but found the bits in between really exhausting. You know, stepping out of the car into the condo, the very tiring fifty-yard walk from the condo to the swimming pool, and so on.

And we learnt about cholesterol and how to fool ourselves that we're not eating such a nasty thing, slimming—and how to pretend that it's okay to pour pints of syrup all over our food, because it's got 50 percent less sugar, cable TV—and how to believe we have choice, and "have a nice day. . . ." And we wondered if that pancake house in a suburb of Boston was typical? "Let's go next door and get ourselves a light breakfast before we get on the road." Time: 7:00 A.M. At that time in the morning, the place was packed, and thinking we might have cereal, orange juice, and coffee, as we were led to our table, we looked around us in a daze of misbelief. There was some serious eating going on with people—adults and kids—eating eggs, bacon, grits, hash browns, sausages, flapjacks, waffles, honey, fruit, ice cream, and maple syrup *all on the same plate*! But we are hooked on America, and who wouldn't be when in a piano bar in Provincetown, Cape Cod (Massachusetts), a member of the audience at the end of the evening suggested everyone stand up and sing "God

Save the Queen" in honour of us—embarrassing, but really flattering.

If we had to name one personal obstacle to vacation home exchanging, it would be swapping cars. We've been reluctant to loan out our car (maybe a British hang-up), and we just have the one. We stipulated with an American exchanger we'd be glad to exchange cars, but we don't want you to do more than a thousand miles on ours because a high recorded mileage would adversely affect the car's trade-in value (what a feeble excuse). They seemed to take it in good heart. When we did a delayed exchange this summer (their second home, too), he told me over the phone we've got the car ready for you, and you've got a thousand miles, right? He said this tongue-in-cheek, but we did feel rather silly.

The most memorable vacation exchange story so far? The retired English couple, who had been living in Minorca, Spain, for twenty years and wanted to use our cottage last Christmas to be near their daughter. They had a great time and extended their stay twice. We are due to go to their place next June, and imagine our surprise and slight shock when we were reading a letter from them the other day which said that after their recent exchange experience back in England, they had decided to return the next month to live in England permanently! They went on to say, however, that our exchange with them was safe, as they could call on a friend in Minorca with a similar property to help out. Okay, it wasn't just our cottage that did it, but it was the opportunity that vacation home exchange provided which led them into making this major change in their lives.

While it's quite unlikely we'll be packing up and moving to America, or elsewhere, certainly we are grateful for the fact that home exchanging has helped to make our vacation weeks both enjoyable and memorable.

Vacations often serve as opportunities for family reunions—get-togethers, sometimes, of three generations of families from near and far. Unique, however, has been the experience of American psychologist Debra Berg, her French husband (an executive with an aeronautics firm in Paris), and their young children. This family has combined family reunions, yachting, and international home exchanging.

Debra J. Berg writes:

We live in Malakoff, which is just one street away from Paris, France. In order to maintain strong ties with my father and mother, we used to have our vacations at their home on Staten Island in New York City. Our two young children (now we have three) enjoyed those visits for many reasons, not the least of which was the fact that we all made frequent trips in my parents' thirty-two-foot Canadian-built sailboat, *Duet*—perfect for sailing in New York waters, on Long Island Sound, and up to Martha's Vineyard, Massachusetts.

Though *Duet* has five berths, the close quarters were a bit trying on the nerves; actually, if we were to continue these annual vacations, it became apparent we would need more space. A vacation home ashore with nearby docking facilities would be ideal. With this in mind, my parents rented a spacious home in Orient Point, at the tip of Long Island, New York. With this home's bedrooms and the boat's berths, we had sleeping accommodations for my parents, my three brothers and their children, and our family as well. It was just great . . . but very expensive—what with the rental of the home and dock or mooring.

In three different magazine articles, we read about vacation home exchanging. Perhaps this concept would be the answer to our more-space, low-cost family reunion dilemma.

We arranged to have our home here in France listed in one of the home exchange directories. Immediately after the directory was issued, we studied it for hours and hours. That's the key, we think, to success in finding home exchange partners: lose no time in perusing the directories, noting potential exchange possibilities, and making the initial contacts. We, of course, were looking for Paris-bound exchangers offering homes in coastal areas within a few days' cruising distance from New York City.

We ended up with twenty different exchange possibilities. From New York, my father contacted eighteen of these exchangers by telephone. Of course, correspondence would have been less expensive, but we were pressed for time. The logistics of organizing a long-distance family reunion, combined with arrangements for mooring and crewing a sailboat, demand lots of lead time. Early on, we decided that initial exchange contacts should be made five to six months ahead of the proposed exchange dates.

As it turned out, only *one* exchanger (that's all it takes!) from our list was a really "live" candidate—yes, she would love to go to Paris, and, in turn, offered us her lovely home in Stonington on the Connecticut shore, with yacht club dockage and moorings nearby. With July now only weeks away, we worked hard to prepare our home for our exchange guest, who came alone but used our home as a rendezvous point for close friends and her family members as well. Finally, the four of us, plus a baby sitter, left Paris for Stonington, where we found our exchange host had done a beautiful job of preparing her home for us. It was an historical home . . . situated in an historic village.

We had a joyful, two-week family time. Really, the best of two worlds: day sailing in coastal waters not previously known to us and on-land sightseeing in towns and vineyards, amusement parks and museums.

Having come through our first home exchange experience with flying colors, we felt like old hands as we arranged for the following year's exchange in Cotuit, on Cape Cod in Massachusetts. "Samson's Folly" was the name of this eight-bedroom, six-bathroom home built nearly two hundred years ago. Again, it was an historic home located in an historic community . . . but, then, isn't everything historic in New England? The house was so big we were able to reunite our whole "gang" again, including all three generations plus a baby sitter and a few friends: thirteen adults, one teenage baby sitter, and eight children under ten years of age.

Together, we enjoyed Thanksgiving dinner and a surprise seventieth "October" birthday party for my mother—all in the middle of August. My husband and I also arranged a guest membership at the local tennis club. I got a public library card, so we could borrow books and video movies as a treat for the children. With that large a group, it was impossible to move around en masse, even if we had wanted to. So we rather naturally split into smaller groups as activities changed from day to day, according to sailing weather and the other marvelous sightseeing opportunities on Cape Cod. Dad must have been a bit disappointed, though, because the use of the sailboat seemed to decrease as the size of our group increased.

Unfortunately, everyone had scheduled his vacation for the exact same period of time, and making satisfactory daily plans for so many of us was both strenuous and time consuming. Probably it would have been preferable to stagger arrivals and departures within the eighteen days we had use of our exchange partner's home. A few overlapping days for all of us to be together would have been ideal.

Our third year of home exchanging also included boating, but on entirely different shores—off the western coast of Ireland. Our friends, Annick and Jean-Pierre, had their sailboat, *Foggy Dew*, on a mooring near Clifden. I set up this exchange by telephone with a family with six children in the charming little city of Galway, Ireland, at the beginning of the wild and breathtaking Connemara countryside. It was a four-hour drive from Galway to Clifden, so, although our house exchange lasted for three weeks, we spent the second full week away from Galway on *Foggy Dew*.

We can't say we sailed much that week. Our highly qualified captain, Jean-Pierre, listened regularly to dismal shortwave radio weather broadcasts. The only advice: sit still and wait it out. Our children and our friends' little girl, Anne, were wonderful aboard and kept busy for hours on end with a few toys and books and a lot of imagination!

It was a relief to arrive back in Galway with most of the cruise under engine. Even on land much of our sightseeing was dashed by gray skies and rain. Now I believe that two weeks is really adequate for any exchange because you spare yourself the disappointment of spoiled vacations should weather or any other factor interfere with plans.

We did make some unpleasant discoveries on our return to France. Apparently, our exchange family's standards of cleanliness were not up to ours, and their children had broken some of our children's favorite (and costly) toys. We had never broken anything more than an ordinary plate, so I was too embarrassed to contact our host family, requesting they reimburse us for damages. Doing it again, I would surely write the family a courteous explanatory letter . . . and then hope for the best. As a special precaution, in the future we plan to store away our breakable items. And perhaps we will ask our guests to employ our housekeeper at least once a week and especially for a few hours following their departure. Prior to our much simplified fourth exchange this past summer, with neither boating nor family reunions for a change, we did agree with our exchange partners in San Sebastian, Spain, to replace such objects as they or we might damage to one extent or another. In San Sebastian, we decided to begin our clean-up efforts two full days before our departure. By so doing, we were not under pressure during our last several days, and we were able to leave their apartment spotlessly clean.

Now we are beginning to dream about our next home exchanges. Hopefully, my husband and I will go to Venice, Italy, alone for one week next year. And perhaps an exchanger with a roomy house in the U.S.A. along the east coast near a friendly yacht club would like to set up a vacation home exchange with us.

We look forward with anticipation to further home exchange arrangements in the short term and the long term as well. We hate hotel living and feel in addition to keeping costs down that home exchange vacations are more comfortable for families with children . . . and what better way to observe, firsthand, how other people really live than actually living in their homes?

I want to reemphasize the fact that vacation home exchanging is not simply a means to avoid hotel living; it's truly a shared step toward converting an unknown house into a familiar place called "home."

9 Putting Out Your Welcome Mat

YOU AND YOUR VACATION home exchange partner have won the battle! With all flags flying, you have scanned and evaluated the home exchange directory listings; made the contacts, in spite of the eccentricities of the postal service; and come to agreements on the dates and all other elements of the vacation home exchange route to your respective dream vacations!

In all likelihood, this vacation home exchange venture will involve the members of your family and your home exchange partners living for a time in totally unfamiliar homes. Hence, you and your partners should make every effort to help familiarize each other with your respective homes. This chapter focuses on two very important elements of home exchanging: the preparation of your home for those with whom you are exchanging and the information you communicate to your guests about your home (interior and exterior) and the services available to them in your community.

A Poughkeepsie, New York, couple with home exchanging experience in Arizona and New Jersey, say, "We always feel more critical of our housekeeping when we know 'company's coming,' so we have our house in 'apple pie' order for our exchange guests."

There are those who view getting their homes ready for the use of exchangers as one huge task! It really need not be such. The burden will be lighter if you begin a month or so in advance of the exchange date *and* involve all members of your family. Look at it as sort of a spring house cleaning, realizing your home exchange partners are going through the very same procedure (hopefully they are!) preparing their home for you.

A Connecticut exchanger reports that one of the home exchange services recommends that exchangers preparing their homes endeavor to view them "through a stranger's eyes." A good suggestion.

Perhaps the most helpful way to deal with preparing your home for a vacation exchange would be to follow a "laundry list" format including many of the steps you can take to make your home a comfortable home for your exchange guests.

Much can be learned from others who have had experience in preparing their homes for use by exchange partners. A retired U.S. naval officer and his wife living in Hawaii, who have exchanged in New Zealand and elsewhere, recommend leaving ample space for exchange guests' clothing and personal items—"at least two large drawers and about two feet of closet space per guest." Another exchanger suggests that the empty drawers—those to be used by the guests—be so indicated by these drawers being left slightly open (or marked with stickers). Also, there should be some closet shelf space available and plenty of clothes hangers.

It is recommended that you remove personal items from the tops of dressers, tables, and other places that contain items not necessary to the functioning of the home.

Cleaning the medicine chest provides a grand opportunity to dispose of all those outdated, half-full bottles of years-old prescriptions! Other medicine-chest items should be placed in a secure location not available to your guests. You should leave a clean medicine chest with adequate space for your guests' personal items.

You will want to arrange for your household staples (toilet paper, extra soap, tissues, paper towels, detergents, dish washing soap, cleaning materials, and so on) to be easily accessible to your guests. As supplies of these household items are depleted, they are generally replaced by your guests. Spot remover is another important item. But use of this can be a problem sometimes bordering on disaster, because certain types of stains and spot removers on certain types of material do not react well. Some home exchangers recommend spot-removing kits that have half-a-dozen different types of liquid for different types of stains—and complete use instructions. Also, help your guests to keep your house as shipshape as you would want them to keep it by having available a vacuum cleaner in good working condition and with replacement bags and instructions, along with a suitable assortment of brooms, mops, and dust cloths. The refrigerator should be clean and empty. (It is quite okay to leave frozen food in the freezer, but do make freezer space available for your guests' frozen foods). The stove and other appliances should be clean and ready to use.

While honesty and truthfulness seem to be synonymous with vacation home exchangers, it just makes good sense to put away jewelry, silver, heirlooms, and other items of monetary or sentimental value. Perhaps your furniture includes some of those "look at but don't sit on" side chairs; these, too, should be stored in appropriate places.

Special attention should be given expensive electronic equipment: word processors, computers, FAX machines, and especially valuable stereophonic systems. Bulky as some of these are, if your home does not have a sufficient amount of storage space, plan to place these items in cartons and ask a family member or neighbor to hold them for your return, or make it clear these pieces of equipment are off limits to your exchange guests.

Do, however, leave a television set or two (along with channel selection instructions), possibly a VCR, a radio. If your area is prone to occasional power failures, a flashlight or some candles will be appreciated.

Some homes have closets that can be locked—great places for a variety of valuables. One exchanger had two such closets. One was for items *not* to be used by exchange guests; the other, for items to be used by these guests: an ironing board, beach chairs and towels, extra linens. A closet key was left for the guests. The only problem was, it was actually the wrong key. The guests had access to a closet full of their host's personal items and valuables, but no way of getting to the things intended for their use!

Of course, a sufficient amount of "everyday" china, flatware, glassware, and cooking utensils for the number of guests in the exchange party should be readily available in your kitchen and/or dining room.

If you have wines and liquors in your home, you will need to decide whether or not you want to make these available to your guests. Many hosts prefer simply to put away their wines and liquors during the exchange period. Others store their costly, special wines and liquors in a safe place, leaving out a few wine cellar basics. (Note: in case your guests do enjoy a bottle of wine now and then, it would be appropriate for you to have available a corkscrew or some other wine-bottle cork remover.)

In this connection, a company director and his wife living in Dundalk, Ireland, write: "We always say to our exchange partners that they have the total freedom of our property and everything in it for the length of the exchange. We tell them to avail themselves of whatever drinks they wish from our drinks cabinet. Prior to leaving on a vacation home exchange, I purchased two bottles of a much sought-after vintage port at a very expensive price. Some months later on a very special occasion, I decided I would open a bottle of that port, only to discover that both bottles were empty! The following Christmas we received a very nice letter from our exchange partners stating how much they enjoyed their holiday in Ireland, and that they also enjoyed glasses of port each evening after dinner."

The handling of incoming mail can be a problem. One host instructed his local post office to hold all mail during his four-week vacation exchange. So the post office dutifully held "all mail," including the letters sent to his exchange *guests*—letters which were, of course, correctly addressed to the guests in *care of* the host! A similar situation confronted an exchanger in New York City. All of her host's mail was sent to a post office box number, along with this

exchanger's mail. But she was given no key to the post office box and therefore had no access to her mail. A phone call to her host rectified this situation. One way to avoid mail problems is for mail to be delivered as usual. Then the guests simply hold mail for their hosts.

Food staples (salt, sugar, flour, condiments, and the like) are left in the kitchen cabinets or in other appropriate places. Guests should be advised that it is okay for them to use these staples and then replace them.

Then there is the matter of home-delivery services. While at a home in England, exchangers from Georgia learned that a newspaper was delivered every day, and milk every second day. Also, a woman appeared at the door with a dozen eggs. When told the eggs were not needed, she said she was "supposed" to deliver eggs to this home every Friday! Another time, a neighbor's boy was quite insistent about washing the car. These exchangers began to get nervous about answering the doorbell! Just prior to the exchange, the host should make proper arrangements for all home-delivery services throughout the exchange period.

Even under vacation home exchange circumstances, life must go on. Fuel oil must be delivered; electric, gas, and water meters must be read; neighbors' dogs and cats will wander through the yard; the world's noisiest garbage trucks will arrive at 5:00 A.M.; aluminum-siding salesmen will ring the doorbell at the very moment you're heading for the hot tub; and, yes, the television will break down just as your favorite program goes on the air. In many respects home exchanging is just like being at home!

"A bed full of *water*? Hey, c'mon, be serious." Yes, in the 1960s the manufacturers of water beds had to overcome a mighty obstacle: water in your *bed*? But their perseverance was rewarded, and to this day in many homes (especially in the U.S.) the beds of choice indeed are water beds. "There was a water bed in every damn bedroom, and I didn't get a decent night's sleep until we got back to our home—and bed!" writes a particularly irate home exchanger. And from a school psychologist/elementary teacher couple in Charlevoix, Michigan: "When we exchanged with a family near Washington, D.C., we slept on their water bed, and liked it so much we went home and bought one for ourselves!" If water beds are a part of the scene in your bedroom, it would be a good idea to mention this fact early on in your correspondence with potential vacation home exchangers.

Assuming you provide the proper materials for your home to be cleaned periodically when it is occupied by exchangers, you can safely assume your exchange guests will do such cleaning up as they feel is necessary. A Los Angeles, California, lawyer and his realtor wife have a woman who cleans their home weekly. "While we are exchanging, the cleaning woman continued to come each week—cleaning the house and changing the beds, so while our exchange guests are occupying our home, we know it's kept the way we like it." Departure clean-up is, of course, more of a task. Generally, each of the exchange partners agrees to handle the thorough cleaning of the home or condo just before the departure date. If a housecleaning service is to do this job, prior arrangements should be made as to when this cleaning will take place and whether paying for this cleaning is to be the responsibility of the host or the guest.

In addition to their vacation exchange home being cleaned and ready for their use, high on the home exchanger's want list is detailed information about the use of your home, inside and out. Leave information on whom to contact in case of need (plumbers, electricians, and others), about the neighbors, and about the shops (food and otherwise), the restaurants, and things of interest to be seen and done in your community.

How do you go about arranging this considerable amount of helpful information so that your guests can make quick reference to it from time to time during the exchange period? Well, first, how *not* to disseminate this information: a teacher from Milan, Italy, writes: "(Our exchange apartment in Spain) was full of posters—including DON'T TOUCH! DON'T SHOWER TOO LONG! DON'T USE TOO MUCH ELECTRICITY! We really needed much more humor than usual to enjoy our vacation exchange home *that* year!"

Occasionally, exchangers' travel schedules permit them to meet in advance of the exchange, perhaps at one of the homes or at the airport. And this is good because after all that correspondence, it is fun (and nearly always reassuring) for exchangers to meet, in person, those who will be living in their homes. If this meeting is to be at one of the homes, then the host has an opportunity to give the guests a tour of the home and property. These pre-exchange meetings, however, in no way substitute for in-depth, written information about your home. Indeed, "a rapid oral blitz of home-related information is wasted on a jet-lagged or car-weary traveler," writes a retired educator in Ridgewood, New Jersey.

All of the home- and community-related information an exchange host wishes to pass along to his guests can be placed in the Home Information Kit—"Info Kit." The material in this kit must be typewritten or printed so that it can be read and reread during the early days of the exchange and referred to by your guests throughout their stay in your home. The Info Kit can also be in the form of an alphabetized ring binder or on 3″ x 5″ cards; an advantage here would be the ease in adding, deleting, and/or revising sections of the Info Kit from time to time. A suggestion from an optometric assistant in Ashland, Oregon, who with her professor-of-marketing husband has had thirty exchanges since 1974: "Type your information pages, placing each in a plastic cover, and this book will last for years of exchanging."

Your guests will want to use the appliances in your home—the refrigerator, stove, disposal, clothes washer and dryer, dishwasher, microwave oven, and so on. Some families keep for future reference the manufacturers' booklets giving full instructions for the use of their appliances. If you have these available, they certainly should be an integral part of your Info Kit, along with such specific 1–2–3 instructions for use as seems appropriate. Because one exchange host in France left absolutely *no* instructions, a Connecticut family found the washing machine to be a "source of amazement; the first six days of our vacation were spent trying to get our clothes *out* of the washer!"

And then a Vero Beach, Florida, exchanger writes: "During an exchange in Sweden, we could not flush the toilet until a neighbor came to the rescue!" These eccentric appliances are not all in Europe. All across the U.S. are appliances that do not do what they are supposed to do when they are supposed to do it! The vacation home exchangers' answers to dilemmas such as this should be found in the Info Kit, which their hosts have carefully prepared.

The operation of home heating and air-conditioning units can also be baffling. A Florida host's exchange guests had nothing but problems with his home's air conditioning unit until he included the following information in his Info Kit under "thermostat for heating and air conditioning."

> The thermostat is located on the wall in the hall. If cold air is desired, place "fan" switch on "auto" and "system" switch on "cool." If hot air is desired, place "fan" switch on "auto" and "system" switch on "heat." In either case move thermostat lever (underneath unit) to desired temperature and be sure all doors and windows are tightly closed. Frequently, at times other than summer, you will be quite comfortable with "fan" switch on and "auto" and "system" switch on "off." Then screened windows and doors may be opened.

While the above may sound just a bit like overkill, with the thermostat before them and these operating instructions in hand, this Florida host's guests now have no problems whatsoever with the heating and/or air conditioning of this home.

One home exchanger vacationing in Cambridge, England, noticed some discolored water seeping through the ceiling of the linen closet of his exchange home. Not *any* plumber, but the plumber who was familiar with *this* home was needed—and *fast*. Fortunately, the home exchange host had left his plumber's name and telephone number in the Info Kit. In an hour (on Good Friday!), this plumber was there, and the problem—a toilet leaking two floors above—was solved, with the repair bill, of course, going to the exchange host, and with the plumber staying for lunch. On returning home later, the exchange host wrote that, somehow, this particular plumber always scheduled his repair work just before the noon hour. And stay for lunch he always did!

So do include in your Info Kit the names of your plumber and your electrician, as well as the names of those who service your appliances, including your garage door opener (if you have one), and by all means list the locations of your home's master electric switch and fuse box (or circuit breaker) and gas and water shutoffs. Additional information which should be included: under "Garbage," where are the plastic garbage bags? On what day is the garbage pick-up? Where is the garbage to be placed? Beside the road? Outside the garage door? "Parking," with complete instructions—In the garage? On the road? Off the road? "Plants" need to be watered, and "Pets" need to be fed (see chapter 14). And where are the pencil sharpener, hammer, screwdriver, and other basic tools for minor home repairs?

A ten-time London, England, exchanger (a retired lecturer) recommends that the Info Kit include the names, addresses, and phone numbers of doctors, should emergency medical care be required. "I once drove for two hours with a high temperature visiting doctors who wouldn't see me without a prior appointment. Eventually, I found a walk-in clinic, which was excellent."

These days an increasing number of homes seem to be equipped with burglar alarm systems. Now burglar alarms can be very temperamental, sometimes making a terrible racket during thunder storms. Or if you are just a few seconds late in deactivating the device after you enter the home, or sometimes for no reason at all, the alarm may go off. In learning how to live with your security system, your guests will need to know how to operate it and care for it, along with the name and telephone number of the security firm that services it. An employee benefits consultant from Minneapolis, Minnesota, writes: "In Boston, as we returned from a day of sightseeing, we entered the house, and not one of us could remember the proper code to punch on the security alarm system. A contingent of local policemen arrived in very short order. I guess they realized we were not burglarizing the place when they saw our six children!"

"While exchanging with [now] friends in Orlando, Florida, we were staying at their holiday home. After having had a number of burglaries, they installed burglar alarms, smoke alarms, and time on/off switches for lights. Great was our alarm when we set off all of these hidden devices by accident! Though our host did warn us about the existence of these alarms and time switches, coming from the very peaceful, rural farm life in South Africa, we had never previously had any use for them."

"Help," exclaimed a Seattle, Washington, couple when a faucet in their exchange home fell apart. "We couldn't find the water main shutoff valve; it turned out to be halfway down the property, encircled by some tropical foliage." When water leaks occur, it is imperative to know the location of that water shutoff. If you do not know where yours is, find out and include this information in your Info Kit.

Those staying in your home will also want guidance from you in case of an emergency—addresses and telephone numbers for police, fire, medical doctors, hospital emergency rooms, dentists, your insurance agent; also do include information about the use of elevators and/or fire exits if you live in an apartment building or a multifloor condominium complex.

Home exchangers in New Jersey learned that "tick-bite fever" was prevalent in their exchange location: Transvaal, South Africa. Yes, their exchange host (a medical doctor) had provided tick-bite fever medication "just in case." A Dorset, England, exchanger carries this matter of meeting the needs of his exchangers' wardrobes a bit far. "Use my clothing," he says, if they have not brought along suitable clothing. (Another thought: it is best to advise your exchange partners in advance about your weather extremes so that they will bring the right clothing!)

Leave information about the exterior of your home. If you have a pool, instructions should be left as to its use and maintenance. Who cares for the lawn, and where is the lawn mower? If yours is a winter exchange, who handles snow removal and where are the shovels and/

or the snow blower? Instructions for the use of this equipment should be included. Experienced home exchangers also provide the names and locations of the supermarket, dry cleaner, laundromat (if no washing machine is available), bakery, butcher shop, and other recommended stores and shops. Since in all likelihood your home exchange partner has never been in your community before, this information is most helpful and useful, along with recommended restaurants and schedules for public transportation in your area. Americans exchanging in suburban Nuremberg, Germany, were glad their host left them complete information about the city's subway system. These guests were in and out of downtown Nuremberg by subway several times a day—convenient, safe, inexpensive travel. Indeed, only twice were taxis used—from and to the airport.

If your community has a private or municipal swimming pool, tennis or racquetball court, or a golf course, and arrangements can be made for your guests to use these recreational facilities, then they will need complete information about these. Depending on the ages of those occupying your home, you should also include suggestions for sightseeing, museums, guided tours, historical sites, special children's activities, and other points of interest in and around your community. A Tennessee exchanger mentions that a trip to your vacation area chamber of commerce will provide you with area maps and enough descriptive brochures to keep your guests reading day and night.

A Colorado couple wrote that their hosts thought of everything: "They arranged for tennis partners, golf partners, and a sightseeing boat trip. It was an utterly *delightful* vacation. Better than we could ever have arranged for ourselves!"

Do include information as to your whereabouts should your home exchange guests wish to reach you for some reason or other. We suggest this because home exchanges are not always simultaneous. While someone is occupying your home, it is quite possible you might be visiting an elderly aunt in Chicago or snorkeling at Key West or perhaps even skiing in the high Sierras or the Austrian Alps.

Home exchangers worldwide agree that their hosts' neighbors, relations, and friends often add great dimension to their vacation home exchange experiences. Underscoring this, a businessman in Des Moines, Iowa, writes: "In our European and U.S. exchanges, we have been fortunate in having wonderful neighbors. They have invited us for meals, they have honored us with cocktail parties, they have shown us the sights in and around our exchange cities, and true friends they have become. We exchange notes and Christmas cards sometimes for years after our meeting each other. And the neighbors have been of real *help* in times when we have faced minor crises, i.e., in Banbury, England, our lights went out . . . we looked and looked ould not locate the circuit breaker box. A phone call to a neigh- lved the problem."

n attorney and his wife from Tampa, Florida, share this experience from their exchange in Austria: "We were met at the train by our exchange partner's brother (a doctor), who took us to his home for a delightful welcome lunch. During our stay, he and his family took us on several outings in the surrounding mountains—also to visit some wineries. This man's father was mayor of our town, so we had tea with him and a tour of the town hall."

A husband and wife (both teachers) from Ripley, Tennessee, appreciated the courtesies their exchange home neighbors extended them: "One friend had us over for tea, and another invited us for dinner. It is always nice meeting people from different states and different parts of the world."

"Our exchange partner did a wonderful job of preparing for our arrival," writes a retired couple from Schenectady, New York. "We were met at the airport by a friend of our host and then driven to our exchange home, where we were met by a neighbor, who later entertained us several times. Other of our host's friends either called or dropped in. On our return home some weeks later, we learned our neighbors and other friends had also been gracious to our exchange partners. This friendliness can add much enjoyment to a vacation home exchange."

Your guests will want to advise their family members and friends how they can be reached while vacationing at your home. If you have one home, of course, from their communications with you, your guests will know your address and telephone number. On the other hand, if you have a second home and your guests will be staying in this second home, you will need to give your guests the address and telephone number of this second home. Then they will be able to give this information to those who may wish to contact them during their stay there.

Before you depart on a vacation home exchange, by all means do tell your neighbors, relatives, and friends about those who will be staying at your home, and suggest that they might enjoy meeting them. One German host made a deal with his neighbor: "If you wish, you can take fruit from our trees and vegetables from our garden if from time to time you will entertain our guests." (This sly maneuver is known as the "VHEFAVAT," Vacation Home Exchange Fruit and Vegetable Arm Twist!)

Within a month or so before your actual arrival date, you and your exchange partner should finalize arrangements for arrivals at your respective homes. Whether it is from the airport by taxi, by train or bus or car, being met by friends, relatives, or no one . . . regardless of the arrival circumstances, these arrangements should be agreed to and thoroughly understood by both parties to the exchange. The plans should be put in writing and should include dates, times, addresses, telephone numbers, driving instructions (with maps), and all other elements of the arrivals of the exchange partners at each others' homes (see chapter 10).

More than likely, some days after you have left your home in the care of your exchange partners, you will wonder how they are getting along. Are they having any problems? Does the Info Kit need any clarification? If yours is a simultaneous exchange, they probably have the same questions. So, by all means, touch base with them by telephone.

Your exchange guests will be appreciative of your preparing your home for their vacation experience, appreciative of your introducing them to some of those living nearby, and especially appreciative of your taking the time to prepare for them that important home Info Kit. Extending your hospitality in these special ways will be just as important to your guests' vacation enjoyment as the key to your home's front door!

A final note: often exchange hosts leave a bottle of wine, a bouquet of flowers, a casserole (for that first meal in your home), or some other appropriate gift to welcome exchange partners to their homes.

10 Getting Off on the Right Foot

"BELLHOP," CALLS OUT THE resort hotel's reception clerk, "here's the key to room 3808. Please show Mr. and Mrs. Hall to this room." And after being shown to room 3808 and tipping the bellman generously, the Halls, of Macon, Georgia, agree that this room is "just fine" for their week-long vacation. "And what does Activities have planned for us tomorrow?"

Countless vacations, for countless vacationers, over countless years have started just this way. There are no problems whatsoever with keys on a conventional vacation.

With home exchange now very much a part of the vacation scene, an often asked arrival question is, "The key . . . *where's the house key?*"

This from ten-time vacation home exchangers in Atlanta, Georgia: "We were to have been met at the railroad station by the key-carrying friend of our host, and then we were to have been driven to our exchange home. No problem, except that this friend was not at the station at the appointed hour, and his telephone number, as given us, was not the correct number. Stranded for a while at the station, finally we took the bull by the horns—in the form of a taxi to our host's home. No sign of the friend; no key for the house. With the help of neighbors, we were able to locate a relative of our host, a relative who did indeed provide us with the elusive key."

A Washington, D.C., area home exchanger was given the key to his California exchange home, but it was the wrong key. "We had to push our daughter through an unlocked window to get into the house."

From exchangers in San Clemente, California: "While in England, when we returned from the city of London, the key to the front door broke. We were advised to call the fire department to help us get in. They arrived and used ladders to get up to the third floor where a window was open. When the fire truck arrived, the lights in the surrounding townhouses went out as people opened their windows and doors a crack, so they could sit in the dark and observe what was happening without being observed!"

"On arriving at our exchange home in London," writes an Easton, Connecticut, exchanger, "We had the key all right . . . but the front door of the house was inadvertently double-locked by a real estate agent who had been showing the home to a prospective purchaser. All other doors and windows were also securely locked. As we sat in a despondent state, surrounded by our luggage, we attracted the attention of two curious boys. After we explained our predicament to them, the boys hurried off . . . and soon various of the neighbors came to help. Chosen smallest in the crowd, I was boosted over the adjacent neighbor's fence, where I had access to a small window. Breaking and entering that window, soon we were inside—but not before we had been made fast friends of the neighbors, who then invited us to a block party celebrating the wedding at Prince Charles and Princess Diana."

Because the driving instructions were clearly spelled out, other exchange guests had no problem locating their condo. Now, the key? It turned out the front-door key was *away* on a three-day vacation with the condo building's janitor!

While enjoying a vacation home exchange in Puerto Rico, a West Coast family locked themselves out of their exchange *car*—"only to find out later that our exchange partner had locked himself out of our Seattle home! Moral: we now make a special point to square away in advance not only the directions to the home, but the matter of extra keys for the house and car."

Somehow, house and car keys are so far down on exchangers' check lists that frequently they are forgotten. It is of critical importance to arrange for the exchange of keys during the latter part of the home exchange correspondence. As mentioned in the previous chapter, keys should be mailed prior to the exchange date. If this is not done, then very specific, written instructions must be given to the exchange partner as to the whereabouts of both the home and car keys.

Among the first things some exchangers do is to have duplicate keys made. Immediately after arriving at their vacation exchange home, key-conscious exchangers in Fieldston, New York, arrange for a duplicate set of keys to be made (about $1.25 per key). Then the extra set is squirreled away outside the home's front door, under a rock, behind a bush—anyplace where it's hidden from view and yet can easily be retrieved by the guest during a key emergency.

Arrival dates can also be a problem. This can be attested to by a Maitland, Florida, family that was all set to enjoy a week's vacation in Baltimore, Maryland. They found their exchange home all right, but it was still occupied by the host. Ooops, these eager exchangers were one day early!

"Have you ever left home and driven 110 miles in the middle of the night," writes an exchange host from Durras, Australia, "only to find on arrival at the airport that your exchange partner from the other side of the world is to arrive the following day?"

One could write an entire volume based on the arrival experiences of vacation home exchangers—some upbeat; others decidedly downbeat, but all *quite different* from conventional vacation arrivals at, say, Club Med, a cottage by the sea, a cruise ship, a dude ranch in Wyoming, or large or small hotels in Whereversville.

Met at the New Orleans, Louisiana, airport by their exchange host's son, Colorado exchangers were driven thirty-one miles to their exchange home across the border in Mississippi. "This home was utterly gorgeous," they write, "all the luxuries—including an indoor-outdoor swimming pool—and a fabulous view of the Gulf of Mexico. A Cadillac for our use, tickets to the Mardi Gras ball, a loaned tuxedo for my husband's use, and, in the fridge, a corsage for me. What a marvelous arrival-welcome!"

"After leaving customs at London's Heathrow Airport, we were met by our host's chauffeur/gardener, who drove us to a small town in the south of England—Stockbridge, our vacation spot for the summer," writes a Florida couple. "It was a three-story, five-bedroom, four-bathroom establishment, beautifully situated on several acres of rolling countryside. A heated swimming pool and 423 rose bushes (we counted them!); a new Citroen station wagon was at our disposal. And, as the ads say, 'much, much more!'"

From San Diego, California: "*Being met* on arrival for a vacation home exchange is a godsend. Our French host drove four hours to meet us at Paris' De Gaulle Airport. We were then driven to his primary home, where he and his lovely wife entertained us royally—a gourmet dinner (duck à l'orange). The next morning our host gave us a car, and off we went to his holiday house on the Brittany coast; this home was situated on a bluff high above the sea. A truly great place for a vacation exchange home!"

University faculty members from Rincon de la Victoria, Spain, suggest vacation home exchange partners share family photographs prior to the exchange date. "Two reasons: first, it helps to inspire confidence, and then also a photo can be very useful to anyone meeting your exchange guests at the station or airport."

New York City exchangers were met on arrival in Mexico. "And—en route to our exchange home—driven down a dirt road, with burros, chickens, and goats everywhere. Fear and trepidation set in, and my elderly aunt was with us, too. The driver assured us he knew where he was going: 'no problem!' It was a mighty long four miles . . . but we finally came upon our casa. Indeed, we had a shaky arrival . . . but a glorious home exchange vacation."

Arriving in Santa Barbara, California, from Virginia Beach, Virginia, exchangers had an unusual 2:00 A.M. reception: "We got our luggage inside, looked over the house a bit, and entered the bedroom

to find one very large man—sound asleep. We nervously and quickly got our stuff without waking him and retreated to a nearby motel." Another day-early disaster!

From Rottwell, Germany: "When we came to the airport to pick up our family from the U.S., we tried to find this family. The father was supposed to have a newspaper in his hand . . . but there were a lot of men carrying newspapers!"

Exchangers from Michigan had been advised to telephone their host on their arrival in Cork, Ireland, some miles from their vacation home. It was pouring rain, and they sought shelter, a telephone, and a beer at the nearest pub they could find. To say this particular pub was less than comfortable would have been a masterpiece of understatement; it was dark and dirty, and the patrons looked as if they had been left over from the night before. On arriving by car to pick up his exchange guests, their host exclaimed, "How did you ever find *this* place? It's enough to give drinking a bad name!"

From Florida: "Our host's name on the door was our clue as to our exchange condo in Cannes, France . . . but the halls in this ten-story building were pitch black (and we didn't then know about the light timer switch in the hallways on each floor). Using matches, we checked the name plates on each condo door, from floor to floor. When we finally exhausted our match supply, we courageously rang a doorbell. Shortly, the door was opened by a lady obviously interrupted from sunbathing on her porch . . . but she was able to give us directions to our host's condo!"

A duo of arrival stories from a family in Ithaca, New York: "On one of our exchanges, we were late in getting out of our home, and we noticed a car driving around in front of our house with a family that seemed to be lost. You guessed it! They were the family with whom we were exchanging. It was fun to meet them and give them some additional information about our home and area. On another occasion, our exchange partners invited us to come the night before for a swim in their pool and to have dinner with them. This was also very enjoyable."

Finally, a suggestion from an eight-time home exchanger, a telephone engineer in Fort Worth, Texas: "We always bring along to our vacation exchange home the correspondence file for this exchange host. This gives us everything we might want to know about this particular home: the telephone number, a description of the home and our host's family, and something about the area in which this home is located. We find this type of information is frequently useful when we arrive and during the days that follow. If you have kids and your exchange host has kids, it helps to know his kids' names . . . and this is in the early letters from this exchange host."

Getting there may be "half the fun" . . . and *arriving* there will also be a pleasure, provided all of the arrival instructions are clearly understood; if not, your actual arrival may well be the source of memories you prefer to forget!

11 Successful Living in Someone Else's Home: Part 1

VACATION HOME EXCHANGING is a living-in experience—living in someone else's home, while, of course, that someone else is living in your home, or will be living in your home at some time in the future.

The Bible exhorts us to treat our neighbors as we would have them treat us. This abiding truth is also a basic element of the home exchange concept: care for your host's home as you would have him care for your home.

Along with applying your own good judgment to home-related matters that might come up during your vacation stay, probably the best guide to the care of your vacation home will be found in the information about this home prepared for you by your host—the Info Kit. In this, you will find everything your host wants you to know about your vacation home, and it is of paramount importance for you to read carefully through this material very soon after your arrival. If, by chance, this is your host's second home, then possibly it might not have been occupied immediately prior to your arrival. Indeed, it might even have been vacant for some weeks, or even months, before your arrival, in which case your host's instructions will be basic: opening the storm shutters; turning on the furnace, hot water heater, and/or air conditioner; and in other ways preparing the home for your use. More than likely, however, this is your host's primary home and, as such, it will have been occupied by him immediately prior to your arrival; hence, the more basic aspects of the home's operation will have been taken care of.

First things first, and if your arrival is in the late evening or during the night, the first thing you and those with you will want to do is get some sleep after the long drive, flight, or bus or train trip. You will not need the architect's drawing to find the home's bedrooms and bathrooms!

When you are ready to sit up and take notice the next morning—perhaps after enjoying breakfast or some other meal from the kitchen staples your host has left you, you and each member of your vacation group should take an exchanger's tour of the home. Check out all the rooms, noting the drawer, closet, and storage space you are to use; explore the basement, attic, garage, and other of the home's facilities; and then take a walk around the property to familiarize yourself with this vacation scene, to get the "lay of the land." While you are thus wandering about, no doubt some of the neighbors (oh, your host has told them all about you) will make themselves known to you.

If you are vacation living in an apartment or a condominium, during your first day or two by all means introduce yourself to the superintendent or those in the condominium management office. After all, if you should have an emergency of some kind, these people and your neighbors could be of real help.

Generally, home exchange hosts leave their guests ample room for clothes and other personal items, but such is not always the case. One family arrived at their vacation home only to find *every* closet and *every* closet shelf and *every* drawer in *every* bedroom filled to overflowing with the host family's clothes and other personal items. This exchange couple and their two teenage sons had brought along golf clubs, tennis racquets, and fishing equipment for all; personal items; and lots of clothes—a whole carful of stuff, and no place to put it! A little creative rearranging solved *that* problem!

Then there was the Australian couple who had a similar challenge on arriving at their exchange home in England: "Our host left us one small closet and two tiny drawers—very inadequate. As we cleared drawers and made closet space for our things, we felt like intruders!" An important reminder: return your host's belongings to their original places before you leave.

On some cruise ships and in most hotels (even New York's palatial Waldorf), there is little space for storage, so on that kind of vacation you spend two weeks stumbling over your empty suitcases! Not so on a home exchange vacation. You simply put these items out of the way in a closet, in the "mud" room, or in the basement (but not on the basement floor, as "statistics prove" that two-thirds of the basement floors the world over are damp to one degree or another).

Your vacation home may not have all the appliances you have in your own home, and it may have some your home does not have, but in due course you will be using most or all of the appliances this vacation home does offer. If you have problems operating any of these appliances—and you probably will—check out the Info Kit and/or the manufacturers' booklets. More than likely, these instructions will provide you with the help you need.

Most exchangers prepare most of their meals at home. ("But not my wife. On vacation, no slaving in a hot kitchen; no self-catering for *her*!" writes a seasoned English vacation home exchanger.) So early on in your stay, after you have familiarized yourself with the house

and its accoutrements, you take stock of the available food staples and get together a shopping list (See? Just like home!). Off you go on your initial vacation food-shopping expedition, perhaps with some where-to-buy-it suggestions from your host and/or the neighbors. You view the shopping situation, getting some ideas on what shops are available nearby.

You may be using many of the food and household staples left by your exchange host. A fifteen-time home exchanger—a wife, mother, and teacher—in Seattle, Washington, writes: "Our arrangement has always been to keep paper and pencil handy in the kitchen to make note of each item (with brand names) we use, so we can replace these things."

Homemakers—wives *and* husbands—often become very attached to their own particular kitchen utensils, attached to the extent that there are just no substitutes for their "good, old, reliable" vegetable parer, set of kitchen knives, wine bottle opener, or some other kitchen utensil that has passed the test of use and time. If you are traveling by car, do bring these items along with you. And do not forget half-a-dozen boxes/bottles of your favorite spices, your scissors, a few plastic travel glasses, an apron or two, and a box of Band-Aids!

In most cases, making the transition from one's own home furnishings to those in an exchange home is relatively simple, like getting accustomed to the furniture in a hotel or a rented vacation cottage. But, as in hotel living, sometimes *beds* are a challenge. The beds in your host's home may be just right for him and his family but too hard, too soft, too saggy in the middle for you. Experienced exchangers have learned that nearly *all* bed problems can be solved by placing a folded blanket or bedspread strategically between the bed's mattress and springs, boxed or otherwise. (This procedure did not solve the bed problems some American tourists had at The Ritz in Paris, so they simply flopped the mattresses off the twin beds and slept on the floor. Yes, it *was* at The Ritz, and the next morning the chambermaid exclaimed, "*Mon Dieu!*")

Home exchangers from New Jersey had a similar experience while exchanging in Nuremberg, Germany. The bed was marvelous—very comfortable. But it was a mechanically controlled "do-everything" bed: the head could be raised, the foot could be raised, the middle could be raised. A push of the control sent the bed into its act. But it got jammed with the head and foot level and the middle very *high*. Off went the mattress onto the floor—a good, firm "bed" in the shadow of the nearby tent-shaped monster! The host later instructed these New Jersey-ites on the proper use of that bed's controls.

Sometimes other elements of the exchange home—furniture or decorative accessories—take a bit of getting used to. For example, prominently displayed in the living room of a London, England, exchange home was a three-foot-high glass case containing a large stuffed *dog*. "What an interesting way to remember a beloved pet," mentioned these exchange guests from the U.S. "No," said the host, "we just have him there to *shock* people!"

While much can be said for taking vacations at times other than the summer months, the survey showed that the majority of home exchangers prefer to take their vacations in July and August. In the northern hemisphere, where most vacation home exchanging takes place, these two months are generally the hottest months of the year. Apparently, there is an unwritten international statute stating that no two air conditioners can be manufactured or operated alike. Yes, *all* air conditioners (or "air-cons," as a Hong Kong home exchange host calls them) are different. But like traveling salesmen who "motel it" five nights a week, the experienced home exchanger becomes an expert in operating air-conditioning equipment. A Phoenix, Arizona, exchange host learned his air conditioner was quite okay, as were his instructions for operating it; his German exchange guests just liked it better with no air conditioning and the windows wide opened. Even the 117°F. high/90° low temperatures did not change their minds!

The following chapter will deal in depth with various other aspects of living in your vacation exchange home.

12 Successful Living in Someone Else's Home: Part 2

YOU ALREADY KNOW THAT your exchange host's neighbors and other friends can play a very important role in the vacation home exchange picture. Hopefully, your host has left you some information about his nearest neighbors, and this will help you as you meet these new friends. More than likely, you will be hearing the most widely used phrase in the vacation home exchange world, one which can be attributed to home exchange neighbors: "Be sure to let us know if we can do anything for you folks."

Floridians, on returning from a three-week exchange in Winchester, England, said: "A highlight in this most recent exchange of ours was the opportunity we had to fellowship with our host's neighbors. Some of these people are retired, while others, younger than we, make the daily commute to London. One of these couples invited us to a dinner party at their large and lovely home just down the street—a party to which they invited other neighbors; people two houses away had us in for cocktails; and a third couple took us on a day-long automobile trip to see something of the sights in and around Winchester. We had only known Winchester Cathedral as a song ("Winchester Ca-theee-dral"), but after having been guided through this cathedral on three different occasions, we found this lovely, historic cathedral to be much, much more than just a song! Not only did these new friends show us the town, so to speak, but they became true friends who added much to our vacation experience."

A Baltimore, Maryland, couple writes: "Our home exchange host in Wales, Great Britain, arranged a family-catered party aboard his beautiful fifty-two-foot motor yacht. Among his many other guests, we were introduced to the Marquis of Anglesie."

A Virginia exchange couple writes: "In Scotland, our host's gardener stopped his work to take us in his car to a bus stop for a day trip to Edinburgh. We worried that perhaps his boss might not appreciate his spending this time with us instead of doing his gardening work. 'No problem,' he said, 'at age eighty-two, I'm my own boss!' "

After exchanging in Switzerland, a Florida physician and his wife wrote: "We won't forget these neighbors; from them we had a daily offering of fresh raspberries!"

From Sunset, Maine, another exchange couple wrote: "We contacted two couples with whom we had negotiated, but not exchanged, in Scotland and in England and met them for dinner. On both occasions we were nervous and wary, but the two evenings were high spots of our trip. The first couple was Scottish and lived in a suburb of Edinburgh. They fed us a great meal, poured endless wine, and educated us in Scottish history. The second couple lived in a stone cottage on the moors in the Yorkshire Dales. He was a rock musician and chatted amiably all evening; she was tall and dressed in black, with long red hair, cooked a wonderful meal, and barely spoke. She wrote Harlequin-style romance books. We have continued a lively correspondence with both of these couples and, actually, each has invited us back for a visit."

A Santa Fe, New Mexico, couple who own a retail shop and have exchanged five times—Hawaii (twice), Florida, England, and New Zealand—write: "We met people who had not previously exchanged, but who expressed an interest in exchanging with us at some point in the future."

"Our vacation home exchange was a trip to England with our two college young people. We made the exchange to save money," writes a Tampa, Florida, couple. "However, other pluses far outweighed the original reason. For example, our exchange family's next-door neighbors invited us over for cocktails. As it turned out, they had young people our children's ages, and these kids had a grand time together. These same neighbors very kindly allowed us to use their membership at the local yachting club for dinners out where, incidentally, we met other delightful people who invited us to their church worship service and also to their five hundred-year-old home."

Pride of ownership is a key factor in the good care you take of your own home and your own possessions. Apply this same practice in the care you take of your host's home. In cases of rain (or threatening rain), do not leave the windows open . . . respect the furniture and use of same . . . do not track mud, sand, or whatever through the house (that doormat is there for reasons other than saying *welcome*) . . . keep the appliances clean and in good working order . . . follow through with the arrangements made for cleaning the home, watering the plants, and caring for the property.

A Vancouver, Canada, business couple arrived at their Minnesota vacation home and found that their host had made ample

drawer and closet space available to them. There were clean linens everywhere, and the entire home had been beautifully cleaned. "But there was an antique silver tea set, sterling silver flatware, and lovely crystal everywhere in the dining room; in the living room, there was a huge selection of expensive wines and liquors and a humidor filled with Havana cigars! And the refrigerator? It was fully stocked—enough food to last the two of us for a lifetime! We found some 'regular' china and silverware and endeavored to replace all of the food items we used. We don't drink or smoke. We put all of the valuables out of the way, endeavoring to return each to its proper spot when we departed."

Those who have had more than a few home exchanges know, sometimes from bitter experience, that occasionally (even with careful use) things do get broken or otherwise damaged. "We had not been in our exchange partner's apartment for ten minutes when one of our kids opened the fridge door too 'exuberantly' and knocked the ceramic kitchen clock off the wall." So writes a Peruvian exchanger. "My husband was mortified, and we set right out to seek a substitute clock. The only store we found did not have exactly the same clock, but we did get one that I liked and left it on the table."

"When we arrived home following a great three-week exchange in Hawaii, we discovered the young couple in our California home had apparently never encountered a microwave oven. They left a note of apology expressing a desire to replace our once fluted plastic bowl that was now a perfectly flat tray. No problem. We still use it."

A Garden City, New York, exchanger writes: "In the 'never take anything for granted' category—we had exchanged with an English family, and upon our return, a neighbor told us how, after having been in our home for over a week, the English housewife remarked, 'I really can't see how they cook very well—with only a pancake griddle.' The neighbor came over, pulled open the pots and pans drawer of the range, and found the usual collection of pans and skillets. The English woman gasped, 'Oh, dear, I thought that was where one lit the oven, and I never bake!'"

Just as most basements are damp to one degree or another, "statistics prove" that many toilets continue to drip water after the water tank has refilled. You can save your exchange host a few dollars on the next water bill by removing the top of the toilet tank and adjusting the ball (or float). Bend it (or set it) down slightly; this will prevent the water from continuing to flow over into the overflow pipe. See? Once again, staying in someone else's home is just like living in your own!

This from a special education supervisor in New York City: "Our 'new' friends from Menlo Park, California, were staying at our condo in Vermont. We got a phone call stating that the television set was not working. They could not understand the problem and therefore called our television repairman. As it turned out, the television set was not broken; it was just not plugged into the outlet. Our exchange partners were embarrassed, but we thought it was quite funny!"

A nine-time exchanger from Kaiserlautern, Germany, (who has a winter home in Fort Lauderdale, Florida), puts it this way: "Be tolerant to your partner's property. And watch the property from partners like their own. Never go wrong. Home exchange vacations, I like it, and I will do it again." If you care for your exchange host's property as if it were your own, usually nothing will go wrong, and you will have a memorable vacation home exchange.

It is customary for exchange hosts to pay for their basic monthly telephone service; however, home exchange guests always pay the charges for their toll (long distance) calls and pay for such local calls as they make if the telephone company serving their area charges for local calls. In the U.S., the various telephone companies provide their customers with monthly statements including date, time, and charges for each long distance call made. So after the exchange takes place, the U.S. exchange host simply mails to his guest a photocopy of the telephone company's statement covering the exchange time; the guest then reimburses the host. Outside the U.S., the telephone companies follow different billing procedures, country by country. If your overseas host gets an itemized monthly statement, the procedure suggested above can be followed. If not, the exchange partners must decide in advance how the long distance charges should be handled.

With access to a variety of dresser and desk drawers, closets, the basement, and the attic, and nooks and crannies throughout the exchange home, exchange guests may be tempted to spread their personal belongings all over the house, never quite sure which item went where. Experienced exchangers keep their clothes and personal items together in various rather obvious places. If each person in the exchange group follows this procedure, things are not likely to get lost, and certainly the packing up at the end of the exchange is a lot less difficult.

When making up the bed in their bedroom some weeks after their exchange partners had returned to Cornwall, England, Florida exchangers discovered a packet of traveler's checks under the *mattress*! Yes, it was hidden, hidden so well the departing guests thought they had lost their traveler's checks and had them replaced.

This story comes from an eight-time exchanger in Albuquerque, New Mexico. "Several months after home exchanging and after the exchange was forgotten, I was moving furniture to clean, when I found an unfamiliar lady's undergarment. My husband was in big trouble until I noticed that the garment said 'Made in Canada,' and our most recent home exchange was with a Canadian couple. She was glad to get it back."

In a previous chapter, burglar alarms (in these 1990s they are known as "security systems") were mentioned. Like air conditioners, every security system is different. Some are operated by keys. You unlock the front door with the regular key, to be greeted by a buzzing sound, then rush inside to the security system control box and deactivate (or, as they say, "disarm") the system with a special key. Other systems are operated by a push-button code, with the device mounted outside the home near the front door or just inside the front door.

A Toronto, Canada, optometrist writes: "Our host had placed a 'barking dog' alarm in his basement. During our autumn vacation stay, the falling leaves from trees next to the home would regularly set off the alarm!"

It is always a challenge to get the system disarmed before the alarm goes off. This piercing sound—both inside and outside of the house—is guaranteed to wake not only the dead, but the neighbors and also the police! Hopefully, your host will have left you very clear instructions on how to operate his security system, if he has one.

Not having the proper key or code number at the proper time, an American who exchanged in England wrote: "No problem"; he climbed through an accessible back window, setting off the alarm. The neighbors were quick to exclaim, "What are those wacky Yanks doin' *now*?"

If your host's home does have a security system, it is important that you activate it each time you leave the home.

An American exchanger vacationing in Barbados, writes: "We were robbed very early on a Christmas morning. We had left everything in the living room of our atrium-style home: presents, purses, and other personal items. Everything was stolen . . . and all because we hadn't bothered to lock the doors. Our advice to other home exchangers-in-residence: when you are asleep (as we were) or away, be sure to lock *everything*. By so doing, you will take a necessary step toward protecting your things and those of your host as well."

A retired U.S. Air Force major, now living in Germany, writes that his exchange home was burglarized during a home exchange vacation. "Fortunately, my insurance covered the things I lost, and my host's insurance covered his losses."

Once in a great while, as a part of the exchange arrangements, your exchange home will have other occupants. An American exchanger writes: "We exchanged with a family with two children. These people had just hired an *au pair* from France who was to remain with us at the home while the host and his family were at our home. As soon as our host left, the *au pair* took over the home—entertaining her friends and always making herself 'at home' in rooms we were occupying; once she even decided to 'borrow' some of my *clothes*. A real horror story!"

Writes a retired senior naval officer in Sarasota, Florida: "On our exchange in France, a non-English-speaking grandmother came with the house, but didn't sleep there. Each day she helped with the cooking, the cleaning, and the laundry. During our stay I decided to take her up for her very first airplane ride. As an ex-U.S. Navy pilot holding many licenses, I was able to rent a little Cessna. My grandmother passenger-friend was thrilled as I conducted a few acrobatics over our little village. Many of her relatives were out waving white sheets, and after we landed, this grandmother got on her bicycle and spent the rest of the day telling her relatives and friends all about her experience!"

In addition to swimming, golf, tennis, walking trips, sightseeing, and other vacation activities, home exchangers often arrange to get together with other exchangers. Before leaving home for their vacations, some exchangers check out their vacation home exchange directories, making photocopies of those pages covering exchange listings in or near the vicinity of their vacation homes. During the vacation, these exchangers refer to their home exchange listing photocopies and contact some of the exchangers listed. It is a good way to meet other exchangers and share exchange stories and a good way to make contact with others who might be interested in exchanging with you. Experienced exchangers never leave home without several Fact Sheets descriptive of their home, as well as an assortment of exterior and interior photographs to be shared with potential exchangers they meet along the way.

An exchanger living in Hawaii writes: "After arranging our England exchange, but about three months before going, referring to the home exchange book, I wrote letters to a dozen interesting looking people living in Cornwall, England, and in Ireland, asking if we could visit with them as we were to be exchanging in their parts of the countries—not to stay overnight, just to visit. Their hospitality was overwhelming. These people couldn't do enough for us."

A Seymour, Tennessee, orthodontist writes: "Our exchange partner instructed us to eat from the garden. The garden was beautifully cared for and the fruit and vegetables so abundant that our family couldn't possibly utilize even a small portion of that which was available. We ended up preserving much of the garden's produce for our very kind exchange partners."

Vacation home exchangers are known to respect the homes in which they live and the communities in which their exchange homes are located. They are good neighbors. "When in Rome, do as the Romans do" is a key phrase in vacation home exchange-ese!

As you leave your host's home, it is suggested you leave a note for your host—sort of an overview of your vacation at his home. Mention any problems you had while staying there: broken dishes, malfunctioning appliances, or whatever.

Also, you will want to follow whatever arrangements you made with the host regarding the final departure cleaning and the disposition of the house and car keys. At departure time, too, one should double-check the home (closets, drawers, and every room) to be absolutely certain no personal items have been left behind. Home exchanging is rife with tales of articles exchange guests have left behind—clothes, clocks, money, and a veritable parade of children's books and toys. Finally, most departing exchangers leave some small gift as a thank you for the enjoyable vacation they had at their host's home.

13 Taking the Kids Along

PERHAPS MORE IN THESE 1990s than in the 1980s and previous decades, dads and moms are bombarded from all sides—schools, churches, service clubs, recreation organizations, health clubs—with vacation opportunities for their children: baseball, soccer, basketball, and other sports camps; wilderness camps; music appreciation camps; happy-jolly-fun camps for overweight underachievers and underweight overachievers; church camps; computer camps; and, yes, even some genuine, old-fashioned *camp* camps! There are also dude ranches, national and international student travel groups, short-term overseas missionary projects, and weeks with relatives and friends—a veritable parade of diverse ways in which to keep children and young people happy, healthy, and *occupied* during school vacations, especially summer vacations.

In spite of all this youth vacation opportunity hype, the fact is that *family* vacations are still very much the "in" thing to do. It is the prospect of doing things *together as a family* that is behind these family vacations—looked forward to and enjoyed by both parents and children.

Confronted by the skyrocketing costs of conventional (hotel-motel-restaurant) vacations, home exchanging is especially attractive to parents who prefer to vacation with their children. Confirming this fact, an exchanger in Minneapolis, Minnesota, who vacations with his wife and *six* children, writes: "This vacation home exchange idea is great. It sure beats hotels, motels, and buying twenty-four meals in restaurants each vacation day!" Infants, children, and teens alike are becoming very much a part of the vacation home exchanging scene. Indeed, the survey underscores the fact that nearly one-half of exchangers residing in the U.S. travel with their children. And with those exchangers residing outside of the U.S.? Exactly one-half.

Living in Churchville, Pennsylvania, with three exchanges in England and France, a college professor husband-and-wife team recommends vacation home exchanging as "really the only way to go with children. . . . Home exchanging has been a great opportunity, allowing us to take vacations with the whole family—vacations we could not have otherwise afforded. On one occasion, we had the child of our French exchange partners stay with us for two weeks before his parents arrived; this was a very positive experience, which led to an invitation for our son to spend some time later with them in France."

B-o-r-i-n-g and *fun* are two of the words most frequently used by children and teens, especially young teens. Watching television in a cramped motel room with parents is *boring*. Waiting to be served meals in restaurants is *boring* ("Why can't we have all our meals—breakfast, lunch, dinner—at McDonald's?"). Hour after hour in the car, driving to see some Civil War battlefield. You guessed it: boring!

While vacation home exchanging does, of course, have some negative aspects, one thing it is *not* is boring. It is *fun* watching TV and playing VCR games "just like at home." It is *fun* helping Dad barbeque spareribs for dinner at "our" vacation home and not having to eat out all the time. It is *fun* taking short, tourist-type car trips while based at an exchange host's home. And it is *fun* making new friends with the family next door and playing with the host's kids' toys.

"While vacation home exchanging, our two kids feel as though they have a new home, in a new place; soon after arriving, our kids view our host's home as familiar surroundings in which to relax and play," writes a teacher in Miami, Florida.

From El Paso, Texas, a physician's wife shares this story—one with a vacation home exchange dividend: "While staying at our home, our exchange partner's little girl learned to ride our two-wheel bicycle; on returning to their California home, this youngster was given her first very-own bike!"

Much has been written in previous chapters about the responsibility vacation home exchange partners must have for each other's homes and personal property. When children of any age are a part of the exchange, a special burden of responsibility rests on the shoulders of the respective exchange partners' parents. More often than not, home exchangers with children seem to exchange with partners who also have children; this makes it easier all the way around. Indeed, within the world of vacation home exchanging a fraternity of home exchangers who vacation with their children has developed. Most in this group are fully aware that "children will be children."

Special precautions should be taken for the protection of the homes and property of both parties to the exchange, and these precautions start with the preparation of the home for exchangers with children.

Ample drawer and closet space should be provided for the use of children—their clothes, toys and games, and other things they bring along with them. Special attention should be given to putting away all treasured family possessions, bric-a-brac, and (especially) breakables—items which might otherwise be accessible to groping, innately curious little hands.

If the child or children involved are infants or youngsters, the host partner should anticipate the needs of these little guests. He should make every effort to provide for these needs, a checklist of which might include:

- crib
- playpen
- high chair
- car seat
- stroller
- rubber bed pad (even a toilet-trained child tends to "forget" when away from his home environment)
- baby sitter contacts

A home exchanging geophysics engineer in Kernen, Germany, writes: "We spent three-and-a-half months home exchanging in New Zealand with our three-month-old son, Jonathan. The reception we got on the part of our exchange host's relatives and friends was magnificent. All the necessities for Jonathan had been made ready. We had the use of a crib (with mosquito netting), a baby's bath tub, a changing table, and even some child's clothing. Our host had registered us for the local baby care program [visiting nurse] and many other services. It took us but a short while to feel completely at home."

If the exchange hosts themselves have (or have had) young children, many or most of these child-related necessities will already be at hand. If not, perhaps some of these items can be borrowed from family members or friends. As a last resort, any or all can be rented from a local rental service, with arrangements being made during the pre-exchange correspondence and the exchange guests being responsible for all rental fees.

If older children are included, rules should be established, in writing, regarding the use of the hosts' bicycles, skateboards, and other family sports equipment, including basket and soccer balls, fishing tackle, and so on. Rules should also be made as to the use of the VCR and stereo equipment. If the host approves of his guests using the VCR, then instructions should be left as to the availability and use of his cassette library, and information should be given regarding local video-cassette rental stories.

Regardless of whether children accompany their parents on a conventional vacation or a home exchange vacation, experienced dads and moms know that one of the most important elements of a successful vacation with children is *keeping them occupied*.

Here again, host partners can be a real help to their exchange guests by providing them with complete information about the ac-

tivities for children and young people offered in their communities. Some host families holding memberships in country, tennis, or swimming clubs arrange for their guest partners to use their club guest cards, enabling them to enjoy tennis, swimming, golf, exercise equipment, video games, and other facilities. Most communities provide a wide variety of recreational opportunities for young children and teens: baseball, soccer, or Red Cross swimming and lifesaving lessons. There are the YMCA, the YMHA, local playgrounds, museums, miniature golf, amusement parks, picnic facilities, boat trips (those exchanging in New York City report the "best sightseeing value" available to teens and adults is the Circle Line's excursion boat trip around Manhattan Island), and fishing—lake, river, deep sea.

Home exchangers vacationing in condos often enjoy a parade of activity opportunities: tennis, swimming, barbeques, recreation rooms, and planned and supervised social events keyed to children of all ages.

"At our Washington, D.C., exchange, each evening my sons and I enjoyed playing table tennis—more fun than sitting around in a motel (wondering what to do *now*)," writes a Minneapolis, Minnesota, exchanger.

Previously it was suggested that vacation home exchange hosts provide their guests with specific information about the home and its appliances—what to do, what not to do—and also general information about their neighbors, neighborhood, shops, and such other facts will help their guests to feel at home in their homes in the communities in which these homes are located. This information should be available in the Info Kit.

A similar Info Kit should detail for exchange partners with children the type of child-related information set forth in these paragraphs. Included in this Info Kit for vacation home exchange partners with children should also be the names, addresses, and telephone numbers of a local dentist, pediatrician, family physician; the nearest hospital emergency room; and the nearest urgent-care type clinic that will accept patients without appointments. Hopefully, this information will not be needed, but having it at hand could be a tremendous help if a health emergency should rear its ugly head. This was certainly true in the case of an insurance company secretary in Hartford, Connecticut, who writes: "While on a vacation home exchange in Dayton, Ohio, overnight our six-year-old daughter developed an unexplained, unusually high fever. Fortunately, our host had left with us a reference to a nearby pediatrician. This doctor saw us on very short notice, treated our child, and in a day our family vacation enjoyment was back on track."

Any or all of the above steps taken by the vacation exchange host will be greatly appreciated by exchange guests vacationing with children.

Now the other side of the vacation home exchange coin: guidelines for the exchange *guests* traveling with children. Heeding these will assure that the entire family will have an enjoyable and memorable (and, yes, fun!) vacation.

First and foremost, it is doubly important that the arrival of the exchange guests with children be without incident. Nothing is as disturbing as arriving at the exchange host's home with the wrong door key at night, in the rain, with two travel-weary, screaming kids! To avoid this or some similar near disaster, both parties to a home exchange involving children must be especially careful in their arrival arrangements—arrangements which must be clearly understood by the host and guest families. In many respects, preparing for a vacation home exchange with children is quite like preparing for a conventional vacation with children. The amount of luggage space will dictate how many child-related items can be taken along—security pillows and blankets, games, dolls, stuffed animals, Band-Aids (a New Hampshire home exchanger's four-year-old son calls these "bump-aids"), and other special things not so important to the parent but sometimes of paramount importance to the children.

Often a child's initial reaction to the exchange vacation home can be somewhat less than positive, putting a damper on the vacation's first day or two. An attorney in Boston, Massachusetts, and his wife, traveling with two young children to an exchange home in France—a sixteenth century home in a small village near Paris—got this reaction from their kids: "'This place is terrible. We don't want to live *here*!' Subsequently they loved the place."

Immediately after arrival at the host's home, guests should look for the home-related, child-related material—the Info Kit left them by their exchange host. Depending on the ages of the children, "house rules" should be drawn up and understood by all, what to do, what not to do, where to go, where not to go: "No feet on the couch"; "Keep the volume on the stereo low enough not to inflame the neighbors": "No Cokes or apple-cranberry juice in the living room" (the room with that deep-pile, bone-colored carpet). And so on.

A retired businessman and physical education instructor and his reading specialist teacher wife in Frackville, Pennsylvania, write: "We exchanged with our five children, all under sixteen, and the only thing we ever broke was an ashtray, which we replaced, and the only thing our exchange partners did was block our toilet, and they paid the plumber's bill."

Teachers in Seattle, Washington, write: "We always put away dangerously positioned bric-a-brac, as bouncing balls have a way of appearing from nowhere. Also, we sometimes put towels on the nice furniture when we get to our 'new' home—an ounce of prevention. Finally, in assessing the house, we look for cracks in the windows and any other apparent damage, so we know what we did and did not do while exchanging at this particular home."

Home exchanging with children should definitely be a family affair—*everyone* has to help in some way so that *all* will enjoy this stay. Depending on the ages of the children, a job schedule should be drawn up—who does what, when—just like at home.

From Coeur d'Alene, Idaho, a four-time vacation home exchanging professor writes: "Contact with neighbors adds security to the exchanger with children." If the neighbors have children with ages similar to those of the exchange children, these kids will get to know each other very quickly—new friends, new toys to play with. Fun!

Here is another thought from a four-time exchanging salesman in Kentucky: "On our first vacation home exchange (in Oregon), we found our ten-year-old son was bored most of the time, so since then we have arranged for one of his special friends to go along with us. Problem solved!"

A nine-time exchanger from Cape Cod, Massachusetts, writes: "On two exchanges, we took along our sitter to help with our two sons. She had not traveled a great deal and so enjoyed the opportunity of seeing all the sights in the Washington, D.C., area and visiting the Berkshire Mountains while staying in a home complete with a horse in the back yard!"

From a child's point of view, vacation home exchanging—a different vacation home every year—can be a marvelous, memorable, mind-expanding experience.

And from the parents' point of view?

Floridian exchange parents report: "With our two children, a vacation home exchange is ideal." Parents from Birmingham, Alabama: "Our kids play with our hosts' neighbors' kids, and we have a grand time!" Parents from Rutland, Vermont: "With the money we save home exchange vacationing, we now take our kids along and spend four weeks on vacation, not the previous two or three." Parents from Tampa, Florida: "With our small children along, home exchange will be the best way for us to vacation for years to come."

14 The Animal Kingdom

A COUPLE FROM KENT, ENGland, writes: "Our two adorable Persian cats spend their holidays at a luxury cat hotel while we do our holiday home exchanging in America."

If five-star "luxury cat hotels" are as expensive, relatively speaking, as five-star luxury people hotels, it is apparent that cats, dogs, and other pets must be a part of many vacation home exchange arrangements, and indeed they are. An appropriate automobile bumper sticker for pet-owning vacation home exchangers might well be "LOVE MY HOME, LOVE MY PET!"

"Yes, we will take care of your pets," a Leawood, Kansas, family wrote their exchange partners. But when these Midwesterners arrived at their first vacation home exchange on Oahu, Hawaii, "a beautiful home overlooking Waikiki, we found a houseful of pets to care for: two inside dogs, one outside dog, a bird, a cat, a pheasant, and rabbits and goldfish. The first morning my husband and I awoke to find one of the large inside dogs sharing our bed. Fortunately, we love animals, and it all worked out well and gave our two school-age children some odd jobs to do during their vacation."

Baltimore, Maryland, exchangers "developed a close friendship with our exchange host's dog. It was a slightly sad parting for both dog and ourselves when the exchange period ended."

Exchanging in the state of Washington, a Eugene, Oregon, family writes: "Our host left his big, beautiful dog for us to feed and care for. This dog was just great, and our teenagers fell in love with him!"

There cannot be very many pet rabbits in London, but a Derbyshire, England, couple had great fun taking care of their London exchange host's rabbit and his cat, as well. The rule of that exchange home: "Keep the cat away from the bunny!"

Just as home exchangers in the correspondence stage must be very clear as to the number of adults and children in their exchange

group, pet-owning exchangers also must share *complete* information about their dogs, cats, and other assorted pets. What kind of pet? How old? How large? And so on. In most instances, these pet details are dealt with early on so that the exchangers know exactly what they are getting into, pet-wise. But, often, sadly, such is not the case, report a Seattle, Washington, retired couple—three-time exchangers: "Our exchange partners didn't tell us they had a dog-sized cat, which darn near scared us to death! Another time, there was a hamster in a cage in an upstairs bedroom, which we discovered completely by accident. It would have died (by the way, do rodents die?) if we hadn't fed the damned thing!"

This from a retired teacher in Jackson, New Hampshire: "I failed to check on the pet situation and found myself with a dog and three cats to be taken care of. However, they were very sweet, well-behaved animals. No trouble at all. I enjoyed them." But this exchanger should not have *needed* to check. The pet situation certainly should have been made clear to her in the first exchanges of correspondence.

A rancher and retired lumberman from North Bend, Oregon, writes: "Soon after we arrived in London, our host's neighbors came to visit and said they were bringing along some friends to see us. These 'friends' turned out to be our host's pets—a dog and a cat—which we took care of, feeding and loving the darned things!"

"On one of our six exchanges in California," writes a secretary in Balzers, Liechtenstein, "the people told us they had no pets, and within a day or two after our arrival we had three dogs and one cat to take care of!"

And, finally, in the "Act of God" category, a Colby, Kansas, "self farmer" (who with his wife and young child have had six vacation home exchanges from Australia to Kenya, East Africa) shares this story: "Our Massachusetts exchanger had made arrangements for his Labrador retriever to be 'pet-sat' while he was gone. The sitter was in a car wreck just before our arrival, and we inherited the dog. My wife was disgusted, our four-year-old son was thrilled, and I was somewhere in between. Our son and I enjoyed some beautiful sunsets walking around Marblehead Harbor with the dog. I guess the above is just a statement that the unusual can always present itself and be accepted in different ways by different people."

Pet care on a vacation home exchange is not usually one-sided. Each pet-owning exchanger cares for the pet (or pets) belonging to the exchange partner. Pet exchanging is an integral part of many exchanges, and exchange pets (especially cats and dogs) are often loved almost to the point of being members of the family.

The care and feeding of the pets would, of course, be among the most important elements of this special, pet-centered material; additional information should be included:

- What does the pet's like and dislike?
- Is this an inside or outside pet?
- Where does he/she sleep, eat, exercise?
- Where does the pet do his/her "business" and what about local regulations related to this necessary aspect of the pet care?
- Who is the veterinarian familiar with the pet?
- If the home exchange guest is to be away for a few days, who is to take care of the pets?
- What about fleas?

A Brooklyn, New York, exchange family writes: "*Cat Fleas!* We exchanged with people in Amsterdam, Holland, who said their cat had fleas . . . 'but only cat' fleas. When our son became covered with flea bites, we realized that our exchange partner's pet fleas were not confined to cats!" And a Larchmont, New York, exchanger writes: "Our London host's home was infested with his cat's fleas. Much cleaning and insecticide at least made the place habitable."

An exchanger in Boise, Idaho, shares this "Foolproof Test for the Presence of Fleas": "Wearing only white athletic socks on your feet, take a walk around the house—basement, kitchen, porch, all the rooms. Then check your socks. If they are covered with little black spots, you've got flea problems!"

Face it. If your pets and/or your home is flea-ridden, you must get rid of those fleas before your exchange date. Then put flea collars on the dogs and/or cats, and leave instructions for preventative measures your exchange partners should take to avoid a future flea episode—flea powder, insecticide, whatever.

These suggestions from fellow vacation home exchangers are in no way intended to disparage pets. Pets can be lots of fun and can provide you with both love and laughs, even if sometimes they do *weird* things. A New Haven, Connecticut, exchange couple enjoying their vacation home exchange in Maine returned to their exchange home one evening and found Nellie (the cat) sitting close up to the garage door, "just like a black ceramic fireplace cat guarding the door. Even when we tooted the car's horn, Nellie did not budge an inch. When we opened the garage door with the car's remote control device, out popped Nellie, whose long tail had been caught under the garage door. Apparently Nellie had been sitting in this spot when the garage door was closed electronically on our departure . . . and she had been stuck there all evening!"

Two retired sisters in Coral Springs, Florida, four-time exchangers, write: "In Surrey, England, our house 'guest' was a large Morris cat. We nicknamed him Henry VIII because when he was displeased with his food, he pounded on the wall!"

From Paris, France, an education system inspector writes: "Our exchange animal was a completely mad cat. Apparently missing her master, every night the cat made such a loud noise she terrified not only us, but the neighbors as well."

"We loved our vacation home exchange cat in Holland," writes a sixteen-time exchanger in St. Croix, U.S. Virgin Islands. This feeling must have been mutual "because one evening Pushkin followed us to a local concert, waited two hours until the performance was over, and then followed us back home."

From Wales, Great Britain, comes this story: "One of our exchangers thought the cat 'flap' in the door was a mail drop." Another couple exchanging in Winchester, England, knew what the cat flap was for—an exit and entry for their host's cat. "And the *neighbors'* cats also knew what the flap was for, because at cat-feeding time each day, three other cats appeared in our kitchen!"

A New Jersey couple agreed to care for their host's cat, Blue. But often at mealtimes there was no sign of Blue, just one of the neighbor's cats at the door meowing, "I'm Peter."

A *sixty*-time (since 1962) exchange couple, now living in Guadalajara, Mexico, writes: "When we had a home exchange in Denver, Colorado, we took our two high school daughters along with us. There was a cat dish on the back porch, so we assumed this was for our host's cat. We fed it regularly. It was ready to have kittens; the

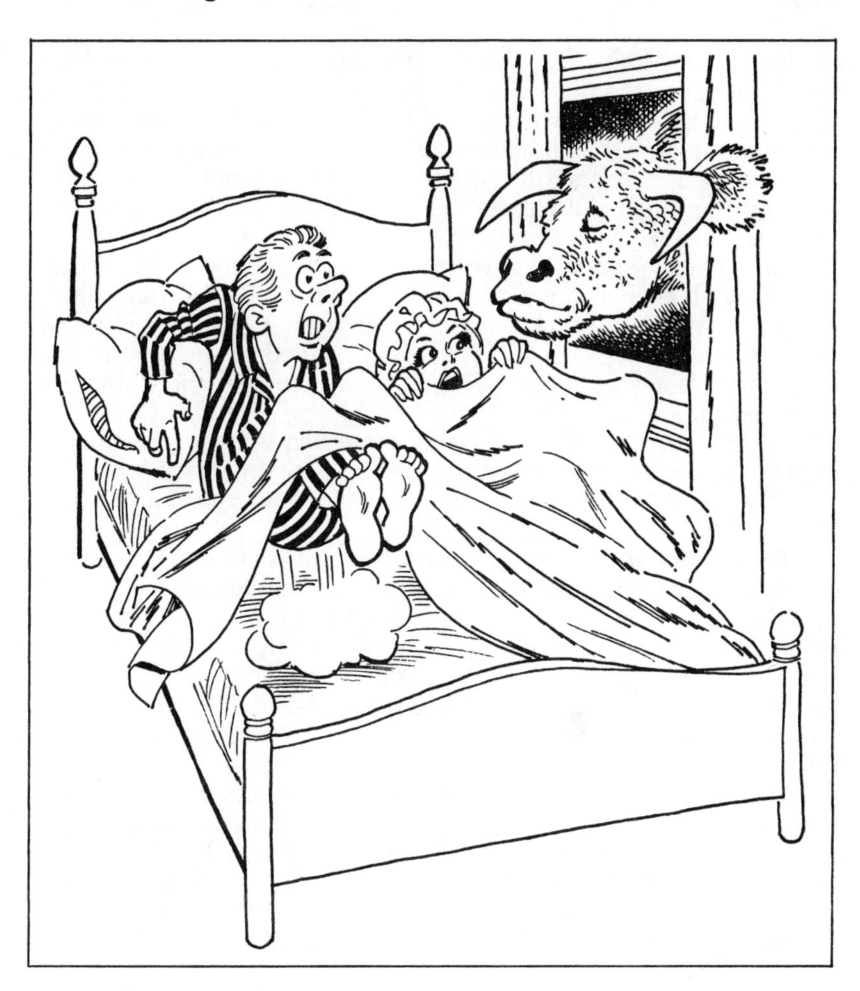

girls were very excited about this! Then one day, no cat, but finally she did show up—no longer a mother-to-be. The girls then followed her and discovered we had been feeding and taking care of the neighbor's cat!"

While cats and dogs seem to be the vacation home exchangers' pets of choice, they are by no means the only pets in the vacation home exchanging community. A vacation home exchanger living in Staplehurst, England, listed their "pet"—an Arabian horse, which was there to be ridden by "experienced horse people."

In Fernandina, Italy, vacation home exchangers from England wrote: "Every day our neighbor took his ferret out for a walk on its leash. And they call us English eccentric!"

Other English exchangers from Shrewsbury write: "In our exchange country home near Nice, France, we were intrigued to hear our three-year-old come into our bedroom talking about a 'crab' climbing the stairs. How inventive! I got up to meet a rather sleepy *scorpion*, which had climbed out of the cellar. It was pretty big! We were later reassured that the sting of a scorpion is not serious, or at least not life threatening; nevertheless, this did not make us all rest particularly easily."

An engineer and teacher couple in Bethesda, Maryland, writes: "Our English exchange partners were watching after our daughter's pet turtle. We forgot to tell them that the turtle was supposed to eat the goldfish in the water tank. When we called to see how things were going, our guests felt very guilty and worried about the fish *disappearing* from the tank."

From Sandwich, Massachusetts, a fourteen-time home exchanging couple writes: "Our worst experience pet-sitting was when we were supposed to take care of some canaries and one escaped from its cage."

From Boulder, Colorado: "Once while staying in London, taking care of our host's two very furry cats, we decided to take a drive out into the countryside to spend the night. I carefully closed our bedroom door, so the cat wouldn't get on the bed and get fur all over. We had a lovely time in the country and on our return, we couldn't find one of the cats anywhere in the three-story house. *Of course*, I had locked her *in* the bedroom instead of *out*—not only that, but inside the closet!"

While not exactly a home exchange pet-sitting story, this one from exchangers in Florida is certainly animal kingdom/home exchange-related: "Several weeks before our exchange in Canada, I had the unfortunate experience of having a corn snake drop over my head, Medusa-style, from our front door ledge. Naturally terrified . . . but finding it humorous *later*, we shared this one-time adventure with our new Canadian friends the night before they departed for our home. We all had a great laugh until a week later, when we received a telephone call informing us that 'Fang' had dropped over the arm of our home exchange partner's husband . . . but, at least, we were somewhat relieved recalling we had forewarned them about this visiting snake."

"While in California," a Somers, Connecticut, exchanger writes, "the couple we were exchanging with had left two dogs at the house. Their daughter down the street would take care of the dogs. However, my two daughters fell in love with the dogs (one a poodle and the other a pup), and that was the highlight of their trip. They didn't even want to see the sights."

"Our twelve exchanges have been relatively free and straight forward. But," writes a Brooklyn, New York, couple, "we just exchanged in Hawaii, and we usually exchange pet care. We have a dog and two cats, but this particular Hawaiian family had a menagerie, for sure—a goat, two geese, two chickens, two cats, and a bird. It was very interesting for us city folks to take care of farm animals. Fortunately, our daughters were with us and did most of the animal-related work. The reward was really fresh eggs, something you do not get too easily in Brooklyn!"

And, finally, from Bologna, Italy: "When we went to Los Angeles, we accepted to take care of the dog of the family we had exchanged with. It was a black wolf dog, and we remarked he was always bad tempered. Then we discovered that its owners had left him only a large bag of dog biscuits and told us not to worry about its food. Once we tried to give him the kind of food we gave our dog in Italy, when we had one. We prepared some recipes we defined 'dog's homemade Italian food'. Later he became very friendly . . . perhaps he liked home exchanging, too!"

In scanning the vacation home exchange directories, smokers pass over "no smoking" home exchange listings, exchangers with children pass over the "no children" home exchange listings, and, of course, many home exchangers prefer not to become involved with pet care and include this fact in their listings.

But, as has been mentioned, most pet-sitting home exchangers are also pet owners and pet lovers, so they are quite familiar with pet-care responsibilities. Moreover, they are accustomed to having pets of one kind or another around the house. Just as their own pets provide loving companionship when they are at home, these exchangers more often than not appreciate the companionship of their exchange partner's pets.

15 Putting Exchange Wheels under Your Vacation

IT IS SAID THAT THROUGHout a lifetime of spending, a person's largest single investment is in a home; the next largest is in a car (or cars). Apparently, these statistics overlook the costs of marrying off daughters, university tuitions, and sneakers for teenagers!

While many chapters of this book deal with exchanging that largest investment, the home, this one is focused on the automobile. Less money is involved than in a home, true, but a man or woman's heart is often where his or her car is. "Take my wife, take my life, but don't take my car!" And yet the survey reveals that three out of four vacation home exchangers worldwide include cars in their home exchange arrangements.

"We thought long and hard about including our car in our home exchange," writes a shop owner in Norwich, England. "Funnily enough, we were *more* worried about someone driving our car than taking care of our home and two cats! But we were going to Germany for a month, and the cost of a rental car would have put us in the poorhouse. So exchange cars we did, and it all worked out wonderfully well. Oh, we did have some right-side traffic problems, but our German exchange friends had to face the hazards of entering clockwise-traffic roundabouts, while driving on the righthand side of the car!"

What about accidents? Insurance questions and problems? Repairs and flat tires? Cars falling short of their owners' somewhat exaggerated descriptions? Car operation problems? Misunderstandings about where, and how far, cars are to be driven?

For each of these questions the answer has to be yes, of course, occasionally problems do arise in the exchanging of cars. But according to the survey participants, the negative aspects of car exchanging rarely rear their ugly heads . . . and on balance, they say the advantages of car exchanging clearly outweigh the disadvantages.

What are the advantages of car exchanging? On Manhattan Island, in New York; in London's West End; and just about *anywhere* in Paris or Hong Kong, a car is an unnecessary burden. But the vast majority of vacation home exchanging is done not in heavily trafficked cities, but elsewhere—where a car is nearly always an absolute necessity. So car exchanges or car rentals are the only ways of putting wheels under your home exchange vacations. And renting (except off-season in some areas) can be expensive. Whether you are talking about a week, a month, or more, in car rental you are talking about big dollars, pounds, francs, marks, lira, or any other currency. While certainly there are many reasons for vacation home exchanging, there is only one reason for exchanging cars: to save money.

Car problems and car-related problems between exchange partners can happen, say experienced exchangers. But preventative measures can and should be taken.

Those who do car exchanging strongly recommend car exchange partners have a written agreement in advance to deal with the most important elements of car exchange.

Aside from providing reliable exchange cars in good condition, adequate automobile insurance coverage is the most important element in car exchanging. Are car exchangers covered by the car owners' auto insurance policies? While car exchangers are not specifically mentioned in auto insurance policies, most insurance agents agree that a car exchanger comes under the general category of those authorized by car owners to drive their cars. If one car owner lends his car to a neighbor or friend—or to a home exchanger—generally that person is covered by the car owner's comprehensive automobile insurance policy—accident, liability, medical, fire, theft, and other standard provisions. The following clause, for example, is an integral part of the policy written by one of the largest insurers of cars in the U.S. regarding who is an "Insured." Among others, after the policyholder, his/her spouse, and their relatives, an insured person is "Any other person while using such a car if its use is within the scope of consent of the insured and his/her spouse."

And the following appears in the auto policies of a major British insurance firm: "Persons or classes of persons entitled to drive, provided that the person driving holds a license to drive the vehicle: any person who is driving on the Policyholder's order or with the Policyholder's permission."

Some home/car exchangers are provided with cars by their employers, insured either by the employers (self-insurance) or by their employers' insurance firms. More often than not, such company-owned cars can be driven only by the employee and by members of his or her immediate family.

Some auto insurance firms require their policyholders to pay a surcharge if cars are to be driven by those other than the policyholder or his immediate family. Exchangers in Cos Cob, Connecticut, for instance, ran into this very situation while exchanging in England. They offered to reimburse their exchange host for this surcharge, but their host did not wish them to do so.

A three-time exchanger in Seattle, Washington, writes: "One concern we have always had has been the possibility of having an accident while using our home exchange partner's car. We have always discussed this with our exchange partners and agreed that, in the event of an accident, we would cover any funds not covered by the owner's insurance company. On our second visit to the United Kingdom, in Scotland, we hit a large oil spill on the roadway (caused by a previous accident) and spun off the road into the ditch. There was damage to the car we were driving, and I paid the deductible (about $100), while our host's insurance company paid the rest."

This car exchanger's experience underscores the fact that all parties involved in car exchanges should carefully check out with their insurance agents all provisions of their car insurance policies as these relate to friends' (home exchangers') use of their cars. Then the car exchanging partners should share this information with each other.

While driving in the U.S., one must have available his car operator's license, the registration certificate covering this car, and a current, in-force insurance identification card. Usually, the latter two documents are kept in an envelope placed in the car's glove compartment, and the operator's license is kept in the driver's wallet. A home exchanging accountant in Raleigh, North Carolina, adds to the glove compartment envelope a "To Whom It May Concern" letter, which in essence authorizes the car owner's exchange partner to drive this particular car.

When the car exchange involves a car outside of the U.S., it is incumbent on the car's owner to be certain the car's documents are in order and accessible to his exchange partner.

Important, too, is the matter of who will be driving the car. Most exchanges, of course, are composed of a husband and wife. Are both to be driving the exchange car? If the exchange is made up of two couples, are all four in the exchange group to be driving the car? These matters should be clarified and agreed to by all parties prior to the exchange date.

Insurance companies in the U.S. tend to be very nervous about their coverage of persons—especially single men—under twenty-five years of age. Indeed, most insurance policies that include persons under age twenty-five are rated up; that is, the insurance premium is considerably higher than would be the case if the car was to be driven only by persons over age twenty-five. A recommended rule of thumb here is that persons under twenty-five years of age should not drive exchange cars, especially in the U.S.

Also to be clarified in advance of the car exchange date: generally speaking, where and how far is the exchange car to be driven? A Vero Beach, Florida, teacher and his wife "put 10,000 miles on our English host's VW camper in England, Scotland, Wales, and on the Continent via Dover—a seven-week exchange. The English couple enjoyed Florida so much they came back to our home the next year, while we vacationed elsewhere in the States. We figured we owed them an additional exchange after putting all that mileage on their camper." Ten thousand miles in seven weeks would seem to be an inordinate number of miles to be put on an exchange vehicle, but apparently this was done with the approval of the camper's owner.

On their first vacation home exchange, a Fullerton, California, retired geologist put seven hundred miles on his Dutch host's car in Europe and returned to California to find that his exchange partner had put 3,000 miles on his car! "Next time," he writes, "I will negotiate a set mileage, like one thousand free miles plus a per-mile charge for excess by either party."

With a difference of 2,300 miles driven between these two exchange cars during a three- or four-week period, one can well understand why the exchanger at the short end of the deal would want to build safeguards into his future car exchange arrangements. Though this kind of lopsided mileage is a rarity in car exchange circles, a ten-time auto exchange home exchanger in Atlanta, Georgia, writes: "I know some exchangers do get taken advantage of in car mileage driven by their partners. Before each exchange I get a rough idea where my exchange partner is going to want to drive, and I tell him what our car-driving plans are. Assuming we are both on the same wave length in this matter of mileage to be driven, as we generally are, I do not check on my various partners' mileages, and if they check on mine, they've never questioned me about it."

More the rule than the exception is this from a Kattskill Bay, New York, retired consultant in the forensic safety engineering field: "Our three-week exchange partner in Cubbington, England, made his small car available to us, while he drove our larger station wagon, touring the New York, Long Island area, and driving down to Washington, D.C. And we went to Stratford, Bath, Wales, and various places in between. It was a fair and square arrangement."

The survey participants had a good deal to say about the cars that have been a part of their various home exchanges. Exchanging in England, a Brigantine, New Jersey, retired schoolteacher found herself behind the wheel "of a large and beautiful Daimler, but I really didn't drive it much; I was afraid something would happen to it."

"There were three Cadillacs in my California host's garage," writes a French businessman, "and a note that said, 'Use whichever cars you want and there are two boats in the canal beyond the swimming pool. Enjoy them all!'"

From a Hong Kong car exchanger: "We still laugh about our early attempts to drive in California. What seemed to be an aircraft carrier with marshmallow wheels was actually a Pontiac!"

On the other side of the home exchange coin, a Californian writes: "We left them a motor home and our car. They were supposed to leave us a new car and a trailer. The car didn't work . . . and there was no trailer!" An exchange car disappointment was also in store for a German family car exchanging in New Orleans, Louisiana: "My partner's car was so bad we had to *rent* an automobile. But, no mind. I let him use my car anyhow." And another disappointment, this from a Massachusetts exchanger: "That load of theirs barely made it through the two weeks!"

On one hand, Cadillacs and Daimlers; on the other, unsatisfactory cars. Great cars, lousy cars. Of course, these are the extremes. According to the survey, most car exchangers are provided with moderately priced cars that are two to five years old. When the exchange partner has two cars, he generally offers the car with lesser value. Given a choice, most exchangers would prefer not to drive a low-mileage, more expensive car. This very choice was given to long-time Florida exchangers when in Wales, United Kingdom. " 'Take our new Volvo, not that old fifty-thousand-mile Subaru,' urged our host. Having driven in England quite a bit, we have no real problem driving on the 'wrong' side of the road under normal conditions. But if confronted by one of those rare driving emergencies, it's just possible we might instinctively react as if we were driving on Interstate 75 in Florida, and we would not have wanted to put our host's new Volvo through that kind of an ordeal. For a month, we enjoyed the Subaru—happily, without any emergencies! Later that year our Welsh exchangers had no problem with the three-year-old Honda Accord we offered them during their Florida stay."

When Americans and Canadians exchange cars, they do not have to play the "wrong-side/right-side" driving game. Also, most cars in the U.S. and Canada have automatic transmissions and are air conditioned. In making arrangements for a car exchange in Europe, Americans and Canadians must realize that many, if not most, exchange cars have manual transmissions (stick shifts), and few are air-conditioned. Most Europeans simply do not feel the need for automatic transmissions, and their few months of really hot weather make car air conditioning an unnecessary expense. Also, many English cars—even late-model ones—do not have automatic chokes, so one must become accustomed to a manual choke during the first few miles of driving until the engine warms up.

A teacher from Stafford, New Hampshire, writes: "The car we exchanged in England broke down on a superhighway. We had to be towed, etc. They had a car club insurance that paid for it. We found out later that the car we had loaned to our exchanger had also died. I guess we had each given the other our 'worst' car!"

Regardless of whether their exchange cars are older or newer models, car exchangers must be sure their cars are mechanically sound, have recently been lubricated and tuned up, and are clean. Car owners must apprise their exchange car partners of whatever ec-

centricities or quirks their cars may have.

Also, the operator's handbook for each car exchanged should be placed in the car's glove compartment. Writes a San Francisco, California, teacher: "One of our car exchangers (a retired utility company vice president with an engineering degree) couldn't figure out how to start my Mercedes 240D. Even with my operating instructions taped to the dashboard, he couldn't get used to the importance of the glow plugs in starting a diesel engine!"

A Denver, Colorado, car exchanger in Hawaii drove at night with his headlights on bright. "Cars coming from the other direction were forever blinking their headlights at us. It was embarrassing, but I could not locate the headlight dimmer switch." A retired electrical engineer in San Diego, California, writes: "On the morning after our arrival in Florida, we went to the grocery store and stocked up, putting all of our food purchases in the trunk of my host's late model car. When we arrived at our exchange home, neither my wife nor I were able to get this car's trunk unlocked. We drove twenty-five miles to the nearest Volkswagen agency, where a mechanic opened the trunk and adjusted the lock. No more problems!" And from a car exchanger in Seattle, Washington: "In Hawaii, we had the use of a gorgeous four-door Jaguar—automatic this and automatic that, from door lock to seat position to sun roof . . . but one of the rear windows would not close. We panicked, knowing that if it were left on the side of the street, the car would disappear. A nearby mechanic solved the problem, but after that, this window stayed closed!"

Problems like these confront not only home and car exchangers, but all car owners. After all, cars are like people; they are just not quite perfect. The operator's handbook can often be a problem solver; if that fails, then an auto mechanic will be happy to come to one's rescue. A measure of good judgment coupled with a little patience can handle just about any minor problem that arises.

For over-the-road problems, there's the Automobile Association of America (AAA) or its equivalent outside of the U.S. These days the AAA covers car towing or emergency repairs for the individual AAA member, not for the car owned by the member. In the U.S., AAA members can telephone AAA for repairs to any car they happen to be driving—personal, rented, or exchange. But the AAA does not serve its members outside the U.S. The auto services comparable to the AAA outside the U.S. have different regulations, country by country. It would be appropriate for all potential car exchangers inside and outside of the U.S. to inquire of each other about such over-the-road emergency repair services as might be available to them.

Once in a while, as mentioned earlier, car exchangers have accidents while driving their exchange partners' cars. "While driving through California's Redwood Forest, a deer jumped out in front of our moving car," writes a teacher from Putney, England. "Unfortunately, the deer was killed, and the front end of the car was badly damaged. Our host worked a good deal with his insurance company, and the car was made like new."

From Sumner, Washington, an eight-time vacation home exchanger writes: "Our most embarrassing car exchange problem occurred one evening when I drove our exchange partner's car right through the back of his garage! As it happened, our partner was a very proper Englishman. He was a very kind and understanding man. He also was in the home construction and remodeling business and had no concern about the damage I had caused. This altercation between his car and his garage didn't interfere with our relationship. We continue to communicate, and we see each other when we are in England or he is in the States."

A college professor from Texas writes: "We parked our exchanger's car at Gatwick Airport, outside of London. The car was in good condition when we parked it. When the owner picked it up, he noticed that someone had backed into it, causing lots of damage. Our car also had been damaged. As it turned out, we found there was a tradeoff in the costs of repairing both cars."

The "accident" that was not an accident occurred in England—just two blocks from Kensington Palace. The car was a large Rover, curbside parked by permit. "Though car exchange was a part of our arrangement with this English family, when in London we use buses and subways, and the Rover just sat there in front of our host's home for the month," writes this non-Rover-driving American. "Well, the day before our exchange ended, we noticed some damage to the Rover's front bumper and fender. There was a lot of home renovation taking place on this same street, so we assumed one of the construction trucks had inadvertently backed into the Rover. Out came our host's in-case-of-a-car-accident instructions. Dutifully, we reported the accident to the police, and we called the insurance company, describing the 'accident' and put in a claim for repairs, figuring we were helping our exchange partner in his absence. A week or so after we had returned to the States, our London host wrote, thanking us for our trouble and mentioning he had forgotten to tell us that the car damage was done some weeks *before* our exchange!"

Finally, in the accident arena, a Las Vegas woman writes: "Then there was the time my husband became confused in the London traffic and had an accident with our host family's Mercedes! Then followed one of the most difficult phone calls my husband ever had to make. Our host was most gracious about all of this, and our insurance covered the damage. Whew!"

British exchangers driving cars in the U.S. do not seem to have problems operating cars in America, probably because British vacationers often take their own cars to nearby France and elsewhere on the European continent. There, though their driver's seat is on the right side of the car, at least they become familiar with driving on the right side of the road, as is the case in the U.S.

It is, however, an entirely different story, reports the survey, for American car exchangers in Great Britain. From Sedona, Arizona, a retired, ten-time worldwide exchanger writes: "When we exchanged with an English family, we picked up their car at Gatwick Airport. It was about fifty miles to Swanley, our destination. The car was a stick shift, with steering wheel on the right, etc. A fog settled in, and a slow drizzle with visibility near zero. New freeway construction and road barriers and roundabouts made for a very slow and interesting trip. We parked the car and never drove it again for the entire month we were there. The train station was only a few blocks away, however, and we had a great time."

"We found the most dangerous situation we were in," writes a retired shop manager in Idaho Falls, Idaho, "was driving in England. It's not easy or even natural to drive on the 'wrong' side of the road. We once went through a circle (over there they call them 'roundabouts') in the wrong direction and met all the traffic coming head on!" Those roundabouts do present a real challenge to Americans driving in Great Britain. A tip from a car exchanger in Lansing, Michigan: "We had a terrible time managing those circles during our Oxford, England, exchange. Finally I got the hang of it: first, determine before you confront the circle which road you are taking out of the circle. Slow down as you approach the circle and turn left as you enter it; (important) the car in the circle—coming from the right—has the right of way (the driver assumes you know this, so he will just keep coming on); signal for a left turn, and take that left turn when you reach your predetermined road out of the circle."

From Salem, Oregon: "At first while driving in London, I found myself endeavoring to 'convert' in my mind each traffic situation from the left side of the road to the right. This was disastrous, because by the time I had completed my conversion process, I had several very close shaves!" Practice, leading up to experience in light traffic and, later, heavy traffic is the only way a driver can gain confidence and become a safe driver in "wrong" side of the road driving.

This from a Florida attorney: "I found driving on the 'wrong' side of the road and in unfamiliar places quite confusing. Therefore I bought a piece of poster paper and a marking pen and put a sign in the rear window of our exchange car: *Please Be Patient—Confused American Driver.* Not only did the horns stop blowing at me, but on numerous occasions people would ask if they could be of any assistance. We even had one dinner invitation because of that sign. I changed the sign from car to car for the next three months while we did a chain of exchanges in England, Scotland, and Ireland."

Provision must be made for parking exchange cars. Generally, garage space is available, assuming this garage is not stuffed with lawn mowers, bicycles, wheelbarrows, and half-filled paint cans—no problem. But if no garage space is available, the exchange partners must make adequate arrangements for the parking of their respective cars.

"Though we had properly parked the exchange car we had been driving," writes a businessman from New Mexico, "our exchange partner left our car in the wrong section of the airport parking lot, and we thought it had been stolen." Just as home exchange arrivals and departures must be carefully planned and spelled out in advance by both parties to the exchange, so must car exchange plans. The partners should understand where their respective cars should be picked up and where they should be delivered at the end of the exchange. And, of course, the location of car keys should also be clearly understood.

"I had a funny car exchange retrieving experience," writes a Phoenix, Arizona, exchanger. "We loaned our home exchanger our blue Taurus, leaving our white Nissan at home. Two weeks later when we returned to Phoenix—tired after a long, delayed flight—out came our photocopy of the airport parking lot showing the general area in which our car was to be parked by our exchange partner. Well, we searched and searched; our car was not to be seen. So, I'm thinking, 'Why did I bother to give that jerk a parking lot map showing where to park our car, if he was going to go and park it wherever he darned well wished?' While criss-crossing the lot one more time, right where it was supposed to be, there was our car—the blue Taurus—and all the time I was thinking we had loaned our partner the white Nissan!"

On some occasions, car exchanges have advantages over and above those planned for, such as the Glen Cove, New York, multitime exchanger who learned to drive in Scotland with a stick shift; the Boynton Beach, Florida, couple whose exchange host in Germany invited them to take his Mercedes station wagon to Vienna, "as we'd planned on renting a car for that trip"; the Nevis, West Indies, exchanger whose car is not dependable and who therefore sometimes rents cars for her exchange guests in return for the use of their cars when she visits their homes in Europe; and, finally, the Canadian physician, who tries to arrange for exchangers to stay in his house for a period longer than he stays in theirs in return for his use of their car for additional weeks of travel.

Immediately prior to the exchange, the car exchanging partners will have had their respective cars lubricated and tuned up and have the tires checked. Assuming this to be the case and assuming each car is driven less than three thousand miles, the partners need only purchase gas and have the oil level, water, and tires checked periodically. If the car is driven more than three thousand miles during the exchange, then the driver should arrange to have the car lubricated and have the oil filter changed.

The fact that the vast majority of vacation home exchangers include cars in their exchanges is proof positive that car exchanging works. But responsible exchangers endeavor to make this element of home exchanging work better, or best, by checking into the matter of car insurance; offering clean, reliable cars in good condition; providing information about AAA or its equivalent; agreeing on who is to drive the car, and where; having proper documents for the car available to the exchanger; making suggestions as to the availability of persons to handle both minor and major repairs; and making clear to all concerned the pickup and delivery arrangements for the exchange cars.

If these elements of car exchanging are discussed and agreed upon by car exchanging partners and if both parties to the car exchange are reasonable and fair, the result is almost certain to be a successful car exchange.

A postscript on car exchanging from a Seattle, Washington, exchanger: "We always leave our partner's car with a full tank of gas, and we nearly always find our car exchange partners do the same."

16 Still More People Who Tried It . . . and Liked It

With a total of forty home exchanges in thirteen U.S. states, plus three in the West Indies and fourteen hospitality exchanges in six states, surely the Fauré family has earned honors as France's number one vacation home exchange family!

Felix Fauré writes:

I am sixty-four years old, my wife, Susan, is in her early forties, and we have one teenage son, Frederic.

In twenty cities in the south of France are located supermarkets I own and manage; our staff numbers seven hundred men and women. Since 1981, at one time or another we have exchanged all four of our homes and condominiums. Our main home is located near my office in Pamiers, forty miles south of Toulouse. This house has five bedrooms, three bathrooms, large living and dining rooms furnished with antiques, a garden, outdoor pool, and a fantastic view of the Pyrenees Mountains.

At 4,500 feet elevation in the mountains is located our ski lodge, great for winter sports and a remote, pleasurable place for year-round vacationing. We have also two elegant apartments on the French

Riviera, located in Cannes, on the famous Croisette Boulevard, overlooking the sea and the beautiful private and public gardens.

With these four properties, I can offer home exchange year 'round in a large spectrum of southern France. With these properties, too, we have opportunities to exchange homes with families almost anywhere in this world we wish to go. I personally answer each of the hundreds of home exchange inquiry letters we receive. Because we have more exchange opportunities than we could possibly accept, occasionally we rent our properties, but home exchange guests always come first!

We love very much Americans and America—especially its sun and its wonderful beaches. We have been north, east, south, and west in the U.S., but we most like California and Florida. During the 1980s, we received in our homes a total of 236 American travelers. Some come back every year, or every two years, and consider my properties to be "their" properties. Mostly our home exchangers stay at my homes longer than we stay at theirs, but I do not keep a strict account of this, since my business limits the time I can spend away each year. But, no matter; we are building up a lot of home exchange "credit" weeks!

Our family likes very much the vacation home exchange system. You avoid the tediousness and the impersonal, sad character of hotel life. You vacation in the warmth of a family home, with all the usual things: books; family pictures; comfortable furniture; basic food items, which we replace scrupulously. You have all the conveniences of your own home, the fun of supermarket shopping, watering the flowers, seeing baseball on television, driving around, and making the acquaintance of neighbors. In fact, by this immersion, you entirely feel American!

It is always a pleasure to meet old (and make new) friends. We are often invited out for dinner at restaurants or in homes. During a recent California home exchange, in fifteen evenings we were invited out by neighbors a total of fourteen times. Many, many times we have seen the red carpet of hospitality rolled out for us. Perhaps the most spectacular example of this we experienced on our arrival at Los Angeles International Airport. Our home exchange host had a limousine meet us with fine champagne served by the driver-hostess, and we were driven to a private airplane that flew us to our home exchange destination in Carmel. Our pilot flew off the route to San Francisco, as he wanted us to view the lovely Bay area from the air.

And then there was the beach home in Hawaii . . . Laguna Beach, with a pool and beautiful garden . . . a Lake Tahoe cottage with a waterskiing boat provided . . . the casual atmosphere of Cape Cod, Massachusetts . . . the penthouse of a New York City apartment building. I could write for many pages about the vacation home exchanges we have had over the years. Of course, when our American home exchange friends are coming to our French homes, we try and be "neighborly" too. We pick them up at the airport and take them to

our homes, host parties for them at home and at fine restaurants, drive them to interesting places, help solve their health and/or money-changing problems, and my car is available to them. In return, we receive letters of appreciation; I have a book full of "thank-you" letters. These home exchangers of ours return to the U.S. as firsthand witnesses of French hospitality and friendship.

Yet another advantage to the home exchange system is to be very unique. Home exchangers do not pay rent or (often) car rental fees, just the round-trip airfare. They find food shopping in southern France is no more expensive than in America, and we in France offer at minimum prices the world's finest wines!

Our son, Frederic, always enjoys getting acquainted with the young people of our home exchange hosts' friends, and his English language-speaking improves with each trip to America.

My wife, Susan, is a very careful housekeeper and likes cleanliness and neatness in her homes. During our early home exchange experience she was somewhat reluctant, fearful that exchangers might not take proper care of our homes; we make our homes clean for our exchange guests, and we always endeavor to leave the home in which we stay clean and ready for the return of our hosts.

In *all* of our home exchanging, we have had only *one* unfortunate experience: this was an especially inconsiderate family who drank most of my old wines, without my permission used my personal cards as access to my private club, and broke—and tried to repair—some of our items without telling us. Did this one negative experience dishearten us? Not at all!

Susan, Frederic, and I are unconditional "partisans" of the vacation home exchange system. With ten years of home exchange experience, we feel this system is a marvelous gateway to inexpensive travel and to making new friends. Finally, I have developed a conviction that the human relations and the knowledge of other peoples are the most important things in life.

Thirty notches on their vacation home exchange suitcases! Since their inaugural home exchange (1977, in Fraser, Colorado), Santa Fe, New Mexico's Jere and Linda Corlett and their children have had a total of thirty different exchanges, a number placing them among the top U.S. exchangers.

Jere has a private law practice, is an elder in the Presbyterian church, a Kiwanian, and leader of Santa Fe's "Red Hot Chiles Dixieland Jazz Band!" With degrees from Ohio State University and the University of Colorado, Linda is now working on a Ph.D. in psychology. Since her "retirement" from teaching, Linda has been restoring old adobe homes and is active in real estate development.

Linda Corlett writes:

A three-story restored Victorian mansion in San Francisco . . . an ancient Irish farmhouse on Roaringwater Bay, Ballydehob, County Cork . . . a beach home in Gulf Shores, Alabama . . . a Lake District restored cow-byre near Penrith, England (with Mrs. Kelly's goat just across the "close" from us) . . . a double-timbered English manor house minutes from downtown Boston, Massachusetts . . . a Hawaiian condominium overlooking Honolulu . . . an ultramodern artist's home in Scottsdale, Arizona, complete with our own wrap-around swimming pool . . . a Wyoming ranch.

You name the place, and chances are we've been there (or near there)! Mountain Lakes, New Jersey; New Orleans, Louisiana; Lighthouse Point, Florida; Denver, Colorado; San Antonio, Texas; Thomaston, Maine; Virginia Beach, Virginia; San Diego, California; Sedonia, Arizona; and many, many other exchange destinations.

We are listed in one of the major home exchange directories. This gives us access to thousands of vacation home exchangers in the U.S. and abroad. In fact, we could probably go anywhere in the world if we had the time and the money.

I begin contacting potential home exchangers a year in advance. That starts it, and then follow a massive number of letters back and forth and some phone calls, too. Each year we also get quite a few letters from exchangers who have seen our listing in the exchange directory. From these communications, we get excellent ideas for future exchanges. I try to be prompt in answering those letters which result from my initial contacts and from those who contact us.

We don't feel there is any "ideal" length for a vacation home exchange. Our exchanges have been from three days or so to five weeks in length, and we've enjoyed them all. We love to exchange for long weekends.

Jere and I have had a most interesting mix, so to speak, of home exchange partners: an engineer, wilderness camp owner, minister, artist, author, real estate man, college professors, lawyers, physicians, a stock broker, an architect, a judge, an English House of Lords member, a plumbing supply house owner, a retired navy officer, a radio station owner, a retired geologist, an avocado ranch owner, an environmental designer, and others.

Though roughly half of our exchangers have brought along their children—all ages—we have found that, without exception, all of these folks have taken excellent care of our 5,000-plus square-foot home. Oh, one exchanger did break the cheapest, ugliest lamp I've ever owned! We try to care for our exchange partners' homes just as we treat our own. And we've had no problems, no complaints.

Often, cars are a part of our exchanges. Here again, no problems . . . except the time we couldn't shut off the heater in our exchange Saab, and my husband ended up with a hot seat. We all got a laugh out of that!

Some of our friends think we are perhaps a little crazy in letting complete strangers "sleep in [our] beds." To them I always say, "When you go to a hotel or a motel, don't *you* sleep in a bed recently slept in by *many* strangers?" Besides, I also think your house is much safer with someone in it, rather than just leaving the place empty.

Many of our friends are interested in—actually, fascinated with—the vacation home exchange concept, and we have met many along the home exchange route who are as addicted to home exchanging as we are. We don't feel home exchanging is for everyone. Successful home exchangers have to be flexible enough to deal with various home exchange uncertainties—in scheduling; in some destinations or homes perhaps falling somewhat short of expectations; in partners who may have different lifestyles than ours. To us, it's one great adventure, and we are able to laugh at anything that goes wrong. I guess a sense of humor, and of adventure, is needed for home exchange success. "People have to hang loose," is a trite and hackneyed expression, but the most successful home exchangers do. I guess the word that most expresses our attitude toward life is *serendipity*, which is a most handy attitude for home exchangers to have. In home exchanging we are looking for a *different* style of living. If peoples' priorities are measured by the sizes of exchange homes, maybe a deluxe hotel might be more appropriate for them.

Our son, Chris, is now twenty, and the young lady of our house, Catherine, is now nineteen. These children were with us during nearly all of our exchanges. They never got bored, and after arriving in a new neighborhood, they would immediately make friends. Many times they would stay with these friends while we traveled around the country. In Ireland, Chris loved helping Mr. Wolfe shovel the manure; Mrs. Wolfe taught our daughter how to make Irish pastries. In a homelike atmosphere, the kids became part of the neighborhoods. They had friends and toys, bikes, and sports equipment. Because they soon knew the neighborhoods, we soon did, too. We think home exchanging made them very independent and adventuresome. My son (at age twelve) had a Rover pass and went all over London by himself. My daughter sang in Irish pubs all over Ireland and visited pen pals in Scotland and France. Indeed, we believe it was because of home exchanging that these young people came to appreciate other cultures, and perhaps this is why they are well-rounded young people today. Home exchanges are more than vacations, they are "stepping into another culture's shoes."

At this point, some suggestions for potential vacation home exchangers come to mind:

1. For a small additional charge, most home exchange directories will include a small photo of your home. Because you want your directory listings to "sell" your home, we feel the inclusion of a photo can be very helpful, *provided* the photo you send is of especially high quality.
2. With the exception of *NS* (non-smoking), *AE* (automobile exchange), and *EE* (experienced exchangers), don't use the directory symbols; rather, describe your home as best you can in the space provided. Words like "modern kitchen," "television," are really not meaningful. Select unique words to describe your

home. In communicating with persons with whom you might be exchanging, your letters should be neatly typewritten. Your letter should be literate (misspelled words turn people off). Talk about yourselves and your home. Potential exchangers are mostly interested in what kind of people would be using their homes.
3. If you are an experienced exchanger, include a few references—partners with whom you have exchanged. If you are a new exchanger, send names and addresses of people who know you and can attest to your character and the way you live.
4. Be as flexible as possible in your selection of destinations and in your vacation dates.
5. Send a lot of letters, and you'll be surprised how many responses you will receive.
6. In addition to helpful information about your use of his home, ask your exchange host to provide you with information about restaurants where the locals go, shopping facilities, and activities which might be of interest to you.
7. While on an exchange, get involved in the community. We have found schools and churches most helpful in this regard. We go to fairs, all kinds of dinners, rodeos, charity benefits, community dances, community centers, musical events (my husband has played the piano in churches near and far). We read the local newspapers and endeavor to get involved just as the locals do.
8. For first-time exchangers, start small—maybe a long weekend or a week.

I've tried to share here something of our family's excitement about vacation home exchanging. Whether we are at home here in Santa Fe or away on home exchange vacations, we talk up this terrific way to vacation. It's mind expanding . . . it's great for kids . . . it's an opportunity to make new friends . . . it's less expensive—and much more adventuresome and fun—than a "yesterday"-type vacation!

Following service in the military throughout World War II, Bob Rapley spent some years with the British Colonial Service in East Africa; later, as an ornithologist, he organized photographic wildlife safaris in Kenya. His wife, Anne, also British, earned degrees in psychology, philosophy, and economics at the University of Edinburgh and held short-term positions in London, France, Canada, and Switzerland; lectured for four years in the Bahamas; served as production assistant on several films in California; and is a writer of cookbooks. Bob and Anne Rapley are now retired, living in Paphos, Cyprus.

Their years of hospitality hosting and being house guests themselves uniquely qualify the Rapleys to serve as the primary resource for this introduction to hospitality exchanging.

One of the great advantages of vacation home exchanging is its flexibility and adaptability to one's individual needs and desires. Perhaps you are an older couple, or two sisters, two brothers—or are a recent widow, or are otherwise single—seeking not only a home away from your home, so to speak, but companionship. Perhaps you do not feel quite ready to turn your house (or car) keys over to someone you do not really know firsthand. What if you want to visit Germany and your only knowledge of German starts and stops with *ja*? Perhaps you long to vacation in a New York City penthouse but have big city apprehensions? Is there no vacation alternative to hotel/motel living or regular home exchanging—living alone in a "stranger's" home?

"Yes," say the Rapleys, "*hospitality exchanging* is the answer to your dilemma!" Hospitality exchangers stay as guests in their hosts' homes while the hosts are there, then serve as hosts themselves in their own homes at another time convenient to all. Since most already know how to entertain house guests—and how to enjoy being house guests—hospitality exchanges offer a comfortable, enjoyable alternative to regular home exchanging. Nevertheless, a hospitality exchange does have much in common with a regular home exchange in that you make your connection with possible exchangers, correspond, exchange photos, and work to find a mutually acceptable date for the visit.

Among the advantages of hospitality exchanging is that both parties do not have to—indeed, cannot—have exactly the same vacation dates. If you want to get away in the winter and they want to visit you in the spring, there is no problem. This leaves you a great deal of freedom along with the possibility of visiting a given vacation destination during its best season, knowing your guests will see your area at its best, too. Yet another advantage is that hospitality exchanges are often for shorter lengths of time than home exchanges—a week or even a long weekend.

There is no need to arrange car insurance coverage for your guests, clean out the master bedroom closet, or put away your grandmother's silver, either! Your guests will stay in your guest room, join you in whatever meals you agree on, and take part in your family life to whatever extent seems appropriate. On your part, there will be more mouths to feed at dinner and some entertaining and sightseeing to organize, but no more than is expected when you have relatives or special friends come for a visit, and it is fun being a "tour guide" in your own hometown! Of course, you do not have to spend every waking moment with your guests—not by any means. Most will enjoy exploring your area on their own, with a little guidance from you, then return for dinner and a quiet evening. You may want to go out to dinner once or twice during the visit or escort your guests to one or two special places of interest, but leave them time to be on their own, too.

There is no need for you to be a gourmet cook! Regional and national specialties—food not normally available in your guests' countries or areas—will always be appreciated. When you are going through the correspondence stage, do find out if there are any particular foods they enjoy or cannot eat, but other than that, there is no need to be overenthusiastic about feeding them. If you have any doubts about their preferences, take them food shopping with you. It can be an enjoyable eye opener for everyone, and they really get to know a country or area by checking out its food stores.

In return for your hospitality, you will enjoy having your vacation as a guest in their home, without worrying about getting lost, suddenly needing to find a good doctor, using kitchen appliances or complicated security systems, or buying food in the local market. You will enjoy home cooking instead of expensive and often uninteresting hotel food, have a comfortable bed every night, and enjoy the company of real "natives" who will be eager to help you enjoy yourself and learn about their countries or areas. All, of course, at much less cost than that of a packaged tour or staying in hotels.

Exchanges of hospitality do involve a little more work on your part before a final agreement is reached, since you obviously want to visit people with whom you will feel comfortable. Making a hospitality exchange arrangement should involve more correspondence than a regular home exchange so that you will know more about each other and feel confident you will not develop any sudden distaste for each other's company. In the most diplomatic manner possible, find out all you can about the family, including the presence of children and pets. In return, be perfectly honest about your own home and family. No one wants to travel hundreds (or thousands) of miles and be unpleasantly surprised, especially when there is always a certain amount of tension involved in being a host or a guest.

You also have to watch out for misunderstandings that may arise from language or cultural differences. It is hard to be a good judge of people who are writing to you in their second or third language. Even a brilliant college professor can sound pretty childish in a language he only studied for two years! To avoid unintended social blunders visit your library and read anything you can find on the other area or country's traditions and etiquette—or ask a friend who has traveled in that area.

People who are willing to exchange hospitality are often open, friendly people, or they would not be doing this in the first place; so do not worry too much about your table manners, as long as you avoid the area or country's most horrible social gaffes! "House rules" about smoking and having (or not having) a cocktail before dinner should be understood and adhered to. It is basically a matter of being as considerate of your hosts as you expect them to be in return.

It takes a special kind of person to enjoy hospitality exchanging, and many people will continue to prefer the more conventional exchange of homes; but the benefit of living with another family can be well worth the special effort involved. If you love to meet and entertain people from elsewhere in your country (or in the world), think about hospitality exchanging. As Anne Rapley says, "Best of all, you may develop a life-long friendship!"

17 "The Vacation Home Exchangers? They Went That-a-Way"

AND "THAT-A-WAY" SEEMS to be a very wide-ranging everywhere. Vacation home exchangers, as a group, tend to have no limits in their choices of vacation destinations.

Much like "conventional" vacationers, however, home exchangers seem to gravitate toward particular areas (or regions) for their vacation experiences.

The survey shows, for instance, that over the years 40 percent of home exchanging Americans who chose to vacation in the U.S. exchanged in the western states—in particular, California and Hawaii. Twenty-eight percent have exchanged in New York; Massachusetts; Washington, D.C.; Pennsylvania; and other parts of the Northeast. And 24 percent have vacationed in the Southeast, notably Florida. This is interesting, because *U.S.A. Today* reports, in a recent survey, that of the 326 1991 trips made by U.S. vacationers surveyed, 29% had destinations in the Southeast.

As regards future vacation destinations—U.S. regions Americans aspire to visit in the U.S. during the years just ahead—47 percent hope to exchange in the West; 25 percent in the Northeast; 15 percent in the Southeast; and, interestingly, 11 percent in the Southwest, especially Arizona. With its year-round dry and temperate weather, Arizona is a real draw for middle-aged to older home exchangers.

Large numbers of Americans have preferred to vacation outside the U.S.; of these, 75 percent have exchanged in Great Britain and continental Europe, 12 percent have been to Canada and Mexico, and 5 percent have had exchange destinations in Australia and New Zealand. The remaining small percentage have been to countries as widespread as Tahiti, Israel, Colombia, Yugoslavia, and Iceland.

Looking ahead to future vacation home exchanges outside of the

U.S., once again about 75 percent of the Americans surveyed have their sights set on Europe, mostly England and France.

How about those home exchangers who reside outside the U.S.? The survey shows that, of those who have exchanged in the U.S., 39 percent have done so in the western states—California and Hawaii, for the most part; 28 percent have exchanged in the northeastern states; and 24 percent in the Southeast, in particular, Florida.

The survey also shows the future U.S. exchange travel plans of those residing outside of the U.S. to be quite consistent with those in the previous paragraph, that is, about two-fifths to the West, 25 percent to the Northeast, and another 25 percent to the Southeast.

Of those non-U.S. exchangers who have vacationed outside of the U.S., 77 percent have been to Western Europe, mostly England,

Germany, and France. And their hopes for future vacation exchange destinations? Again, three-quarters would choose Western Europe, while the rest are thinking about Australia and New Zealand, Canada and Mexico, and elsewhere.

Like most vacationers, home exchangers generally have a reasonably good idea of their vacation destinations; they know where they would *like* to go. Even so, a surprising number of exchangers—mostly those who are retired and/or have both the time and the airfare—play what is known as "vacation home exchange roulette." These exchangers (experienced, for the most part) have absolutely no preconceptions as to their vacation destinations. When the various annual home exchange directories are issued (usually early in the year), they pore over the home exchange listings, making notes of potential vacation home exchange partners *anywhere*. This roulette game has only two rules: first, to select interesting-looking exchange possibilities in interesting places and, second, to be sure the listings cover people who indicate they would like to vacation in the area in which the game player has an exchangeable home. One such exchanger writes: "We never know where we are to vacation until the directories come, and we get out a bunch of home exchange letters; each year another vacation 'surprise!'"

A seven-time vacation home exchanger in Boca Raton, Florida, and his wife are also sold on the home exchange "roulette" concept. In 1990 they listed their three-bedroom, two-bath home (with swimming pool and spa) in the two largest home exchange directories. This exchanger's semi-retired status, and their two homes, make it possible for them to include, "We'll go anywhere, anytime," in their listings. They had twenty-two responses to their listing, and off they went to Australia and New Zealand.

So, twenty-two responses in 1990 and (with virtually the same listing in the same directories) how many responses in 1991? Sixty-one! [21 from France; 18 from Great Britain; 7 from Germany; 4 from the U.S.; 2 each from Holland, Canada, and Spain; 1 each from Austria, Brazil, Ireland, Zimbabwe, and Sweden.]

Where in a given country or region would one find home exchangers vacationing? Nearly one-third of American exchangers seem to prefer places with some historic significance; 23 percent head for the seashore; 15 percent, lakes and/or the mountains; 4 percent ski resorts; and 26 percent are happy to exchange "anywhere."

And those who reside outside the U.S.? One-third of these prefer the seashore; 25 percent, places with some historic significance; 22 percent, lakes and/or the mountains; 1 percent ski resorts; and 19 percent are in the "anywhere" category.

In summary, vacation home exchangers travel the world—limited only by time and travel expense. In the vast majority of cases, through their own research, home exchangers are able to fulfill their vacation destination desires through arrangements with other home exchangers.

18 Coping with Culture Shock

IN THE PRECEDING CHAPters, much has been written about the global nature of vacation home exchanging—that by adopting the home exchange concept, vacationers from *everywhere* can literally go *anywhere* in this world. According to the survey, they do just that—vacationing in hundreds of cities and towns located in nearly fifty different countries.

Prior to and in the years immediately following World War II, most international vacationers stayed in hotels situated in tourist-oriented cities or in resort areas, which often featured swimming, golf, tennis, skiing, or other sports-centered activities. This type of vacationing was expensive, especially for families traveling abroad with children. What about cruises? Only the idle rich could afford cruising the seven seas.

The vacation world was ripe and ready for "package" tours, with a fixed fee covering travel, hotels, and in many cases, meals as well. Initially these tours were relatively expensive, but with the advent of the airbus, carrying three hundred or more passengers, and forty-five-passenger, living-room-comfort motor coaches, the tremendous growth of international recreational facilities, and keen competition among the packagers, international vacationers everywhere could benefit. Also, in the past ten years or so, large cruise ships, each carrying a thousand or more passengers, lowered the costs of cruises. So today Europeans, Americans, Far Easterners, and others in all parts of the world are able to enjoy longer and better-value vacations, with no muss, no fuss.

For a wide variety of good reasons detailed in these chapters, international vacation home exchanging is a viable alternative to package tours, cruises on the sea, and other more conventional vacations outside of one's native country.

Culture shock, to one degree or another, is inherent in international vacation home exchanging. Ours is a world of differences: in home-vacation accommodations quite different from one's own home; homestyle cooking on a "foreign" stove, quite a different experience; a home full of unique appliances, each with its own built-in eccentricities. A parade of other vacation differences includes currency, modes of dress, neighbors, friends, customs, shopping for food and other necessities, church life, languages, telephones, emergency services, and possibly even pets!

These and a hundred other aspects of international vacation home exchanging are the underlying causes of what some refer to as culture shock. It is how one *handles* these differences that makes or breaks a foreign-country home exchange vacation. "Sometimes my wife and I go mad," writes a home exchanging Brussels florist, "when we are on exchanges outside of our native Belgium—in Canada, the States, even in Holland—everyone seems to dance to a different tune! But then, in the early days of each holiday, we always get used to it . . . and once back home, we can't wait for the next year's holiday exchange directories (we list our home in three) to arrive!"

This from a multitime exchanger in Northampton, England: "What impresses the English (or Welsh in my case) about the U.S.A. is the scale of everything—houses, residential developments, roads, and cars big enough to carry three British families. The service and the politeness, albeit a touch plastic, lick ours hollow. Combine that with good old American know-how, 'the nobody-does-it-better-folks,' and the *sun*—always the sun—and you have an irresistible holiday exchange experience. Our American friends tell us that the lack of stress, the flowers, the greenery, the flowers (again), and the sheer storybook 'feel' of England combine to make them want to settle here. Maybe we should just swap homes permanently!"

"The house in Austria was situated in the Alps," writes an Espergaerde, Denmark, exchanger who assists judges in a court of law. "Leading to the house was a steep path crossing a wooden bridge over a whirling mountain stream. Our nerves were itching, going up and down. The house was very nice, and our children—we travel with two teenagers and two youngsters—were thrilled with the surroundings. The neighbors had a little deer kid (*Bambi*), tame and lovely, to the great pleasure of our children." Further, "We expect to keep on home exchanging in the future and have given some thought to the possibility of 'child exchanging' meaning exchanging our teenage kids for the experience of living in other countries and learning other languages. These parts of international home exchanging are very important for citizens of a small country like Denmark."

An author-artist in New York City writes: "Our first exchange, in 1973, and two subsequent ones, were in a fifteenth-century Irish castle. In the years since then we have had seventeen other exchanges in England, France, Portugal, Spain, Mexico, Canada, and seven U.S. states. Wonderful life experiences for us and our two (now grown) children."

Those who are a part of the growing number of international vacation home exchangers view their other-country experiences less as culture shock and more as challenge and adventure, an exercise in international living and learning.

Home exchangers who travel abroad report that consummating international home exchange arrangements calls for more homework on their parts and on those of their exchange partners. A year is not too soon, they say, to begin setting exchange plans into motion. Mail delays, especially in overseas contacts, are a major problem.

Michael Almond, an attorney with Parker, Poe, Adams, and Bernstein, in Charlotte, North Carolina, makes frequent business trips to Europe and offers these excellent suggestions regarding money and foreign travel: (1) do not exchange U.S. currency for foreign currency in the U.S.; (2) take along travelers checks purchased in the U.S. and change these into the currencies of the countries visited; (3) whenever possible, use major U.S. credit cards for all types of charges; and (4) carry as little currency as possible, as there is always a charge for changing one country's currency for that of another country. These are words of wisdom for international vacation home exchangers and for all others traveling abroad.

There are two schools of thought regarding telephone use in making international home exchange arrangements. Some say resorting to the telephone should be limited to emergencies and last-minute stages of exchange arrangements. Others recommend telephone use throughout. In this connection, a retired, thirteen-time international home exchanger (formerly a personnel official with the U.S. government) now living in Carmel, California, writes: "I would emphasize using the international telephone system to call good home exchange prospects—this assuming the people have just received their new home exchange directories. Better to nail down a good prospect immediately, rather than to resort to a letter. One, of course, follows up with one or several letters and photographs of the house. But 'strike while the iron is hot.' The cost of the phone call is trivial compared to the savings and fun involved. Don't worry that you will have language difficulty. Most European exchangers have someone in the house who can speak a little English, or one can use his broken French, Italian, or German enough to make the first contact—and quickly!"

A retired teacher in Corpus Christi, Texas, writes: "Right after the annual exchange directory is received, we get busy—scrambling for exchanges. The competition is fierce, but we are finally gaining on California and Florida, as Europeans find out there's something in between—like Texas! In four days we leave for a month each in the Netherlands and Germany and two different fortnight exchanges in England."

Along this same vein, a Danish lawyer (who has exchanged in France, England, and Wales) writes: "Especially in Denmark and other Scandinavian countries, it's very uncommon to swap houses. Maybe also because of this, other European families' attention to Denmark is low, so we have sometimes found it quite difficult to find a European family interested in swapping. But we are very enthusiastic about this way of spending holidays, and we are sure exchanging will become more popular here in the years to come."

Danish home exchange hopefuls apparently face the same basic problem as those in Elkhart, Indiana: too small a pool of potential exchangers. Once again, the way around this dilemma is the "two Ls": *listings* in as many directories as possible (a half dozen or more—see pages 197–201) and *letters*, many more letters, including some to those whose listings do not specify Denmark. In working with the vacation home exchange directories, the Danes should not give up hope because there are so few who list Denmark as destinations; they should watch for *northern Europe*, or *Europe* and give special attention to the many listing which simply state *anywhere* as their destination.

If Texas is finally gaining on California and Florida as a vacation home exchange destination for Europeans, then there certainly is real hope for Denmark!

Many home exchanging Americans traveling to Europe arrange for a chain of exchanges. "After all, once you decide to go to Europe," writes a Riverdale, New York, exchanger, "you might just as well line up several (or more) exchanges. Last year, we had two weeks each in London; Geneva; the south of France; Javea, in Spain, and the Algarve region of Portugal. Sure, this takes a lot more advance planning and arranging. But we figure, listen, why not? Yesterday they said, 'Join the navy and see the world'; today we say, 'Grab a vacation home exchange directory and see the world.' We are long since retired and not going to live forever. Culture shock? No problem!"

All hosts of vacation home exchangers from foreign lands face an additional communications burden. These hosts must spell out clearly—in typed or handwritten form—*step-by-step* instructions for the use of all appliances in their homes, especially stoves, clothes washing machines and dryers, dishwashers, microwave ovens, disposals, and TV-VCR sets. The survey revealed that whenever home exchangers get outside of their own countries, they almost inevitably have appliance problems of one kind or another.

An American in Spain "nearly blew up the house trying to ignite the darned stove's pilot light." In Washington, D.C., a Munich, Germany, exchanger "could not get the air conditioner to make the air cold." A French first-time exchanger was "mystified by the microwave oven's computer panel; it left me in confusion, and the instruction booklet in English worsened the situation." An American exchanging in Holland "couldn't figure out why the washing machine left the clothes soaking wet, until we discovered the spin dryer was a separate, temperamental appliance." From South Africa: "The plumbing arrangements in European cities can be rather baffling. We couldn't figure out how to operate the sink-stopper gadgets. Also, the flushing systems in toilets are rather interesting: some are plungers, knobs to press down or pull up, and some are cunningly concealed."

From Canada: "We beat the English attitude about ice cubes (always too small, too few) by taking along a lightweight, plastic ice tray. One twist and out pop twenty-one full-sized ice cubes!"

Another American writes: "Our host's washing machine got stuck on one of its cycles, and we had to cut off the electricity to stop it." Exchangers in England "had a real hard time getting used to the clothes washing machine. If the hot water did not come in hot enough, the machine would just wait to heat the water. It took us some time to figure this all out." A couple from Paris, exchanging in England, were "perplexed by the dishwasher's strange behavior. We put the dishes in after dinner, pushed the buttons and turned the knobs just as the instructions said. And nothing happened. We went through the procedure a second time. Again, nothing. So we gave up and went to bed. In the morning the dishes were washed and dried! It seems the dishwasher was not just being temperamental but actually was electronically timed to operate during the night, when the utility rates were cheaper."

A Jacksonville, Florida, retired postal supervisor writes: "The house we went to had no hot water. In Scotland, during April, having no hot water is a disaster. I could just barely handle the sixty-five-degree water, but not my wife! She wanted warm bath water. 'Nonsense,' I replied, '*this* is how *these people* live.' The next day my wife discovered an appliance that looked like a hot-water heater. 'What would they have *this* for, if not to heat water?' We found the water heater was on a separate electrical circuit, and in thirty minutes she was enjoying a nice, hot bath. Gloating, she said, 'Now *this* is how the Scottish live!'"

A Vancouver, Canada, hairdresser is not too disturbed when things go wrong with exchange home appliances. "We figure it goes with the territory." Not so. Appliance problems can almost always be stopped before they start, provided the exchange host leaves for the exchange partner detailed instructions on how to operate the appliances. In addition, as is the case when exchanges take place within the partners' own countries, the host must leave names and telephone numbers of electricians, plumbers, and others who do various home repairs.

When the host has not left proper instructions, neighbors can be a real help. This is especially true in foreign-land exchanges, where the language barrier comes into play. Until the world has one international language (and don't wait up for this!), English will have to do, as international home exchangers can nearly always find someone around who speaks English. Apropos is this experience of a Spanish family exchanging in Holland: "Something went very wrong with our plumbing, and although our exchange host had left us the telephone number of his plumber, we were wondering how to explain the problem to the man. However, we were amazed to find that this plumber spoke English, as do we."

But speaking English does not answer *all* of the language questions. A retired naval officer living in Peasenhall, England, writes: "The children were amazed by the apparent strange diet found in Germany. 'Spaghetti' turned out to be multicolored ice cream put through a mincer, providing a spaghetti-like mix topped with strawberry sauce. Also, they drank 'diesel' which was the local name for a mix of Coke and lemonade."

"During the past ten years, we have exchanged in England a number of times," writes a retired St. Louis, Missouri, salesman's wife, "and we have always found our hosts' neighbors and friends to be helpful in every way. And we've made friends, too, through regular church attendance on these trips. In Cornwall several years ago, for example, for three weeks in a row we were two of a twelve-member church congregation! And this year in Suffolk, we were a part of a family-centered worship service (during which the pastor asked my husband to share a bit about church-family life in the States) and a wonderful barbeque following the service. We find ourselves very 'comfortable' in these church-related situations and feel it is a real blessing to be with fellow believers."

In international home exchanging, arrival instructions are of crucial importance. Foreign hosts must be certain their guests know how to reach their exchange homes, especially if the guests are arriving by automobile. A Swiss artist had this experience on her family's arrival in southern Portugal: "My husband took our car, and the children and I followed by air. After a six-day drive, my husband finally arrived in Tavira. In seeking directions to our holiday exchange home, several locals insisted my husband go to the post office. A language problem, he thought. At the post office he finally met a man who did speak some English. The 'address' my husband had was no address at all; it was our exchange host's post office box number! In this instance, a police officer came to the rescue and helped to reunite our family."

Generally speaking, Europeans, Far Easterners, and families elsewhere in the world seem to employ domestic help—maids, cooks, gardeners—to a greater extent than is true in the U.S. In England, some of these domestic servants are called "dailies"; working by the day (or half day), these ladies clean the houses regularly and sometimes do the clothes washing and ironing as well. "Our London, England, host," writes a five-time exchanger (an account executive in New York City), "engaged the services of a maid once a week. An Italian, this woman did a great job, but she was terrified of the vacuum cleaner, so we stepped in and helped with that part." Six-time exchangers from Florida write: "Some of our exchangers had cleaning services—daily maid service in Portugal and twice-weekly service in Spain and in England. This was a nice luxury feature, and we appreciated the fact that our hosts continued these services while we were in their homes." True, but reliable domestics are hard to come by . . . and if these hosts had let their maids go for two or three weeks, it is likely the hosts never would have seen them again!

In the Far East, large numbers of homes have live-in domestics. In Hong Kong, for instance, these "live-ins" are frequently from the Philippine Islands, working under two-year contracts. "Our Hong Kong host said the live-in maid would do the food buying, cooking, cleaning, and washing," writes a Nuremberg, Germany, exchanger, "and if you leave your underwear lying around, don't be surprised if it's washed and ironed within the hour!"

When domestic help is a part of the home exchange arrangement, it is important the host makes it clear to his exchange guests just what the maid's responsibilities are—what she does, what she does not do. Also, is the host or his exchange guest responsible for paying this domestic's wages?

Some Europeans with very young children engage the services of *au pairs*, usually young women in the eighteen to twenty-four age group. Generally, the *au pair*'s responsibilities are to take care of the children and, in some cases, to do light housework. They get their room and board free and live as a part of the family; learning the language is often a part of the *au pair*'s experience.

Connecticut and Florida vacation home exchangers write that their recent exchange guests from England brought along an *au pair* to take care of their children—a *real* vacation for Daddy and Mummy!

Now, selections at random from some survey participants—thoughts of international vacation home exchanges:

From Lexington, Massachusetts: "In Folkstone, England, our exchange home was a stately, four-story Victorian home. Coming home on a Sunday evening after a lovely drive through Kent, we found water gushing like a waterfall over the side of the house! This set off the burglar alarm, screeching through the neighborhood. We found a ladder and, with a small pocket pinchlight, located the problem: a leak in the water tank above the top floor. Meanwhile, the alarm kept going and going—no way to turn it off. Finally, after an hour, the neighbor's son shut off the alarm. Somehow, the leaking water tank was patched up. A *late* dinner that night!"

From Sparta, New Jersey: "While we were in Australia, our hosts took us to their second home, 185 miles west of Sydney, to the 'bush in Mudgee.' At this home ('Land's End') there was no electricity, telephone, or plumbing . . . but there was a river in which to bathe and swim, gold miners' fallen-down shacks, kangaroos bounding around, and a sense of being in the Australia of a century ago. This was a highlight of our trip and something we would have never experienced had we been 'regular' travelers."

From London, England: "Vacation home exchange is the greatest way to travel, provided everyone realizes the mother of a traveling family doesn't completely shed the kitchen cares. But how else can a family of five enjoy five weeks in the Caribbean for something less than $4,000?"

From San Diego, California: "While we were home exchanging in Milton-Under-Wychwood, England, my wife became very ill. The neighbors were such compassionate and caring people. They made certain I was invited to share meals in their homes. My wife was in an Oxford hospital for three-and-a-half weeks, and the neighbors sent beautiful floral arrangements from their gardens. They treated us like 'family.'"

From Spain: "In Holland, my daughter leaned on her bedroom sink—to get closer to the mirror—and this sink came crashing off the wall. The copper water tubing bent but, fortunately, didn't break. It being vacation time, there was not a plumber to be found. We never did locate the water main shutoff and had to leave the sink in pieces on the floor. Naturally, we left money for a new sink to be installed, and our host was very nice about it."

From Baltimore, Maryland: "Our most delightful exchange was our first in 1981, when a young British couple and their three-year-old daughter lived in our house in Norfolk, Virginia, and we lived in their house near Bedford, England, a charming, two-hundred-year-old groom's cottage with low ceilings and a thatched roof. Our hosts had added a modern wing with living room downstairs and master bedroom and modern bathroom upstairs, but the ambiance was definitely eighteenth century, especially when the horses were being exercised in the driveway area shared with the stable. Neighbors invited us for drinks, and other friends invited us to dinner at their homes or to drinks at their favorite pubs. We also were able to take advantage of the 'away-day-return' fares on the railroad (off-hours excursion) and spent several long, tiring days antiqueing in London. Meanwhile, our English guests were enjoying our neighbors, and their daughter was playing with our neighbors' small children back in the States."

From Fayetteville, Arkansas: "We have taken various tours in the past but *no more*. Now we are all for vacation home exchanging. Last summer we took our daughter and three grandchildren to Germany. We had a marvelous time. The children played soccer and computer games with the neighbors' children. Even though neither side could speak the other's language, somehow they managed to understand each othei perfectly. So, with luck, back we all go to Germany next year!"

From Switzerland: "For us, home exchanging is the best way to make holidays. We have met many, many interesting people. We felt at home in the holiday house and town or village. Our children love 'their' new playroom with many exciting new toys. Usually, we have had contact with neighbors and friends of the holiday exchangers, and so did our exchange family while they were staying at our place. We always had very exciting weeks, saw many interesting places, enjoyed the beautiful landscapes, and met new and friendly people. We saw the real country and not always the same tourist places and hotels. We always tried to arrange it to come to the new place a day or two before the exchange family left their place. So we got to know each other, exchanged tips and ideas of nice places to see, and explained everything in the house. We feel very strongly that vacation home exchanging is a good way without prejudice to view a different country and culture. We always try to read different books about the country before we get there."

From West Wales, United Kingdom: "Our first home exchange in 1988 was a great success. A retired couple from Florida spent a month in our house in Cornwall, and later in the year we stayed in their lovely holiday apartment on Sanibel Island, Florida.

"The contrast with a conventional holiday was enormous. Our hosts, who lived nearby, introduced us to their friends, took us fishing, sailing, to a concert, and generally made certain we had a marvelous time.

"Apart from having to abandon the apartment due to a threatened hurricane (it petered out later, to become nothing more than a tropical storm), there were no problems. The possibility of the odd alligator crossing the road at night just meant it was advisable to drive to our local restaurant rather than walk.

"Now our friends from Florida are staying with us again. This time they are in our new home in Wales, whilst we live in a self-contained annexe. In October we shall be off to Sanibel once more.

"We are completely sold on home exchanging and next year will have three couples from the U.S., each spending four weeks at our home. This will enable us to spend February/March and October/November in different locations in Florida.

"We are already planning for the following year and hope to do a round-the-world home exchange trip, taking in Hawaii, the North and South Islands of New Zealand, and Sydney and Perth, in Australia.

"The world of international home exchanging has been a most exciting discovery for us and has made a great change to our way of life."

Culture shock? Reviewing this chapter, one must observe that international vacation home exchangers seem to be able to cope very nicely with culture shock . . . and to go on from there to totally enjoy the positive aspects of vacationing in "foreign" lands.

Meet Ambassador and Mrs. Belden Bell

Since they have traveled extensively, Belden and Rae Bell are unconcerned about culture shock. The Bells have exchange homes in a Washington, D.C., suburb and on the West Indies island of St. Kitts. Dr. Bell was a one-time Republican congressional candidate from the state of Indiana and served in a number of Capitol Hill executive agency posts, including that of deputy assistant secretary of state. Later, he was named ambassador to the Federation of St. Kitts and Nevis; indeed, in 1985, Dr. Bell opened the first Organization of American States Embassy in St. Kitts.

Because it preserves the architectural integrity of St. Kitts, "Lavington," the island home of Belden and Rae Bell, was selected by the island's postal authority to be pictured on a St. Kitts postage stamp. Without a doubt, a vacation home exchange first can be chalked up to the Bells: the *first* home exchangers to use a postage stamp showcasing their own home on envelopes of their home exchange correspondence!

Until mid 1990, when they reached the point of semi-retirement, the Bells were very active in the life of their island nation; their St. Kitts home often hosted memorable events of diplomatic and charitable importance.

With fewer government responsibilities these days, the Bells report: "Offering our homes in Virginia and on the island of St. Kitts, we are now looking forward to and are excited about becoming serious national and international vacation home exchangers!"

19 The Upside . . .

WHAT WOULD *YOU* GUESS IS the primary reason many people like home exchanging? From the Vacation Home Exchange Survey, this is what emerges: Spaciousness, comforts, and facilities of home . . . cooking meals and avoiding the expense of restaurants and hotels . . . having a base from which to travel, leaving suitcases behind . . . not staying in a sterile tourist accommodation . . . convenience of extra amenities such as sports equipment, a tennis court, a piano . . . the privacy of your own bedroom and separate bedrooms for children, relatives, or visiting friends . . . always knowing you have a place to stay at the end of the day . . . being able to sightsee without the hurried pace of a tour. Home exchangers in Leawood, Kansas; Glenhead, New York; Venice, Italy; Big Sky, Montana; St. Andrews, Scotland; Hemet, California; Balzers, Liechtenstein; El Paso, Texas; and many others around the world agree with a social worker and accountant in Las Vegas, Nevada, that this type of vacation is "Home away from home . . . what more could one ask for?"

Special diets can be catered to . . . children kept busy with hosts' children's toys or playing with neighborhood friends. One can shoot a game of pool or swim in a pool . . . watch the video made yesterday of that fabulous castle . . . do a little gardening . . . go on a picnic with appropriate equipment . . . decide to take the day off and relax with one of your host's good books . . . even send the kids to school. An architect in Nairobi, Kenya, looks forward to "room to carry out my hobby, painting," and a lecturer in Shrewsbury, England, appreciates the "generous sort of human nature that emerges in facilities one is left; people make a personal effort to help you to enjoy your stay." A business executive in France writes that he likes home exchanging because "you can avoid restaurants, which are murder with small kids wreaking havoc." In short, just about anything you can do at home, you can do, perhaps even better, in a home exchange.

"It makes good money sense!" claims an exchanger in Sunset,

Maine. An elevator safety inspector in Puerto Rico states: "It is a tremendous bargain all around." Here is a list of the things "liked best" by an exchanger in Stockholm, Sweden, who rhapsodizes: "(1) free of charge; (2) free of charge; (3) the same as above; (4) it's a new 'home'; (5) meeting the people we exchange with; (6) comfortable; (7) you feel at home, free to do everything; (8) last, but not least—*free of charge*!"

Money saved if a car is included in the exchange is also very high on many people's "like best" list. An experienced exchanger writes: "We travel a lot when we exchange, and access to a free car is almost as important as the house." An exchanger in Minneapolis, Minnesota, appreciates "being able to go places that perhaps might not be a first choice if you didn't have the cost savings." How about traveling with *six* children? Or getting two trips for the price of one with the absence of hotel, car rental, and taxi expenses? Return visits to special places are often made possible once a relationship is established with exchange partners. Exchangers in Valparaiso, Indiana, and Longmont, Colorado, sum it all up: "The price is right to have a long, easily affordable vacation experience."

Once an inexpensive vacation in comfortable surroundings has been realized, home exchangers around the world also are in agreement about the next-best aspects of traveling in this mode. Semiretired business executives in Chevy Chase, Maryland, reply to the survey question on what they like best: "Immersing ourselves in the culture of the country; marketing, keeping house, and mixing with people on a totally different level; making wonderful new friends; sharing local experiences." Exciting social adventures . . . new points of view . . . entrée to a neighborhood and to homes that might not be otherwise available . . . hospitality of the host's family, relatives, or friends . . . getting to be in a quiet, residential area, and meeting "real" people . . . to be honest, seeing how other people live, their foibles, their likes, and dislikes—for exchangers from Alabama to Utah and from Tahiti to Istanbul, the opportunity to feel less like tourists or holiday makers and more in tune with the lifestyles of those whose part of the world you are visiting is a very important factor. A couple in a retirement community in southwest Florida exchanged with a family in East Anglia, England. Shortly after their arrival, the Floridians participated in a walking tour of the gardens in the English village, starting with the beautifully landscaped acre where they were staying. Neighbors met on the tour invited these Americans to join a barbeque after church the following Sunday. The proceeds of this barbeque went toward the restoration of the unique, nine-hundred-year-old round church tower. A farmer/civil engineer and his teacher wife in Caledon, South Africa, also attended a church barbeque—but in Germany. Barbeques are obviously great places to make friends! And a couple in New England writes: "During our exchange in England we were invited to a neighborhood 'garden party,' which gave us a great look at that cultural phenomenon."

A doctor and his wife in Ormond Beach, Florida, exchanging in

England, reaped the benefits of home exchanging not only while they were away, but when they returned home: "The mother in our partner family was a culinary artist if there ever was one. During their stay in our home, we had several of our friends entertain them with dinner, a boat ride, and a picnic. When we returned, we learned that our talented exchange partner had a fabulous dinner party and entertained a dozen or so of our friends and took care of our social obligations for the next year. Also, in true British form, when we arrived home, there was our table—perfectly set for six, British style!"

A Cape Cod, Massachusetts, mother summarizes her family's orientation in a home exchange: "We like getting to know a new area. We have our routine: hit the bookstores and get the local papers; find a vegetable and fruit stand; find out what music is being performed nearby . . . what historical sites are in the area . . . pick out two or three great restaurants."

Added to enjoying all the perks of a "live-in" experience in a community is the equally fascinating opportunity to build friendships through contacts with one's exchange partners. After the initial letters are productive, phone calls, photos, additional correspondence, and, hopefully, being able to meet each other forms a bond of friendship that often lasts for years, according to the survey participants. Children's weddings are attended, Christmas gifts exchanged, return visits encouraged . . . one often acquires a new extended family!

A couple in Mojave County, Arizona, exchanged with a family in Hannover, Germany, who "appreciated our place to such an extent that they purchased the lot next door to us. Upon retirement, they plan to move to the U.S. and build a home next to ours. They come each year to visit their 'lot' and stay with us for a week or two. We have become lasting friends." Perhaps your partners will not become next-door neighbors, but an airline engineer from San Francisco, California, remarks: "I think it's most important to have good friends or neighbors to welcome and help your exchangers. We have been extremely lucky in that we have marvelous friends living next door, and they have been more than kind to all our exchangers. They have enjoyed our visitors, and all our exchangers have been most impressed by the kindliness and hospitality they have received in our home."

If at all possible, experienced exchangers try to spend a day or two with their partners, either before their exchange or afterwards. A real estate broker and his wife in Colorado shared the unusual experience of "being able to attend English court in London with our lawyer host (complete with wig, black robe, and square-toed, buckled shoes) the day before we left for our home." A Scottish local government officer regretted that one *usually* does not have the opportunity to meet the exchange family, but then went on to say: "Because of bad weather, we terminated our holiday in Switzerland two days early. Of course, we arrived back before our exchange guests had left. We stayed with my parents, but it was amusing to be served dinner in our own home as our exchangers' guests for an evening. They served us a traditional Swiss dinner! It was an added advantage and pleasure to meet our exchange partners, and we still correspond with them."

Several references have been made to the presence of children during a home exchange, and chapter 13 dealt with this in depth. The survey further emphasizes that the ability to take children makes home exchanging attractive to many. Traveling with children is always more complicated and more expensive, but with a substitute home to provide plenty of room, diversions not available in hotels, and the ability to rest between excursions without feeling guilty, a lot of the difficulties disappear. Not only do home exchangers travel with *younger* children, but a retired college professor in Connecticut writes: "It's an opportunity to have your grown children and their spouses visit an area with you before they may be financially able to do it on their own." A health planner in New York City does the opposite: "We love the ability to bring parents and grandparents on an exciting vacation."

A New York City couple with many exchanges to their credit have made a final refinement: "Our Italian exchange partner has become our best friend. We also have exchanged our children . . . my kids skiing with them in Cortina, their son visiting us every summer." A Minnesota exchanger believes "showing the children how to care for other people's things" is a benefit—and certainly *all* home exchangers would say "hurrah" to this!

Upon settling in a new "home," exchangers need to know how it functions: appliance instructions; repair service numbers; hairdressers and barbers; doctor, dentist, and veterinary (if there are pets to be cared for) phone numbers; shopping and restaurant locations; and, especially, places of interest to visit in the area. The Info Kit should contain this material, and when it is carefully prepared, exchangers itemize under "like best": "great tourist information from hosts" . . . "full information on the area and its facilities left for our use" . . . "appreciated partners' compilation of booklets, telephone numbers, and general how-to-helps."

Once many exchangers get past the *practical* aspects of "like best" in the survey, they begin to wax lyrical. From Dublin County, Ireland, an aircraft engineer and his wife, a registered nurse, report: "The adventurous spirit of it is what we like best"; and from Tyrone County, Northern Ireland, a brick plant manager also enjoys being "adventurous." Journalists in Bradenton, Florida, share the Irish viewpoint as they appreciate "the adventure in trying something different"; and an engineer in Cranbury, New Jersey, further elaborates: "The adventure of finding one's way and making one's own arrangements appeals to me."

"Adventure" covers a lot of territory, and the ability to stay longer in one place and explore it fully at a leisurely pace appeals to many. A teacher in Stroud, England, enjoys "visiting places off the beaten track"; and a "feeling of new discoveries" is the number one item for exchangers in Aspen, Colorado. A physician and his wife in

Honolulu, Hawaii, write: "We want to experience foreign culture, so we will only exchange in foreign countries. We like to get off our island and immerse ourselves in culture, history, museums, etc." "Coming from New Zealand where one's country's history is only 180 years old, we love experiencing the historical depth of older cultures," says a secondary teacher in Auckland. He continues: "In southern France, we camped next to a lorry driver from Paris, who was only too happy to introduce us to both local and other regions' wines and foods. On the other hand, I was able to cook a 'hangi' meal [a Maori earth oven specialty] for his family, using iron brake shoes instead of volcanic stones to heat up the earth oven." Flexibility and ingenuity are a big help when home exchanging!

An insurance agent in Elverson, Pennsylvania, lists "new experiences in different foods" and "shopping in other countries," as major pluses. A sales manager and his publisher wife in Sedalia, Colorado, had this cross-cultural experience: "In England, expecting our groceries to be sacked, we waited several minutes before realizing that in England one sacks his own groceries in his own bag. Our partners from England, in Colorado, on the other hand, thought some young punk was sacking *their* groceries with the intent to steal them!" A teacher in South Africa confides: "Shopping for groceries becomes an adventure in a foreign country; even my husband enjoys it!" One exchanger even went beyond "adventure" to "intrigue" (but did not elaborate further).

The expansion of self . . . widening of horizons . . . art galleries . . . antique shops . . . architecture . . . unique geographical areas . . . educational spots . . . and different climates were all listed as "like best" in the survey. An exchanger in Vancouver, Canada, put into words the main goal of many people around the world: "to go to warm, sunny places during cold, rainy winters." Meet a home exchanger, and you will find a person who knows what he or she wants and loves to talk about it! For instance, a hotelier and BBC correspondent couple from Chateau-d'Oex, Switzerland, are world travelers and emphatically state: "seeing the sea or oceans!" Some look for hiking trails or just access to the outdoors. Skiing exchanges are increasingly popular. A retired businesswoman with a condominium in southwestern Florida on the Gulf of Mexico also has a ski lodge in Sun Valley, Idaho. *Her* possibilities for exchanges are myriad!

Once the logistics are completed, the tickets purchased or road maps readied, and Mr. and Mrs. Homer Exchanger and all the little Exchangers are actually on their way, whole new categories of "like bests" emerge. (Interestingly, the survey showed that exchangers in the U.S. and exchangers around the world almost always came up with the same order in which they listed preferences.) Upon arrival at a strange airport, or train or bus station, "being met is a godsend!" Stories abound about weary travelers wending their way to unknown destinations in the dead of night, but somehow they always seem to arrive safely. (Being taken to the point of departure at the *end* of an exchange is also much appreciated.)

As the adventurous exchangers approach their destination, the *big* question looms paramount in their thoughts: what *is* our home away from home going to look like? Although photos may have been exchanged, descriptions written in detail, and mental pictures formed, the moment of truth is awaited with some degree of apprehension. A retired payroll auditor and teacher couple in Westport, Connecticut, write: "We assure the doubters that the homes in which we have lived on exchanges were more luxurious than ours." A homemaker with a large, beautiful Edwardian (1897) house in Hampstead, England, has enjoyed these exchanges: "A very modern, completely glass-walled house in Holland; a modern house in Denmark; a house in Pebble Beach, California, as well as this host's summer home on Lake Tahoe, Nevada; a house in a small town by the sea a hundred miles inside the Arctic Circle, in northern Norway, where it never got dark all night and reindeer roamed the hills behind us; an Alpine chalet-style house located in a forest just outside of Jackson, Wyoming; and a house looking out over Galway in the west of Ireland."

Some people particularly enjoy seeing how others live and getting new decorating ideas. However, what you *see* may not always be a true reflection of your host's life style, as a public relations executive from Seattle, Washington, relates: "Receiving our exchangers' Christmas letter to their friends in which they described their experience in our home, they described *our* travels on the basis of our home decor. 'They've lived and traveled extensively in the Far East and have a wonderful collection of art pieces!' Actually, our 'art pieces' were all bought in Seattle or picked up in antique stores!"

A farmer in Idaho is concerned about "the uncertainty of approaching people who have more desirable homes or locations than ours," but an experienced exchanger from Florida writes: "Homes are not equal, and one should not worry about whether one is swapping a large house for a smaller one or any other superficial inequity. It's the *experience* that counts."

Having finally found their sometimes elusive exchange homes, many fortunate exchange partners are greeted with extra hospitality, as was a man and his family in Duluth, Georgia: "Once a nice Jewish lady left the refrigerator full of great food she had bought and prepared. A nice surprise and good eating during our stay." A business counselor in Kaneohi, Hawaii, *really* had the red carpet rolled out: "Our English partner left all her best china and crystal available and told us to use it. We elected not to. Our Swiss banker exchange gave us the key to his wine cellar and told us to use all we wanted. We 'borrowed' one bottle and replaced it." Other amenities include: food for two meals . . . flowers . . . a greeting from the hosts . . . being made to feel very welcome. A retired college professor from Florida shares this unique experience: "In Bridge of Allan, Scotland (beautiful town, lovely home, great neighbors) during the annual Scottish Games, we were welcomed over a speaker system; we were the only Americans in the town, and they all seemed to know us!"

On departure, many exchangers leave small appreciation gifts, thank you notes, and even flowers to welcome their hosts back home. A rather unusual twist is shared by a couple in Brookline, Massachusetts: "We had a lovely letter from an Australian couple and decided to let them use our vacation home in Vermont. At some future date, we would use one of their two homes in Australia. They had a wonderful time in Vermont, left a lovely gift, send cards, and so on. We feel we are friends, although we've never met and have no immediate plans to visit Australia. Our friends cannot believe it!"

Chapter 14 dealt thoroughly with the joy/despair of sharing pets in a home exchange. Pet care can be a plus or a minus, but it is a real part of the picture for many exchangers. A couple in a Washington, D.C., suburb comments: "We had a particularly pleasant exchange with a family from Miami, Florida. Their kids were fascinated with snow and three-story houses; ours, with their parrot."

For some reason, exchangers outside of the U.S. do not seem to be as worried about leaving their pets with strangers as are Americans. They like the convenience, as do Americans, but are more optimistic about results. However, one retired couple, originally from Mahwah, New Jersey, may have added a new "beware" for pet exchangers in England. They are sad to report: "We were left in charge of a huge white rabbit and a smaller, black and white rabbit. The gardener mentioned one day that the white rabbit looked a bit sickly and suggested we take it to the vet. We put the ill bunny in a carrying box and drove to the vet's. Unfortunately, the bunny was too sick and could not be helped. Then the *other* rabbit started to show signs of runny eyes and was quickly whisked off to the vet as a precaution. All *he* needed was some ointment applied to his eyes twice daily . . . thank goodness! Breaking the news of their pet's demise to our host during a trans-Atlantic phone conversation was the hardest part of all."

Individual preferences often play an important role in the perfect home exchange. Some listed are: "Near golf course" from exchangers in Barbados; "membership in local sports clubs—we have played tennis in Spain and on Cape Cod," from England; and "exchanged clubs and golf clubs" from Hilton Head, South Carolina. A retired sales engineer in Birmingham, Alabama, writes: "Our Australian partners had a sister and brother-in-law who entertained us at least once a week and made us honorary members at their country club for the month we were there." Additional perks that enhanced some exchanges were: entrée to yacht clubs and even use of hosts' boats; tickets for the opera; an invitation to attend a Mardi Gras ball; tickets to Disneyland; or, in England, an invitation to the Christmas Ball at the Pump Room in Bath.

A vocational rehabilitation counselor in Winter Park, Florida, had these unusual experiences: "Arriving in England the day before the royal wedding of Prince Charles, we met a stranger at Hove Railroad Station who turned out to be a former employee at Buckingham Palace. On the day of the wedding, he escorted us around the palace grounds! Later in our trip, we were able to pick up a hotel reservation and two tickets for the Tattoo performance at Edinburgh Castle in Scotland on short notice due to the cancellation by a stranger standing with us at the King George Hotel reservation desk." Pursuing a hobby (aside from golf or tennis) can be exciting, too, as a central Florida exchanger discovered. "I was sitting in the driveway of our exchange home in Sedona, Arizona, making a sketch of that fabulous place, and a roadrunner darted across the expansive front porch." (A roadrunner is a long-tailed, crested desert cuckoo bird that runs swiftly. Seeing one is a special treat.) These were all special perks that enhanced home exchangers' experiences.

Special circumstances of those wishing to do home exchanging also need to be considered. Handicapped people are able to exchange if understanding exchangers with suitable facilities can be found. For example, a retired teacher in Durham, North Carolina, can walk only short distances and uses a wheelchair in an airport. "I have been able to travel in ways that would otherwise be closed to me," she says. "I get a house with a kitchen, and I can cook a meal if I don't feel up to going out." Some who have lost a spouse agree with a former resident of Jackson, Michigan, who writes: "My husband of forty years, who had all these adventures with me, died about four months ago, but I still think I will do another exchange. I plan to look for a flat in London and exchange partners who would not mind if I had some company, and then I can invite my adult children to share this trip with me. Or I could take a friend for a 'holiday.'" An English widow adds: "My husband died recently, and if I do visit the U.S. or Canada again, it will be to stay with friends I have made through home exchanging." A retired businesswoman, also a widow, from Houston, Texas, frequently exchanges her West Indies vacation home on Nevis with partners in the U.S. as well as abroad. Traveling as a single *can* be fun after all!

Novice and experienced exchangers often plan around an event when seeking a place to go. Do you have a child away at school or college? One exchanger stayed overnight with a former partner while visiting his daughter away at school. Others swapped to attend a World's Fair . . . the Olympics . . . a college graduation . . . a music festival . . . or a wedding. A former resident of Pottsville, Pennsylvania, recalls: "My son caught his first fish at the same time the space shuttle took off at Cape Canaveral; we had to choose which to applaud over the other. My son and daughter took advantage of the location of our second Florida exchange on a golf course to seek daily golfing free of charge! A South Carolina exchange at Hilton Head found us in a villa next door to Chris Evert and enabled us to see the Family Circle tennis and the Heritage golf tournaments."

One woman had to go to another city for an operation and arranged a home exchange for the time she had to be there. A YMCA director in Montclair, New Jersey, writes: "The people we exchanged with were a lovely couple and their two children. They had lived in a community near Montclair and were transferred to London. They wanted to return to the area to be with old friends." The best part of all is that all of these visits were possible without a single hotel bill. One family even arranged a home exchange for their daughter's honeymoon!

Home exchangers around the world find that language can be a problem, but not too serious a one. A retired teacher in Columbus, Ohio, remarks: "We had never been to Mexico until the summer of '88. Neither my husband nor I knew enough Spanish to carry on a conversation, but that didn't matter because through pantomime we got our thoughts across." This would not have helped another frustrated housewife, however, who could not read the labels on food in Spain. A family in Illinois "learned a new vocabulary—a bathroom in England contained a 'loo' and not a 'john.'" A gentleman in Kent, England, remembered his "first meeting with an American ten-year-old who talked so *fast*!" A physician in Brooklyn, New York, finds "speaking the local language" a "like best" item, while a Somers,

Connecticut, couple relates this story: "While we were vacationing in England, a neighbor constantly tried to get in touch with us, but we were not around. She finally left a note inviting us to dinner. The meal was to finish with 'spotted dick,' which is a special dessert. It was the first time that we knew there was a language difference." Generally speaking, home exchangers enjoy the challenge of coping with a foreign language and even learning to speak it better.

Are you worried about too much good living and not enough exercise while you are enjoying your home away from home? How about the perks of a modern home in Holland, as reported by a London, England, couple: "We rode their bikes along the canals and past windmills with a child on the back of each bike." If you do not have to consider the calories, take a hint from an attorney's wife in Tampa, Florida: "My husband loved getting on his bike every morning to go to the butcher, baker, and grocery—wonderful specialty shops." A "like best" from a university library director, also from Florida: "Riding a bike to the bakery for rolls."

Home exchangers even *disagree* about "like bests." "A maid" is a number one item for a South Carolina housewife. A physician from the east coast of Florida enlarges on this theme: "Our two-day-a-week housekeeper thought that not only did our Welsh exchangers 'talk funny,' but they had some strange ideas. Having breakfast in bed is apparently a treasured luxury, so Lula Bell cheerfully complied by serving our guests coffee and Danish in bed twice a week!" *However*, a couple in Hawaii says, "no maids, no bell captains," and an attorney and his jeweler wife in Coos Bay, Oregon, enjoy "sleeping late, undisturbed by a maid."

In the rush of getting things organized for your home exchange partners, you sometimes neglect to get things repaired. No problem, according to a professional reader in Arroyo Grande, California: "On our return after a super vacation, we found that the husband had been a regular 'fix-it' with a couple or so little household jobs (a drawer that stuck, for instance), that *my* husband just hadn't gotten around to. Lovely surprise!" Everyone should be so lucky!

Divergent lifestyles make home exchanging unique. People find certain things they "like best" that no one else does. One such exchanger appreciates "saving money on 'happy hours'" and a journalist from California *loves* "the goose-down 'puffs' in England."

Although only a couple of exchangers listed it, many other survey participants must agree with a Tarpon Springs, Florida, couple who write: "Our condo is not being used by us, so it may just as well be occupied," and others do remark that home exchanging turns a second home into a greater advantage.

During personal and telephone interviews and when they put pen to paper, vacation home exchangers share enough thoughts about the upside—the "like best"—aspects of home exchanging to fill a dozen large volumes.

20 . . . and the Downside

IN THE SURVEY, VACATION home exchangers were also asked to list six things they liked *least* about home exchanging.

A Colorado exchanger puts it succinctly: "I don't *have* six things I like least about home exchanging!" The director of a foreign student program in Washington and a couple in California are on this same upbeat wave length, declaring, "Having to go home," and "going home again" as their like-leasts. Two teachers in Michigan do have *one* like-least: "Having to do housework, that's all!" "No like-leasts," says a London homemaker. "Can't think of any," write exchangers in Nelson, New Zealand. A teacher in England did not even bother to list the things she does not like about exchanging.

Are these people really being honest, or do they just overlook the usual home exchange glitches? "I see virtually no downsides," writes a gentleman in the state of Washington, but then he goes on to elaborate: "One needs to make assumptions, i.e., the home will be relatively clean, etc." Or maybe they are like the insurance agent in Elverson, Pennsylvania, who, after five exchanges, says, "Thank God, no bad ones as of yet!" And a Mill Creek, Washington, business consultant and her stockbroker husband further refine this positive reaction: "Nothing we like least. What we had to offer was 'better' than what we got. This was the only disadvantage, but it wasn't a concern to us."

Amidst all of this worldwide acclaim, there is that small voice that says, "Yes, but . . ." Surely, there are aspects of the home exchange concept that irritate and worry exchangers—first timers and multitime exchangers as well. Surely, exchanging homes cannot *always* be sunshine and roses.

Many home exchangers feel an ever-present concern about "strangers in our house." And, as has been pointed out in previous chapters, there *are* other important questions, concerns, and actual problems that home exchangers have—although, judging from the overall picture gathered from the survey, there are only a very few exchangers who would not "do it again."

The initial steps necessary to get a home exchange underway are time consuming, often frustrating, and sometimes nonproductive. A couple from Pennsylvania is *really* turned off: "We discontinued home exchanging because of the difficulty and the time consumed in deciphering the new home exchange directories." These folks go on, however, to say, "Actual exchanges have been very satisfactory." "People who make the first contact and then no more letters or contact" annoy a St. Thomas, U.S. Virgin Islands, exchanger. A Huron, South Dakota, businessman is "not fond of the paperwork" and is "never sure what you are getting into." A plant manager in Northern Ireland is "afraid of disappointment over the choice of a swap" and also feels there is "not a large enough range of swaps in some countries." Some of these concerns can be dealt with by approaching them in ways described elsewhere in the book, but others just have to be patiently worked out if the exchange goal is to be realized.

Once the initial contacts have been made and it *looks* as if a mutually beneficial exchange can be arranged, second thoughts bring more worries. "More problems if you have to cancel," says a farmer in the Rocky Mountains. A Florida doctor dislikes "the risk of last-minute cancellation," but goes on to report, "It has never happened to us."

Setting ground rules for payment of telephone bills, repairs on houses or cars, exceptionally high electric bills, and so on, can also be tricky. A northern New Jersey exchanger makes a contract available and dislikes exchangers "who fail to comply with the terms and conditions agreed upon." A clergyman in Bradenton, Florida, laments that "the people from England seemed to have no conception of how expensive air conditioning is in Florida, and we had one huge bill. I think they must have air conditioned the screened-in porch!"

From a retired costume designer in Brownsville, Vermont: "I learned the hard way never to exchange my home for someone's 'business apartment' and to definitely limit the number of people occupying my home. An office group took over my home for a ski weekend and it was disastrous!" Some suggestions for dealing with these situations can also be found elsewhere in the book.

Another necessity is preparing one's home for exchangers with all the cleaning, emptying drawers and closet space, making those necessary lists of information, being sure all appliances and household equipment and cars are in working order . . . in short, getting things ready for one's exchange partners. At the other end of the exchange, of course, the cleaning up (if you are responsible for it) is another downer! General agreement around the world was that cleaning before you go away and before you come back are listed as number two under "liked least." Several exchangers noted, on the other hand, that preparing for an exchange forces them to clean up their own homes, and others discovered the same thing a retailer in

Dallas, Texas, did: "On one exchange, we arrived back home to find our house actually cleaner than when we left!"

Unfortunately, when one arrives at the exchange home, things are not always as perfect as they may have been represented to be during the initial contacts. The logistics of actually getting into your vacation home may be frustrating if keys are not in the place agreed upon. This situation can lead to the necessity to *break into* the house! Chapter 9 deals with these desperate situations and some possible solutions. Once inside, however, there may be even more unwelcome discoveries. A Sacramento, California, real estate broker and his wife report: "The home we exchanged in was left extremely dirty; there was even food in the broiler pan in the oven. However, after we cleaned it to our standards, we adjusted quite easily to other inconveniences, such as plumbing and appliance differences. We are pretty adaptable!" Another couple in San Francisco, California, ran into some of the same problems: "Our one really dreadful experience was a flat in London, which was in no way ready to be exchanged; it was in the process of being remodeled, and the exchange host said it would be ready, but it was far from done—horrible bathroom and kitchen. We left her flat in much, much better condition than we found it, and we even had to purchase a lamp, towels, light bulbs, and so on! *However, our home was left in perfect condition by the exchanger!*"

A self-employed businessman and his senior bank official wife in Kirkcaldy, Scotland, said: "Arriving at our exchanger's holiday home in New England, we found no washing machine/dryer, no pressing iron, no stereo/video, portable TV only of poorest quality, cycles rusted, fleas in furniture, poor, unclean car. We returned to our home to find it dirty and our car's clutch worn out! However, despite this, we made the best of it and had a most enjoyable holiday. We assumed it was their first exchange, and it was ours, too. However, we forgave and hope they learned by experience." And a couple in Colorado had a similar experience: "One exchange, scheduled for a full month, was a dump. We reviewed the correspondence, and it was described accurately, so we just made do. The roof leaked, and the place was dirty. It had been renovated (in 1937), but it was bad news. The exchanger did take good care of our place, and we talk about our month in his place all the time." Obviously, home exchangers are a resilient breed, or they would not keep on home exchanging.

Once settled in, college professors in Pennsylvania voiced the feeling of many that they "like least" having "to take care of problems arising from the care of the house, the car, or the pets." The Info Kit is of vital, paramount importance . . . and it must be *understandable*! Utter chaos can otherwise ensue, as a Boston, Massachusetts, lawyer and his wife found out when they arrived at their suburban Paris exchange home: "We were trying to understand and absorb the information and instructions regarding the operation of major appliances, household security system, etc., in half French, half English by our frantic hostess, who was also supervising her children's packing, saying good-bye to neighbors, and so on. In our jet-lagged condition, we were overwhelmed, and our children (who subsequently learned to love the place) were looking grim and disappointed at the fourteenth-century house in a small village, muttering it was *terrible* and they didn't want to live *here*!"

A high school teacher in Yadkinville, North Carolina, remarks: "The second English couple and the Canadian couple with whom we exchanged didn't know about garbage disposals, and each time they 'blew' my disposal. The Canadians left a loose fuse, probably thinking they had messed up other appliances. When we returned, the refrigerator had been off for about two weeks. I didn't think I would ever get the smell out of the freezing compartment!" A woman in Zimbabwe laments: "Visitors do not realize that any appliances we have are imported and *not* replaceable."

Chapter 15 goes into detail about exchanging cars, and this is another major item of concern. An Oxfordshire, England, school teacher worries about "the anxiety of driving another's car and vice versa." Once a car is understood, getting around in unfamiliar territory can be quite a challenge. A Colorado couple exchanged with a Chicago couple. On their first day in Colorado the Chicagoans headed for Pike's Peak. After hairpin turns and overheated brakes, they returned to their exchange home and never used the car again for two weeks!

A Birmingham, Alabama, couple ran into the problem of unfamiliarity with distances in another country: "We corresponded with our Australian vacation exchangers and discussed their travel plans. They had decided to fly to Los Angeles and then drive to Birmingham. They didn't know that Birmingham is three thousand miles from Los Angeles! We convinced them to fly to Birmingham, and then we met them at our airport." Remembering to send or leave adequate information about distances and driving times is very helpful, as driving conditions vary so much from one country to another, or even from one state to another in the U.S. A gentleman in central Florida has this unusual advice about driving in another country: "A lovely, vivacious hostess in Mexico told us, 'Don't turn right on a red light and, if stopped by police, offer a bribe.'"

Sometimes exchangers find they're not going to be entirely alone in their new home. The "like least" of a couple in Connecticut is "having family members remain in the home during our stay." Further surprises met a Kansas couple: "In San Francisco, we found we were sharing a nice big old house with a woman on the third floor, who only spoke Chinese and took care of a very new litter of Pekinese puppies that lived in the basement."

Another vexing problem can be exchangers arriving early or returning early. A California couple relates: "On our first exchange to England, the young man from England came to our home five days before we left, and it was very hard trying to get things ready." Sev-

eral instances of exchangers becoming ill and having to return home while their exchangers were still there were mentioned in the survey. However, these were worked out satisfactorily for all parties. After all, home exchangers have to be adaptable!

Although a Boston homemaker's only complaint was that "We ate out seldom, and it was too much cooking and housework for Mother," an Italian couple discovered that if they wanted to cook in Montana, the closest food store was thirty-five miles away. Shopping hours different from those at home can also be disconcerting, and when combined with a language deficiency, things can really get tough. A Dallas, Texas, exchange couple wrote: "We found the frustration of language ineptitude more critical when home exchanging than when staying in a hotel."

A university professor in Colorado agrees that his "inadequate knowledge of French and German" is a drawback. Even when people speak the *same* language, confusion can happen. A couple in the U.S. Virgin Islands exchanged with an English couple: "In a conversation about where things were at the home in London, we discovered that 'jumpers' weren't for the *car*, but actually were *sweaters*. We had told them the *jumpers* were in the trunk of our car, and they had looked surprised that in tropical St. Thomas we would ever need jumpers (sweaters). A big laugh was had by all four of us."

Arriving at airports can be a problem to some exchangers, especially when cars are left there for them to pick up. A journalist in Madison, Connecticut, writes: "Arriving at Heathrow Airport outside London, we had to find our exchange partner's car in the car park and follow directions to their house only forty-five minutes away. It took us three hours! Horrendous ride, getting used to right-hand drive and stick shift with *my* left hand. We kept getting lost at roundabouts and stopped to ask directions of a deaf mute. What's a 'flyover' [an overpass]? We used to think we spoke the same language—no more!"

A disappointment to some exchangers is not being able to meet their exchange partners, especially during a simultaneous exchange with no overlapping time. Hurried meetings in the rush of airport departures or arrivals are also unsatisfactory to many. An extra effort is often made to solve these problems.

Interestingly, a few exchangers felt that being in a home was *too* restricting. A Covent Garden, London, resident says: "The tendency to 'stay put' curbs the urge to travel further afield." An educator in Idaho comments that "not always being in a part of town where kids have immediate facilities, as in a hotel" is something he does not like. And last, but not least, in these days of global crises, a retired teacher in Ohio regrets "not being able to find U.S. magazines and newspapers!"

On the upside and the downside—an insurance agent in Chester County, Pennsylvania, was enthused: "We love our vacation exchanges. We have met many beautiful people and have made wonderful friends. It makes the whole world much smaller and gives us a better feeling when traveling. It is great to have so many friends in places so far away." A business couple in the northwestern part of the U.S. "love the idea of exchanges. It is one way to allow each of us to know at a deeper level that there are more commonalities than differences among people." But an American couple was disappointed: "We had an exchange in Guadalajara, Mexico, but no one was there when we arrived—total loss! But we aren't letting that stop us one bit!"

From the east coast of Florida: "You asked what we enjoyed most about exchanging. I seem to be interested in the way people live their lives. I enjoy going to the supermarkets and sometimes being surprised at what we buy . . . seeing how they bring their own bags to the supermarket and bag their purchases themselves. It is fortuitous to think we live our lives there as they do, but we come closer than you would in a hotel room." And from Pennsylvania: "In many ways, no matter how simple the accommodation, it is a most luxurious way to travel." Perhaps all home exchangers would applaud a gentleman from Hawaii who sums it all up: "My main problem with home exchanging is *I can't do it fast enough*!"

All sunshine and roses? Well, not quite. Like life, liberty, and the pursuit of happiness, there *are* problems—some large ones, some small ones—that confront vacation home exchangers. While admitting that home exchangers do occasionally have to roll with the punches, a Springfield, Massachusetts, multitime exchanger says: "My wife and I have learned to deal with the few negative aspects of exchanging. We seem to be able to focus on the *positive* aspects—too many to list here—and by so doing, we look forward to enjoying home exchanging 'til death do us part!"

21 And Still More People Who Tried It . . . and Liked It

With military service in the German army during World War II, which included some years as a Russian prisoner of war, Karl-Heinrich Himburg's life work was in the insurance business. In 1983 he retired as a director and manager of the Life Insurance *Allianz* with headquarters in what was then West Berlin. For many years, Rose Himburg had her own career—working with her father in the family's building construction and renovation company. After retiring, the Himburgs moved to Nuremberg, in Bavaria, where they refurbished a large townhouse.

Karl-Heinrich (called "Henry" by his overseas friends) and Rose have two daughters. Daniela is an architect living in Berlin. She has played an important role in the conversion of unused building lofts and other appropriate space to help meet the living needs of persons who have moved from what was East Germany to Berlin. Caroline is engaged in a "forwarding apprenticeship" and attends a commercial school.

The Himburgs' second home is in Javea (Alicante), Spain. This villa, with its private pool and lovely garden, was recently featured in a widely viewed European television commercial.

Rose Himburg writes:

We were intrigued with holiday home exchange concept when we first read about it in a 1983 national magazine article. Initially, we listed our home (with an appropriate photo) in one of the largest holiday home exchange directories. Inexperienced as we were, in our listing, we stated "anywhere" as our hoped-for holiday location. Yes, we listed anywhere, and we got letters from *everywhere*! (I answered every inquiry, but that experience taught us to be specific in stating where we want to go.)

To date we have had thirteen different hospitality and home exchanges in seven U.S. states and in Australia and New Zealand. While each of our exchanges has been about two weeks in length, we always seem to make a "chain" of exchange destinations. Why go from Germany, say, to Arizona for only two weeks? We think that four to six weeks is about right for the exchange chain, though we did have one that was ten weeks in duration. We always enjoy doing hospitality exchanges, but these are usually for shorter periods of time. Especially, we remember a hospitality exchange in Los Angeles. The lady of the house was German, and she gave us red-carpet treatment. Though our plane arrived at midnight, off she took us to the top of the Bonaventure Hotel for a get-acquainted drink. Helga prepared breakfasts and dinners for us; well do we remember those delicious meals! She had a marvelous home in the hills, with an unforgettable, panoramic view of L.A. During the first three days, Helga showed us all of the important things to see in the L.A. area; then we took her car for another three days, sightseeing throughout southern California.

Our very first regular exchanger had a large home in Cambria, California, quite near the famous San Simeon. An after-exchange problem: while we never personally met this California home exchanger, on returning to Spain, we had to collect about two hundred cigarette butts from our garden!

We love both California and Florida; in the latter, our condominium was right on the beach near Fort Myers—perfect for shelling, swimming (both in the Gulf of Mexico and in our pool), and just plain relaxing. Also, of course, Florida offers Walt Disney World, Epcot Center, and the other wonders of Orlando.

We have also lived in condos and houses in various other Florida locations (note I say "lived in," not "stayed in." One simply stays in hotels or motels, but one *lives* in exchange homes. Big difference!) Caroline had her seventeenth birthday party in a Captiva Island, Florida, restaurant—a special event arranged by our home exchange partners; in Orange Beach, Alabama, we stayed in a beautiful five-bedroom home, where our host "fished" with his totally blind dog in the water chasing the fish into his nets . . . and *we* (not the dog!) got to enjoy our fill of trout and mullet!

Our hospitality and home exchange partners' ages have ranged from forty to seventy. Among these exchangers have been accountants, teachers, technical managers, retired bankers, a publisher, an insurance manager, a leisure-park manager, a fish scientist in Wellington, New Zealand, and a ship captain in Australia. Generally they come to our home as a couple, but some have children or several friends accompanying them.

As we think over our exchanges to date, we believe we have been very, very fortunate in every part of our holiday exchanging. A large part of the reason for this is the home we offer in Spain. It's large, with ample bedrooms and baths to accommodate an average-sized family. We have the pool, of course, and a blooming garden (a poolman and a gardener help here) and the home is on three levels—with open decks and glassed-in porches, as well. Our villa is situated on a cliff, called Cabo La Nao, with spectacular views of the Mediterranean and—on clear days—the Balearic Islands. While we make this Spanish villa available to home exchangers the year round, we like to do our part of the exchanges in May or June. We do not have to have simultaneous exchanges, you see, because we have the two homes.

We have never had any of the home exchange disasters which sometimes one hears about. Oh, there are, of course, some things we don't like: being put in a bedroom with an uncomfortable, pull-out bed—sofa or otherwise; not being provided with a sufficient amount of wardrobe and drawer space (and too few clothes hangers); and pets. We don't like cats trying to discover our belongings and leaving fur hairs everywhere, and dogs doing their urgent needs all over the garden—attracting flies, and making it necessary for us to jump between littered spots. Henry calls it "avoiding treadmines!"

With now some years of experience writing holiday home exchange letters, I have learned to ask the right questions; thus we do not often have to confront things which annoy us. If we do run into a problem after we've arrived, we can usually deal with it early in our stay. Also, I have developed a good filing system, so I know what we have told people about our home and what they have told us about theirs. This is important! You just can't have copies of letters and notes and memos floating all over the place. After all, it's the exchanges of correspondence that really do set the pace for the exchange itself. And I always make careful notes of telephone conversations with those we might (or do) exchange.

While we know many exchangers list their properties in more than one directory, we find that our listing in just the one more than meets our needs. Again, our home in Spain does appeal to many potential exchangers. I can see how some exchangers "off the beaten road" would be well advised to list their homes with two or three clubs, thus giving their homes exposure to many more potential holiday home exchangers.

Occasionally we do rent our second home, and like other exchangers we've talked to, we find exchangers definitely take much better care of our home than renters. We arrange for a maid to clean

the home after each guest departs. No, we have never had any problem with the care of our home or property.

I think Henry and I are "people" people. Years ago, we used to holiday on cruise ships and in hotels, and we still do bed and breakfasts sometimes, on short visits. But we feel our very best holidays have been while hospitality exchanging or home exchanging. On the former, we make friends with our hosts, while on the latter, our friends are the neighbors of our home exchange hosts.

Currently, we are in the planning and correspondence stages of arrangements for future vacation home exchanges in Hong Kong and Tokyo and additional visits to the U.S.

Some of our German friends ask, "How can you travel abroad—only to countries where English is spoken?" Well, my English is now quite adequate—much better than when we started exchanging with English-speaking people . . . and Henry's English improves with each passing home exchange in the U.S.

Reading that article about holiday home exchanging back in 1983 started Henry and me (and sometimes our daughters as well) on what we believe to be the world's best kind of holiday: home exchanging—inexpensive, relaxing, and stimulating.

The Lewis family—David, Susan, and sons Matthew and Duncan—live in Hampstead, London, England. *Vacation* and *home exchanging* are synonymous in this family, as the Lewises have enjoyed vacation home exchanging every year now for more than a decade. The boys were ages five and three at the time of the Lewis's first home exchange. Teenagers now, Matthew and Duncan look forward with anticipation and excitement to each new summer's vacation home exchange.

Down through the years the Lewises have been successful in exchanging their home—a three-bedroom converted stable in the fashionable London suburb of Hampstead, just a two-minute walk from Hampstead Heath and the home of renowned poet John Keats, who wrote "Ode to a Nightingale" while sitting on a hill that overlooks what is now the Lewis home. Among their immediate neighbors in Hampstead are artists and writers, rock star Boy George, and Michael Foot, left-wing politician and fervent nuclear unilateralist. The Lewis home is particularly "exchangeable" because it offers quiet country living only a stone's throw from London's West End.

David and Susan Lewis are both writers and currently operate their own book publishing firm. They first learned of vacation home exchanging in 1978 when David, then financial editor of a national newspaper, was commissioned to do a newspaper article about the growing trend toward vacationing, home exchange style.

Their first home exchange was in the U.S., in California, in a three-bedroom house overlooking Santa Barbara and the Pacific Ocean. On arriving in America after an eleven-hour flight, then five-year-old Duncan asked, "Are we going back home now?" They most definitely were not! This first vacation home exchange encouraged the Lewises to take many, many more: two each in California and Florida, one in Massachusetts (high in the Berkshire Mountains), and six to different destinations in Italy.

The professions of those with whom the Lewises have exchanged homes have varied from schoolteachers to a banker and a lawyer. Two couples were retired. "Teachers and retired folk," says Susan, "have the advantage of being able to take lengthier and more frequent vacations." Their earlier exchange partners were families with young children and/or teenagers, but subsequent exchanges have been with families of grown-up children and with older couples who leave their young people and grandchildren far behind.

One exchange was with a marvelous woman of nearly seventy who stayed in their London home with a traveling companion. If she was worried about the Lewises' then seven- and five-year-old boys ruining her luxury condominium on Sanibel Island in Florida, she certainly did not say so. As it turned out, nothing was harmed or broken.

"Very rarely has there been any damage done to property, either to our own or to the homes in which we have stayed," says Susan. "People are extremely careful living in someone else's home. They may have broken the odd cup or plate. And one time an exchanger broke something in our car, but he put it right at his expense.

"When someone breaks something in our home, we say that we could just as well have broken it ourselves. This has never been a problem. When the boys were little, we would move around our 'new' homes taking breakables off low-lying tables and putting them safely away into cupboards. If we know small children are coming to our home, we do the same and lock anything we do not want touched into a small room we use as a study. This includes family-related documents and other items of a personal nature."

Because of the long distances involved in their exchange locations, the Lewises prefer vacations three or four weeks in length during the summer. They also have had Christmas and Easter exchanges.

"One strange experience," they say, "was during our first exchange. We were looking through a photograph album which belonged to the people we had exchanged with. There, in black and white, was our lady exchange partner, a few years younger, standing outside the *very house* we had lived in when we first married. The house was in a distinctive street, so it was easily recognizable. Until our exchange, we had not known each other. She had obviously been attracted to our *first* home, so it made sense she would like our *current* one! It was as if we were meant to meet."

One exchange in Italy was particularly memorable. A local farmer and friend of the Lewis's exchange partners invited them to a Sunday dinner party to celebrate his son's twenty-fifth birthday. The farm was over two hundred years old, built of stone, and one wall was covered with perches where pigeons sat. "There were at least twenty guests," says Susan. "A long table with a white cloth was laid out in the courtyard. A bonfire was lit, and chicken was barbecued on embers taken from the fire. Everything we ate was grown and made on the farm, and after dinner three guests brought out their musical instruments. We danced until the early morning. We could have been living two centuries ago and could not have been made more welcome."

Have the Lewises ever had a home exchange disaster? Well, not *really* a disaster, they say, but one experience they have not forgotten. While on an exchange in southern Italy, they awakened one night to the greeting of a mouse in bed with them! Out of the bed they jumped, catching the mouse in a shoe box. A repeat performance the following night led them to determine the mouse parade was entering through a bedroom window. The solution: coating the windowsill with lavatory bleach. By the end of this particular exchange, the Lewises had reduced by eight the Italian mouse population! "More fun to reflect over, than running around the house chasing mice with a shoe box!" says Susan.

Are the Lewis boys bored with following their parents around the world? The answer is emphatically no. Matthew says, "We enjoy sunbathing and swimming, eating out in restaurants, and just being lazy." Duncan enjoys sightseeing and visiting old castles, of which there are many in Italy. The chance to be in a hot climate (a prerequisite to the Lewis's exchanges) makes all of the travel worthwhile.

Occasionally while holidaying in Italy, the boys have found language to be a barrier. But they manage to play cards and talk in broken English and sign language with other youngsters of their age. "I suppose we are lucky in that the boys are close in age and get along very well together," says Susan. "They make their own company to a certain extent. If they get stuck on communicating with other children, they come to me to help them out. I speak Italian, which is a major asset if you want to exchange in Italy, because not many Italians speak English. Oftentimes, Italians want to exchange with English families because the Italians want their children to learn English and because they are interested in the historical aspect of the country."

One recent outcome of exchanging homes was a letter to the Lewises from Marseille in France, asking if they had a teenage son they might wish to send to France in exchange for their son staying in London. As Susan and David had planned to visit that area, they took the opportunity to meet this French family. The boys were introduced and exchange visits were arranged. Both boys had to learn the other's language for school examinations.

"One of the nicest aspects of vacation home exchanging," says Susan, "is that you are really amongst a local community and get to see how other people live their ordinary, everyday lives. Also, vacation home exchangers oftentimes visit nontourist locations; are introduced to friends and neighbors of their hosts; enjoy cost saving as compared with a more conventional vacation; have accommodations of a better quality than most rental homes, the use of a free car, and an independence in their vacation living experience, which is not usually found in tours and more structured vacations."

Reflecting over the Lewis's many years of vacation home exchanging, Susan says, "We have thoroughly enjoyed every single one of our home exchanges to date, and we look forward to many more in the years ahead."

Having been introduced to vacation home exchanging in a 1978 magazine article, the Sandy Lyons-Sam Evans family of Melrose, Florida, enjoyed seven different exchanges during a five-year period. A 1983 vacation home exchange resulted in Sandy and Sam's redirecting their exchange efforts from their *own* enjoyment to that of *others.*

It is a widespread opinion that architects should be lumped in with doctors, corporate presidents, and lawyers when speaking of pay scales. But six years of vacationless marriage had proven that the Lyons-Evans family could not take lavish vacations on Sam's architectural salary. Sandy set out to search the newspapers and magazines for supersaver vacations that their family of three could afford. Four-year-old Ryan was about to enter school, and five-year-old Kim Soo Young (now known as Becky) from South Korea was about to join the family. Adoption fees had depleted their savings, and Becky's medical reports indicated she had cerebral palsy and mental retardation. There was no telling what their future would hold.

An article about vacation home exchanges caught Sandy's eye, and a family conference brought a unanimous yes for listing in a home exchange handbook and beginning to search for the perfect vacation exchange. This novice family was quickly initiated into the process, learned from their mistakes, and finally landed a firm home exchange commitment after a year of letter writing. During the summer of 1980 the family set out for an historic home in a small community in Maryland, near the nation's capital. Future exchanges would take them to the Pennsylvania Dutch country; music-land Nashville; the future Winter Olympics city of Calgary in Canada; the mountainous grandeur of British Columbia; and to Knoxville and the 1982 World's Fair, not to mention several weekend getaways in their home state of Florida. Perhaps their most unusual and fateful home exchange took place during summer 1983, when Sandy and Sam decided that a trip to Mexico was just what the stress doctor ordered.

Several contacts produced no exchange, but Jaime and Lucy Fernandez responded with an invitation to call them upon arrival in Mexico City for a get-together. The Fernandezes had already made arrangements for another Florida exchange. Sandy jotted a similar invitation to the Fernandez family, and several weeks later the Fernandez family took them up on their offer.

A day of lakeside activities at the Lyons-Evans home quickly led to special feelings between these two families, and a few months later in Mexico, Jaime returned the hospitality while Sam and Sandy enjoyed Mexican culture.

A year passed with the customary exchanges of holiday greetings. Sandy was surprised one midwinter day when a hefty envelope from Lucy was delivered. A quick scan of the enclosed paperwork and letter revealed the birth of Amistad Mundial—Foreign Friendship, a nonprofit home/friendship exchange for children between nine and twelve years of age (age requirements now extend to fourteen years and exceptions for eight- and fifteen-to-sixteen year-olds are common). Lucy's home exchange experiences had convinced her of the need for cultural and friendship exchanges for this forgotten age group, which traditionally has had only Grandma's house or camp as a safe vacation destination away from home.

Sandy's initial response was negative, since she had a busy schedule and was not convinced American parents would be willing to part with their precious heirs for three long weeks in a foreign country without their supervision. An urgent call from Lucy in May 1985 thrust Sandy headlong into the program. An additional eight host homes were needed for unmatched Mexican children. Could Sandy find them in one week? Yes? Good!

Sandy contacted several close friends to seek their positive response. A couple of firm "maybes" encouraged her to call some referrals. Originally planning to take one or two boys close to son Ryan's age, Sandy discovered at the end of a week that she had *nine* potential host homes, not counting her own!

An express package arrived from Mexico with directions for interviewing the families and children. The goal of Foreign Friendship is to provide safe, compatible homes for children of like sex, age, interests, and background. Home interviews confirmed that all the families were acceptable, meeting rigid, high standards. Lucy matched each child with a family. Children would arrive a month later with a Mexican chaperon, who would remain in Florida for the entire three weeks. Special T-shirts were distributed, applications and pictures shared, and communication exchanged between the two matched families. The big day arrived in late June, and Florida hosts greeted their new "family members" at Tampa International Airport. Thus began a three-week odyssey of learning for nine Mexican children (Lucy recruited another girl)—weeks of a new language, different foods, new friends, shopping, planned tours, and a large pool party for everyone involved.

As the children boarded the airplane to return to Mexico, a common question was, "Are you going to do this again next year?" Sandy had been convinced she would, and she had only just begun her public relations work for Foreign Friendship (F.F.).

Five years of F.F. have seen Ryan matched with four young men, and a new world has opened up to him. Now thirteen years old, he looks forward to several more years of practicing firsthand his newly learned Spanish. Sandy and Sam have established close friendships with Ryan's new families and enjoyed hospitality in their Mexican homes when they traveled as chaperons with F.F. in 1988.

Sandy has seen F.F. grow from nine hosted-only exchanges in 1986 to as many as seventeen full exchanges per year in recent years. Given three options—host only; travel only without reciprocal hosting; or full exchange, which involves two to three weeks in one friend's country and then two to three weeks in the other—"over a hundred children have participated." A small core of parents train and work with Sandy each year to promote the program across Florida and Georgia, interview families, and schedule program activities while her counterpart, Lili Arroyo, does the same in Mexico. Prices are considered each winter and have fluctuated between a high of $650 to $575 in 1990. Since some parents work with the program, costs are kept low for everyone, and workers get special discounts for their children. Sandy has learned Spanish and teaches children's classes, with her fees funding her F.F. scholarships. Revised application papers provide better information to the workers who match the children. All workers have their own children involved in the program, so they have a vested interest in the success of each exchange year.

Sandy's new exchange job came by surprise and is often time consuming and frustrating, especially during the spring recruiting and flight scheduling to accommodate such a large group. However, rewards have far outshadowed the problems. She remembers eleven-year-old Hector sleeping on a sofa (after his first lawnmowing experience), a pet cockatiel perched on his head. Nine-year-old Ingrid called her parents in Mexico to request more money because she had spent most of hers at McDonald's. Twelve-year-old Paula parasailed off Acapulco beach, and thirteen-year-old Joe got top billing on the Pueblo newspaper's sports page for kicking the soccer tournament's winning point—and he was allowed to take home the trophy! Vibrant memories like these help to keep the program alive.

There hasn't been time since 1985 for the Lyons-Evans family to pore over vacation home exchange listings, nor have they gone on anything but Foreign Friendship trips to Mexico. But they are not complaining! Instead, Sandy says she is inviting parent coordinators in other countries and states to join the Foreign Friendship family, opening up other areas of this great world to their sharing of international friendship and home exchange.

Note: Those readers wishing to know more about Foreign Friendship may write to: Foreign Friendship, Route 1, Box 1289, Melrose, Florida 32666.

22 The Ultimate Disaster!

EVERY WORTHWHILE FIELD of endeavor has its very own parade of catastrophes, and in this respect vacation home exchanging is no exception. Among the catastrophic aspects of vacation home exchanging: an American turning *right* into an English traffic "roundabout" (circle) in his host's brand-new Mercedes; a French wine expert lost in a sea of Gallo wine bottles at his host's local Grand Union; a nonsmoking exchange host who returns home to find his living room curtains have been yellowed by his exchange partner's smoking a dozen cheap cigars daily; the American exchanger who, in corresponding with the owner of the *perfect* exchange home in Spain, failed to put airmail postage on his exchange-deal-closing letter and thus lost out to another exchanger who did not make the same postage error; the Portuguese exchange host who failed to leave proper instructions on lighting the bottled gas oven and returned home to find his oven had blown up. Yes, catastrophes aplenty in some vacation home exchanges!

But the *ultimate* disaster—the really bad one—in vacation home exchanging is to be confronted and dealt with in this chapter and is perhaps best described by a ten-time home exchanger in Atlanta, Georgia: "A French family backed out of our exchange only days before we were to leave for Europe. We were stuck with airline tickets for my wife, our three children, and me. It was a *dreadful* disappointment!"

A four-time exchanger in Brisbane, Australia, writes: "I know one exchanger who had finalized all details of a U.S. exchange, booked travel tickets, got travelers cheques—only to learn the exchange had been canceled. Not once, but *twice* within a period of three months."

A Sutton, Ireland, aircraft engineer, his registered-nurse wife, and their three children share this unfortunate story: "We had exchanged two letters, very positive, and all we had to do was arrange for car insurance covering our exchange partners. We were expecting a reply to our second letter, but it never materialized. About five weeks before we were due to exchange, I telephoned them, and they shocked us by saying they had changed their minds and were going to Spain instead. They said they had written a letter of explanation, but somehow we never received that letter. At that stage, it was too late for us to make alternate arrangements, so our exchange holiday was ruined."

A retired Eastern Airlines captain in Bradenton, Florida, writes: "We had two great vacation home exchanges set up, and then about a month before the exchange dates, both of our 'partners' changed their minds—leaving us in limbo. We do wish such 'nonexchangers' would always offer some alternate plans."

"Our disappointment was being canceled out two days before our home exchange date on what (to me) was a very flimsy excuse," reports a Virginia home exchanger.

"A dreadful disappointment" . . . "exchange had been canceled" . . . "holiday was ruined" . . . "leaving us in limbo" . . . "a very flimsy excuse." Fortunately, "disappointment," "canceled," "ruined," "in limbo," and "flimsy excuse" are words only rarely associated with vacation home exchanging.

These five exchangers were careful each step of the way in their vacation home exchange planning and correspondence and looked forward to their respective vacation home exchanges in France, in the U.S., in Spain, and elsewhere, only to learn that their exchange partners had become "nonpartners." Again, these five disastrous experiences underscore in the best possible way the vital importance of vacation home exchangers fulfilling their home exchange commitments to each other. In the normal course of events, there is no place for "Dear John" letters in the world of vacation home exchanging!

But on rare occasions plans *must* be changed. People *do* die, children (and adults) *do* become seriously ill, and people changing jobs *do* have to change vacation plans, home exchange or otherwise.

So, you get the bad news. You have some evil thoughts about your nonexchanging partners and give vent to a few expletives. After a restless night's sleep, in the light of a bright new day you realize that it could have been *you* who had to cancel the exchange plans ("there but for the grace of God go I").

To compensate for last-minute cancellations, airlines and hotels oftentimes "overbook" reservations; obviously, such overbooking is not an option open to vacation home exchangers. But it *is* surprising how often a jilted home exchanger can pick up the pieces of an exchange cancellation and arrange alternate exchange vacation plans. There is a dichotomy here in that the person canceling out on you may very well be your best key to the solution of your vacation dilemma. This certainly was the case in the experience of these exchangers in Maryland: "Our exchange partner in France changed his mind, but fortunately he had a second home, which he let us use."

And here is another second-home-to-the-rescue example, from a retired New York school guidance counselor: "We were enjoying our exchange in Spain, while our exchange partners were also enjoying their vacation in our New York apartment—enjoying it, that is, until a telephone call advising our partner his father had died back home; this fact, of course, necessitated our partner's immediate return to Spain. Fortunately, we were in our partner's second home, so we did not have to move . . . but we felt terribly sorry for this Spanish couple, not only because of this man's father's death, but because their New York vacation exchange had to be terminated so abruptly."

A New York City family with a decade of successful exchanges (London, Paris, Israel, Mexico City, and elsewhere) were disappointed when a call came from Rome: their exchange partner had to cancel his trip to New York. What to do? "The upshot of the story was that our exchange host was able to go to the seashore in Italy, while we spent a month in his home in Rome—housekeeper and car provided. Later, these Italian exchange friends came to visit us in New York, and we have been great friends ever since."

If *you* have to cancel a vacation home exchange arrangement, here are two suggestions, each of paramount importance: (1) advise your exchange partner by telephone (if you have no telephone, wire or cable) *immediately* after you know you will not be able to carry through with the exchange plan, giving your exchange partner the maximum amount of time to make other arrangements; and (2) make every effort to help your partner by providing an alternate plan. In this connection, perhaps you have an available second home; or perhaps you have a relative or a friend in your area who has an available second home or whose main home might just be available due to his being on vacation at the time your partner is expecting to be at your home; or perhaps you could arrange a hospitality exchange for your partner; or maybe you could locate an inexpensive rental for your partner, perhaps even offering to split the rental fee. Remember, your exchange partner has been planning to be at your home, so it behooves you to pull out all the stops in endeavoring to arrange a substitute exchange for him or possibly a rental arrangement. In a situation like this, *any* port in the storm could conceivably be instrumental in solving your partner's problem.

This story from an exchanger in Arlington, Virginia: "Just before one of our four vacation home exchanges, my wife became seriously ill, so our home was not available to our exchange partners. As it happened, our next-door neighbor was to be leaving town at the same time that our partners were coming here. These neighbors generously offered to have our exchange partners come to *their* home. It all worked out well."

Exchangers in Portland, Oregon, and in Washington, D.C., had hopes of spending a month in each others' homes—a spring vacation, actually. "We had the exchange pretty well worked out. Then because my mother (who was to travel with us) became critically ill, we had to abort the exchange—hated to do this, but we had to. Happily, Mother recovered, and we were able to complete the exchange

the following spring."

If your exchange partner cannot go through with the exchange and leaves you with no acceptable alternate plan, reach for a yellow, legal-sized writing pad and draw up a "laundry list" of possible other plans—the key element here being the amount of time you have to make such alternate arrangements.

1. By telephone, communicate your plight to some of the "near misses" you might have had in the weeks or months before the cancellation—persons with whom you had correspondence but were not quite able to firm up an exchange; it is just possible one of these persons might not yet have fixed up plans for his own exchange.
2. If there is time, go back to square one: get out your exchange directories and, by telephone, endeavor to put together, in short order, a substitute, satisfactory exchange.
3. Perhaps you will be able to postpone your exchange to a later

date—a date that might be convenient for you and for the exchanger who canceled out on the original plans.
4. And (a last resort), if you have the resources, endeavor to arrange a "conventional" vacation at a hotel or rented facility at some appropriate vacation destination.

Yes, get creative. Make every conceivable effort to hold together your plans for this vacation.

This from an eight-time exchanger, a retired engineer in New York City: "When our exchange partners canceled out on us, we had already purchased nonrefundable airline tickets, so we wrote to a bunch of people in home exchange directories in England, asking for their help. We got two offers of vacation homes at a very cheap rent. We took one . . . in Lyme Regis."

Those who are experienced in vacation home exchanging year after year often have gut feelings that sooner or later some emergency situation will cause a cancellation. They are prepared to roll with the punches. Exchangers in Eastleigh, England, confronted a genuine act of God: they had to leave their Myrtle Beach, South Carolina, vacation home exchange one day early, but by so doing, they avoided Hurricane Hugo, which struck Myrtle Beach with a vengeance!

Anticipating that someday he might be confronted with an exchange cancellation, this same Eastleigh businessman writes: "We were able to extend the usual holiday insurance to include the expense of substitute accommodations in the event that the exchanger could not complete the arrangement. Our experience shows how vital this insurance is, yet no one in England appeared even to have heard of such coverage, and it took a great deal of time on my part before we found a company willing to provide it. Is this peculiar to the United Kingdom, or does everybody doing an exchange take the risk of the other party pulling out at the last moment?" As has been stated already, vacation home exchange cancellations are few and far between, but exchangers might just wish to contact their insurance agents about this exchange-cancellation coverage.

An exchanger from Colorado writes: "On two different occasions, our 'hoped-for' exchanger backed out on us. Each time, my husband said, 'What a revolting development! I'll *never* do another home exchange!' But then we've had such great fun vacation home exchanging that we arranged another and another and another. Now we are in the process of putting together two exchanges, one to follow the other—the first in Santa Fe, New Mexico, and the other one in Tucson, Arizona. If these two work out, we will have completed twenty-one exchanges. And next year we hope to do a six-week chain of exchanges in Holland and Belgium."

On this upbeat note, a reminder: with a reasonable mix of understanding, patience, and flexibility, any person, couple, or family group can look to vacation home exchange as the answer to that perennial question, "What'll we do for a vacation *this* year?"

23 That Inevitable Question

As ONE CAN SURMISE FROM reading previous chapters of this book, to say vacation home exchangers are enthusiastic about the vacation home exchange concept would be a masterpiece of understatement. Actually, the vast majority of vacation home exchangers are *ecstatic* about this vacation concept—so much so that they rarely miss an opportunity to talk up home exchanging and to endeavor to make family members, friends, and others they meet along the way converts to the vacation home exchange experience.

As vacation home exchangers go about their soft- and often *hard*-sell efforts, sooner or later those without vacation home exchanging experience will confront these enthusiastic exchangers with the inevitable question: "Aren't you nervous about having *strangers* actually *living* in your home?"

Certainly this is a very logical question motivated by fear—fear of how "stranger" guests might mistreat their homes: spill red wine on their sand-colored carpeting, bust up their china and glassware, wreck their appliances, burn cigarette holes in their bedding, keep their neighbors awake with all-night drinking parties, and—perhaps even worse—actually *steal* things, that is, the family jewels, the microwave oven, the VCR, the snow blower. Yes, for those who have not yet caught the vacation home exchange "vision"—for those uninitiated into this unconventional vacation concept—these and a hundred and one other questions are totally understandable.

As regards this matter of out-and-out stealing: the survey—really, the foundation of these chapters—failed to turn up even one case of stealing. Remember, this survey covered approximately 2,400 different vacation home exchanges, worldwide. "People interested in exchanging homes are not 'criminal types,'" writes an IBM computer analyst in Ithaca, New York. Apropos, too, is this, from a Stockholm, Sweden, exchanger: "I don't think anyone would rob me during his holiday. Even *thieves* take holidays from stealing, don't they?"

The closest thing to thievery reported were those two or three instances in which the exchange hosts' wine and liquor closets were "abused," and in every case these problems could easily have been avoided had the exchange hosts not made their finest wines and/or liquors easily available. Again, these hard-to-replace items should always be stored away.

Regarding the *care* of the hosts' homes and personal property: of the more than 600 survey participants, nearly *500* reported their exchange guests took "excellent" care of their homes and personal property, 90 reported "very good," and only a handful reported "less than good" care.

On the other side of the home-care coin, without exception, vacation home exchange hosts feel that when they are exchange *guests*, they take excellent care of their hosts' homes and personal property. Not realizing that vacation home exchange partners do take excellent care of each others' homes and personal belongings, those outside of, but inquiring about, the "wonderful world of vacation home exchanging" still ask that inevitable question: "Aren't you nervous about having *strangers* actually *living* in your home?"

"I do think the *first* time you hand over your house keys to a complete stranger, it can be unsettling! Our first exchange," writes a retired airline engineer in San Francisco, California, an eleven-time vacation home exchanger, "was in Hawaii. We arranged to meet our exchange partners in a hotel, exchange keys, drive them to the airport, and then go to their home. My stomach was in a knot; I thought, '*What* are we doing?' But when our partners arrived, they were just like us, and by the time we got to the airport, we were like old friends."

Having enjoyed vacation home exchanging in Holland, Switzerland, and in Jerusalem, an Israeli couple have not yet come to agreement on this "stranger" issue: "I am only a little apprehensive, but my wife *is* nervous about it, so we exchange our second home, situated in Ein-Hod, a beautiful artists' village overlooking the Mediterranean, near Haifa."

So, this initial *fear* of home exchanging is real—very real, indeed. A three-timer exchanger, a university professor in Mexico City, writes: "We were a little nervous before our first exchange, but not at all since then."

From an automobile mechanic in Cleveland, Ohio: "A vacation home exchange friend kept telling us 'try it—no problem'; though we were hesitant the first time, we did try it once, and once again, and again. Now, after six vacation home exchanges in the States, we've never had a problem, and we hope to go 'international' next year."

"We do home exchanging in England," writes a retired schoolteacher in Genk, Belgium. "While we are still afraid of giving our house to strangers, we hope to conquer that fear soon."

"Nervous about having strangers living in our home?" asks an exchanger associated with an architectural firm in Winchester, England. "I'm far *more* nervous that I would let down my home exchange guests by our house not suiting them or by our cat being a nuisance!"

Writes a home exchanging insurance man in Indian Wells, California: "In twenty-seven years of vacation home exchanging, we've never had anything damaged or missing!"

"The key word is trust. We trust them to care for our home, and they trust us to do the same," writes a St. Croix, U.S. Virgin Islands, artist, an enthusiastic "survivor" of sixteen different vacation home exchanges—in three U.S. states and in six European countries.

A businessman in Hampshire, England, writes: "There is a large degree of trust and honor involved."

"Going through the process of blind trust prior to the home exchange and then the pleasant discovery of new friends is a wonderful experience, both as an example to our children and as a renewal of our faith in people," declares a Portland, Oregon, teacher who, with her husband and her two children under twelve, has had six vacation home exchanges since 1980.

This from a marketing manager in London, England, who, with his wife and two young children, has vacation home exchanged in Spain, France, and Italy: "We are not worrying types. Home exchanging is a matter of mutual trust."

"What nonexchangers sometimes fail to realize is that both parties to an exchange appreciate the trust placed in them by their hosts, and they are damn well not going to betray that trust," writes a retired exchanger in New South Wales, Australia.

Among the most frequently used words in discussions about vacation home exchanging is *trust*. Home exchange partners seem to develop a sufficient amount of trust in each other to exchange keys to each others' homes and often the car keys, too. How does a potential vacation home and car exchanger acquire this degree of trust in a "stranger"?

This trust comes as the end result of "talking with other home exchangers," "correspondence exchanges," "sharing photographs," "telephone conversations," "recommendations from previous exchangers," "meetings [when convenient] between exchange partners," "doing your vacation home exchange partner 'homework.'" "After our communication and research, we don't feel our exchange partners are strangers anymore; they become true and trusted friends, and our home exchanges always are cases of two friends enjoying each others' homes for family vacations. No big deal!" These survey comments are from exchangers in Konstanz, Germany; Sanibel Island, Florida; Brisbane, Australia; Dundalk, Ireland; and Prescott, Arizona.

Collectively, vacation home exchangers report that "communication" is the keystone of this trust—the most important factor in the relationship between vacation home exchange partners. This trusting relationship is not simply a letter, a phone call, and here we are—kids, bikes, baggage, and key in hand. No, it is a great deal more. All of the elements of in-depth communication are essential to genuine trust. In an almost uncanny fashion, this communication (which more often than not goes on for months) makes friends out of strangers, trusted vacation home exchange partners out of apprehensive ones. Often, this pre-exchange communication and the exchanges themselves result not only in friendships and in trusting home exchangers, but lifelong, close relationships.

There are those who answer that inevitable question in other ways . . . .

"We find that psychologically people take better care of exchange homes than rented homes because they are looking after each others' homes," says a London, England, fashion consultant who has exchanged twenty-five times since 1970—in seven U.S. states and four other countries.

From a Hong Kong English Schools Foundation husband-wife teaching team and their two children (who have vacation home exchanged in the U.S., Australia, and Germany): "No, we aren't at all nervous. We treat other people's homes with greater respect than we treat our own, and it seems our exchange guests do the same! Maybe we have just been lucky."

"I think a certain type of person goes to the trouble of trying for a vacation home exchange. I guess we have quite a bit of faith in the human race and think the best of people until proven otherwise," writes a teacher on the Isle of Mull, Scotland, who with her husband and (now) four teenagers has enjoyed ten vacation home exchanges since 1974.

This from a retired furniture store owner in Kiryat Ono, Israel: "We are not nervous having 'strangers' in our home. We believe those who connect with us are serious and correct people."

An architect with a family of four, in Warwick, Bermuda, writes: "It's a matter of trusting other people. And besides, life is a gamble. In order to have new and interesting life experiences, you sometimes have to take chances."

If people are *really* nervous about having so-called "strangers" vacationing in their homes, then vacation home exchanging is probably not for them! This feeling, specifically expressed by home exchangers in Connecticut, England, and California is shared by many others—those new to the vacation home exchange game and multi-time exchangers as well.

A few other pertinent comments . . . .

An attorney from Lake Havasu, Arizona: "Although we have nice things in our home, we do not idolize material effects; after all, our things are insured, and besides, you can't take them with you!"

Second-home ownership can help to ease this fear. Those engaged in vacation home exchanging who own second homes not only

have more flexibility in vacation date scheduling, but in most cases have second homes that are modestly furnished and contain relatively few of their owners' more valuable personal items.

"Actually, we feel very secure having our home occupied while we are on vacation," writes a retired DuPont development manager in Wilmington, Delaware. And an upstate New York vacation home exchanger, a computer analyst, agrees: "We feel it's safer to have someone occupying our home when we are away."

Those who have had vacation home exchange experiences—a few or a lot—are by far the best resource for answers to all who ask that inevitable question—"Aren't you nervous about having *strangers* actually *living* in your home?"

24 A Funny Thing Happened . . .

UNLIKE THOSE WHO TAKE conventional vacations—in hotels, lakeside cottages, or ten-day European tours for $1,999.99—vacationing home exchangers sometimes encounter strange, memorable, humorous experiences.

Washington, D.C.: Prior to departing for an exchange, we wrote ourselves a note and pasted it on the front door so it would be the last thing we would see before leaving the apartment. The note said "Hide the Wine" (because we had some nice bottles of wine on our wine rack). However, in our haste to depart we forgot the note, and upon our return the first thing we saw *after* we returned home was our note still pasted to the front door! Embarrassed? You bet we were!

Somerset West, South Africa: We returned home from our Zimbabwe exchange only to find all of our potted plants drowned—watered to death!

Forest, Virginia: Of the five members of the family we exchanged with, only the ten-year-old had not begun to study English in school and spoke no English. We met them on their return to the Netherlands. Rutger, the ten-year-old, had learned a fair amount of English during his four-week stay in the U.S.A., but it was not all good. His father was relating their happening upon a suicide in New York City, in a fall from a high-rise building. He described their approach to the crowd that gathered around the dead man. A native New Yorker began to tell them what had happened. Rutger interrupted his father with, "You know what that man said? He said the man jumped out of the f—— window!" My wife quickly explained to Rutger that he had just learned his first *bad* English word—one he should promptly forget!

London, England: As usual, we went to a lot of trouble leaving information about the home, shopping, restaurants, transportation, and so on. Our exchange partners assured us they had done the same, but all we found at their home was a large sheet of paper on which they had laboriously converted centigrade into Fahrenheit!

Satellite Beach, Florida: During an Alexandria, Virginia, exchange, our host had recommended several restaurants, and we had tried a couple of them and agreed with his choices. So we decided to try another for lunch. We had our two youngest sons with us and to make a long story short, our "lunch" cost us ninety-five dollars. Our sons said, "You *really* know how to show us a good time!"

Tel Aviv, Israel: It takes a while to operate equipment and appliances belonging to someone else. One of our less humorous experiences was during an exchange in New Jersey, U.S.A. While we were parking the car in the garage, the automatic door closed down, and we found ourselves groping around in the dark, trying to get out of that garage!

Nairobi, Kenya, East Africa: "No problem. We have an adequate water supply." This was the assurance given us by our European exchange partner. In actual fact, I had to bribe a municipal driver to bring us water in a tanker!

Torrey, Vermont: One house we stayed in had an actual *tombstone* for their coffee table.

Vitre, France: In Miami, Florida, the police came the first night of our stay in the house. They knew our hosts were away and took us for "squatters."

Cranbury, New Jersey: While on vacation home exchanges, one usually gets or receives phone numbers of friends or relatives to call if unforeseen problems arise. An occasion arose in Italy where we called such a person. He was very helpful and afterward invited my wife and me out to dinner. Somehow my wife suspected that his companion was not quite his wife. This was later confirmed when my wife (who speaks some Italian) had occasion to call his home. When a lady answered, my wife said, "Hello, Sophia?" Our friend called back rather excitedly shortly afterwards and said, "Please do not call my home and ask for Sophia!"

Oran, Algeria: My wife and I were in Glasgow, Scotland, exchanging. Every day I was used to locking the door. One day, as I was going out to pick up the newspaper, I noticed that there were other keys beside mine on the table. I thought about burglars, but nothing was missing. I asked my wife whether it was she who put the keys there? She replied that she had not. I was astonished because I had not seen those keys before. My surprise was great, when I met upstairs head on a young man wearing pajamas! He seemed to stand as amazed at the situation as I was. I asked him how he entered the house. He asked me the same question; then he added that it was his parents' home. I breathed a sigh of relief, hearing that. I introduced myself to him, but I noticed he was not satisfied. I finally explained to him *why* I was in his parents' home. He explained to me that he had been abroad in India and wanted to give his parents a surprise! What a surprise. He felt like a stranger in his own home!

Chardon, Ohio: Our very first exchange in 1980 was for a vacation home on Sanibel Island, Florida. The home was nestled on a canal in the midst of much undergrowth. It was dark when we arrived, and the key was not where it was described to be. My wife and son and I clattered around—trying to figure out a way to get in and fearing we would walk into a canal in the dark and become an alligator's snack. Finally, we noticed an unlocked transom over the front door. My son was boosted up and wriggled through—falling with a loud bang on the other side. When he looked up, he saw an elderly man and his wife, standing there absolutely convinced it was their last moment on earth! They were the *previous* week's exchangers who got their departure-date signals crossed. Profuse apologies were exchanged, and we withdrew to the car and went off in search of a motel. There was none available on Sanibel Island (it was late February)—a very inauspicious beginning to what turned out to be a great vacation home exchange week!

London, England: We arrived in Capetown, South Africa, to find the house we were to occupy had just been burglarized. We called the police and found the policeman at first quite puzzled at our presence in this home. He then became very interested in the home exchange concept, asking if I thought anyone in England would like to swap homes with a "lowly" South African policeman!

Potomac, Maryland: During an exchange in a beach home (our host's second home) on the Connecticut shore, where we had once lived, we held an open house for some of our area friends. Our hosts arrived back early—staying at a friend's—and were surprised to find their house full of strangers!

Chaponnay, France: I have a funny experience, but I speak so bad English!

Las Vegas, Nevada: When we were exchanging homes with a London family, we had the services of their Chinese housekeeper. Several days after our arrival, my brother came to visit. He was un-

aware of the housekeeper's presence in the home. When he heard noises and went to investigate, he discovered a person dressed in black emerging from the salon with two filled shopping bags. She tried to leave the premises by scurrying past him with her head down. He grabbed her and held her, yelling for us to call the police! When we were able to sort it out between the shouts and tears, we found the shopping bags filled with ironing she was taking home to finish! Both parties were embarrassed and apologetic, but the rest of us were limp from laughing.

Coral Springs, Florida: The family who had come to our home (then on Cape Cod, Massachusetts) telephoned us (in prime time on our telephone) to whine a question: "We went to the beach, and the tide was out. Can you tell us where there's a beach where the tide is in?"

Northampton, England: Just picture the scene—it's a hospitality-exchange afternoon swimming party on a beach in Virginia. Huge waves . . . and the deafening Atlantic surf. Linda (holding hands with her exchange host and another male friend) accepts the challenge of a massive wall of water . . . and bobs to the surface—minus her bikini top. Later, many comments from Americans about our European swimming habits!

Mahwah, New Jersey: While researching future home exchange possibilities in London, we visited a home that had no microwave oven, but most of the other amenities, plus (in the kitchen) two thriving marijuana plants! We quickly eliminated this one from our list.

Venice, Italy: During our exchange in Montana, U.S.A., it was unusual having baby grizzly bears in the garden for breakfast.

Ocean Ridge, Florida: In Ireland, the long, narrow road was lined up on each side with a rock wall; it was here that we (in our exchange host's small car) came face to face with a large bus. With no place to pull off, the problem-solving bus driver and some of his equally brawny passengers simply picked up our car and moved it to within one-half inch of the rock wall; then the bus squeezed past, and the bus and we were each on our way.

Cardiff, Wales: Our first exchange was with a Dutch couple who were appalled at the way we treated our goldfish (they thrived on neglect). Our friends left us a note telling us how it ought to be done. Within a week after our arrival home, all of the fish were dead—killed with kindness!

Washington, D.C.: A vacation home exchange slogan: I'll pretend to trust you, if you'll pretend to trust me!

Sanibel Island, Florida: Well, I tell my friends home exchanging is sort of a hostage situation: your exchange partner's home for mine!

Honolulu, Hawaii: Our European exchanger was perplexed by the garbage disposal. "How do you empty it?"

Stockholm, Sweden: Home exchanging is cheap. You meet interesting people. Your hear your house is wonderful. Well, that's all.

Reference Center

Organizations That Serve Vacation Home Exchangers

Having heard about vacation home exchanging from friends or read about it, today many people are asking, "How does our family get started?"

Chapters 6 and 7 deal in depth with the steps one might take in making vacation exchange arrangements. First and foremost, of course, are the resources home exchangers utilize in contacting each other. Happily, the world-wide home exchange community is well served by organizations—sometimes called "clubs"—that compile, produce, and release listings of vacation home exchangers in directories, booklets, and newsletters generally distributed during the early months of each year. Most of these organizations make their listings available both to subscribers of their services—that is, those listed in their directories—and to all interested in securing copies. Having one or more of these directories is the starting point for anyone who wishes to begin home exchanging.

The authors highly recommend the following firms. Each is totally independent and has no affiliation with the other services.

Loan-a-Home
2 Park Lane, 6E
Mount Vernon, NY 10552
U.S.A.
contact: Muriel Gould
phone: 914-664-7640

Home Base Holidays
7 Park Avenue
London N13 5PG
England
contact: Lois Sealey
phone: 081-886-8752

Kimco Communications
4242 West Dayton
Fresno, CA 93722
U.S.A.
contact: John Kimbrough
phone: 209-275-0893

Teacher Swap
Post Office Box 4130
Rocky Point, NY 11778
U.S.A.
contact: Glen Hameroff
phone: 516-744-6403

Worldwide Home Exchange Club
15 Knightsbridge Green
London SW1X 7QL
England
contact: Mildred J. Baer
phone: 071-589-6055

Trading Homes International
Post Office Box 787
Hermosa Beach, CA 90254
U.S.A.
contact: Ed Kushins
phone: toll free (USA only)
1-800-877-TRADE
Outside USA
1-310-798-3864

The Directory Group Association (DGA) and the International Holiday Service (Intervac) produce vacation home exchange directories. Each directory includes thousands of vacation home exchange opportunities the world over. While affiliated with the DGA or Intervac, each of the associates that follows operates as a totally independent organization. Each associate also provides home exchange listings from its respective region to a central point, at which these listings are compiled prior to the production process. Then the completed directories are produced and distributed, world-wide. (*Note:* associates of DGA are printed in boldface, while those of Intervac are in italic).

Australia

International Home Exchange
76 Regent Street, South
Post Office Box 7107
Hutt Street
Adelaide SA 5000
Australia
contact: Aaron & Andrea Brett
phone: 61-8-232-3733

Intervac Australia
% Drive Away Travel, Level 2
17 Sydney Road
Manley, NSW 2095
Australia
contact: Geoff Harvey
phone: 61-2-977-4688

Austria

Intervac Austria
Amselweg 4
A 9100 Volkermarkt
Austria
contact: Ingeborg Winkler
phone: 43-4232/2147

Belgium

Taxistop
Onderbergen 51
B-9000 Gent
Belgium
contact: Jan Klussendorf
phone: 32-91-232310

Intervac Belgium
Keukenlaan 7
B1600 Sint-Pieters-Leeuw
Belgium
contact: Paul Sion
phone: 32-2/3773256

(Dutch-speaking provinces)
Intervac Belgium
Lindenberglaan 26
B 1960 Sterrebeek
Belgium
contact: Jempi & Nancy de Cooman
phone: 32-27315202

Brazil

Intervac Brazil
Avenue Rio Branco
245 Roan 1805
CEP20040 Rio de Janeiro (RJ)
Brazil
contact: Denise Capella
J. V. deAlmeiro
phone: 65-21-274-3521

Canada

West World Holiday Exchange
1707 Platt Crescent
North Vancouver
British Columbia V7J 1X9
Canada
contact: Jack Graber
phone: 604-987-3262

Intervac Canada
606 Alexander Crescent N.W.
Calgary
Alberta T2M 4T3
Canada
contact: Suzanne Cassin
phone: 1-403-284-3747

Cyprus

Homelink International
Post Office Box 3110
Limassol
Cyprus
contact: Rose-Marie Adamou
phone: 357-51-54371

Finland

Intervac Finland
Kellosilta 7
SF00520 Helsinki 52
Finland
contact: Pentti Jankala
phone: 358-0-1502484

France

Sejours
Bel Ormeau 409
Avenue Jean Paul-Coste
13100 Aix-en-Provence
France
contact: Lilli Engle
phone: 33 42384238

Intervac France, Algerie, Maroc, Tunisie
55, rue Nationale
F 37000 Tours
France
contact: Lucien Mazik
phone: 33-47/202057

Germany

Holiday Service
Ringstrasse 26
D-8608 Memmelsdorf 1
Germany
contact: Manfred & Sigrid Lypold
phone: 49 951-43055

Intervac Germany
Verdiweg 2
7022 Leinfelden-Echterdingen
Germany
contact: Helge & Dieter Gunzler
phone: 49-711/7546069

Great Britain

Homelink International
84 Lees Gardens
Maidenhead,
Berkshire SL6 4NT
England
contact: Jim & Heather Anderson
phone: 44-628-31951

Intervac Great Britain
6 Siddals Lane
Allestree
Derbyshire DE3 2DY
contact: Hazel Nayer
phone: 44-332/558931

Greece

Intervac Greece
Fintiou 20
Athens 11253
Greece
contact: Despina Anagnostopoulos
phone: 30-1-8678917

Hungary

Home Exchange Hungary
6 Tinodi Street
4200 Hajduszoboszlo
Hungary
contact: Laszlo Sovago
phone: 36-5262376

Intervac Hungary
Triton Kft/Str. Bognar 3/H
1021 Budapest
contact: Janos Rusz
phone: 36-1760494

Iceland

Intervac Iceland
Nybylavegi 42
200 Kopavogur
Iceland
contact: Elisa M. Kwaszenko
phone: 354/1/44684

Ireland

Holiday Exchange International
95 Bracken Drive
Portmarnock, County Dublin
Ireland
contact: Marie & Paul Murphy
phone: 353-1-462598

Intervac Ireland
Phillipstown,
Ballymakenny Road
Drogheda
Ireland
contact: Frank Kelly
phone: 353-41/37969

Israel

Holiday Service-Israel
c/o M. Kuhn
44 Louis Marshall Street
Tel Aviv 62000
Israel
contact: Janny Kuhn
phone: 972/3-445507

Intervac Israel
Post Office Box 2045
Herzliya 46120
Israel
contact: Dan Barel
phone: 972-52/556729

Italy

Casa Vacanze
Via San Francesco 170
1-35121 Padova
Italy
contact: Fiamma Tarchiani
phone: 39/49-38664

Intervac Italy
Via Oreglia 18
40047 Riola (BO)
Italy
contact: Gaby Zanobetti
phone: 3951/910818

Japan

Intervac Japan
12-27-401 Yocohomachi
Shinjuku
Tokyo 162
Japan
contact: Alain Kregine
phone: 81-3-33587546

Luxembourg

Intervac Luxembourg
Boite Postale 3
L 8201 Mamer G.D.
Luxembourg
contact: Lone & Jens Lauritzen
phone: 352310724

Malaysia

Homelink Malaysia & Singapore
Post Office Box 12697
50786 Kuala Lumpur
Malaysia
contact: Irma Mosimann

Netherlands

Land Org. Vakantie-Woningruil
Kraneweg 86A
NL #9718 JW, Groningen
Netherlands
contact: Renger & Tom de Ruiter
phone: 31-50-132424

Intervac Netherlands
Paasberg 25
6862 CB Oosterbeek
Netherlands
contact: William & Roel Eissen
phone: 31-85-341187

New Zealand

Vacation Corporation
Post Office Box 38615
Howick, Auckland
New Zealand
contact: Craig & Viv Pellet
phone: 64/9-522-2933

Norway

Norsk Boligbytte
95 Kjelsas
N-0411 Oslo 4
Norway
contact: Henning Halvorsen
phone: 47/2-158019

Intervac Norway
Fagerlivegen 9
N-2800 Gjovik
Norway
contact: Ivar Solli
phone: 47-61/79185

Poland

Intervac Poland
Al. Kalningradzka 43m55
10437 Olszton
Poland
contact: Lech Przybylski
phone: 48-89/3332464

Portugal

Homelink International
100 Rua Vasconceles & Castro 2-d
4760 V. N. Famalicao
Portugal
contact: Julie de Wolff
phone: 351-5257160

Intervac Portugal
Rua Inacio de Sousa 23, R/C Do.
1500 Lisboa
Portugal
contact: Antonio St. Aubyn
phone: 35-1-1-785179

South Africa

International Home Exchange
Post Office Box 188, Claremont
Cape Town 7735
South Africa
contact: Connie Booth
phone: 27/21-614334

Spain

Viages Calatrava
Cea Bermudez 70
E-28.003 Madrid
Spain
contact: Jose Luis Arraco
phone: 34/1-5494797

Intervac Spain
Consell de Cent 226
1, 3a, Barcelona
Spain
contact: Maria Angeles Sas
phone: 34-3/2533171

Sweden

Dansk Boligbytte
Hesselvang 20
DK-2900 Hellerup
Sweden
contact: Peter Eberth
phone: 45-3160405

Intervac Sweden
Box 33,
55112 Jonkoping
Sweden
contact: Anke & Kalle Gemfeldt
phone: 46-36/128205

Switzerland

Holiday Exchange Club Schweiz
Asylstrasse 24
CH-8810 Horgen
Switzerland
contact: Joop van Rijn
phone: 41/1-7251047

Intervac Switzerland-Liechtenstein
Zilstrasse 74A
CH 9016 St. Gallen
contact: Heinrich Niedermann
phone: 41-71/354910

USA

Vacation Exchange Club
P.O. Box 650
Key West
Florida 33041
contact: Karl & Debby Costabel
phone: toll free (USA only)
1-800-638-3841
Outside USA
1-305-294-3720

Intervac U.S.
30 Corte San Fernando
Tiburon, CA 94920
U.S.A.
contact: Paula Jaffe
Lori Horne
phone: 1-415-4353497

USSR

Sejours Moscow
Arcademician Korolev Str. 12 (TTC)
127427 Moscow
U.S.S.R.
contact: Nataly Lavrentieva
phone: 7/095-200-0562

Yugoslavia

VCA Exchange
P.O. Box 3968
Newport, Rhode Island 02840
U.S.A.
contact: Larry King
phone: 401-846-9849

Suggested Letters for Use in Vacation Home Exchange Correspondence

In various chapters of this book, it has been made abundantly clear that once a contact has been made, the quality of the correspondence is the determining factor as to whether a particular home exchange is a go or a no-go.

To aid home exchangers in communicating with one another, here is a selection of suggested letters focused on the Fact Sheet, the Initial Contact, Hospitality Exchanging, and other subjects that might be a part of home exchange correspondence.

Exchangers, of course, must write their own letters. It is hoped these suggested letters will be useful in underscoring some of the topics that are dealt with in home exchange correspondence. Also, these letters demonstrate the spirit of honesty, thoroughness, and flexibility that seems to characterize successful home exchange correspondence.

Fact Sheet

The Fact Sheet is an overview of the exchanger's home and the area in which it is situated. It also includes pertinent information about the exchanger and his family and/or others traveling with him. Some exchangers say this is the most important single document in the exchange correspondence because (see Chapter 6) the Fact Sheet is really a *sales tool*—"promoting" a particular home and home exchange family. Always enclosed with the initial contact letters, the Fact Sheet should motivate potential exchangers to exclaim, "Hey, here's one we should follow up!"

Regarding the Stedman's condominium on Sanibel Island, Florida . . . .

For thirteen years now, we have owned a luxury condominium on Florida's Gulf Coast. This second home is occupied by vacationing home exchangers, family members, and, occasionally, by ourselves.

Our condo is at Loggerhead Cay, a large, first-class resort on Sanibel Island, near Fort Myers, Florida. This condo is one of the two most desired condos at Loggerhead Cay—this because it is on the top floor, Gulf front, and faces south with a 180-degree, panoramic view of the sandy beach below and the Gulf of Mexico.

A few steps from the parking space, you will take the elevator to the fourth floor and find the condo has a large master bedroom with a king-sized bed; a second bedroom with twin-sized beds; two baths; and a large living room with a couch that converts into a queen-sized bed. The dining area is connected by a pass-through to a full, modern, eat-in kitchen—one including a microwave oven, a dishwasher, and a disposal. The condo's large screened in porch overlooks the Gulf of Mexico and miles of sandy beach; its sun balcony overlooks the garden and a private swimming pool.

Further, the condo is newly furnished and fully air-conditioned. It has two cable television sets, a radio, and a VCR. Finally, it has ample linens, cooking utensils, dishes, flatware, and all amenities required for comfortable vacationing for a family of up to six persons.

Loggerhead Cay has a beautiful beach, a large private swimming pool, and private tennis courts. There are several public golf courses nearby. In addition to being an ideal, year-round resort, Sanibel Island is famous for its beaches (#3 in the world for shelling); its surf, bay, and deep-sea fishing; its wildlife sanctuary; its miles of cycling paths; and its fine shops and restaurants, in every price range—fast-food to gourmet. The island's lack of high-rise, high-density buildings and its preservation of tropical trees, plants, and flowers help to make Sanibel one of Florida's most beautiful islands.

Sanibel Island is just thirty minutes by car from Southwest Florida International Airport at Fort Myers—one served by most major airlines.

Recent vacationers from Geneva, Switzerland, write: "We have just had the best home exchange ever—at Loggerhead Cay, Sanibel Island, Florida!"

Now in our early sixties, Harry (a retired airline executive) and Alice have had many home exchanges in the U.S. and in Europe. Generally, there are just the two of us traveling, though occasionally we do have another couple along. Because this condo is our second home, we have flexibility in our exchange scheduling. We are non smokers . . . and have three married children and eight grandchildren.

Very cordially,
Harry and Alice Stedman

Initial Contact

This letter is designed for use by the person who hopes to arrange an exchange with another person after seeing the latter's listing in one of the exchange directories.

Enclosed with this initial contact letter should be a Fact Sheet, several photos of the home to be exchanged, and photos of those persons to be a part of the proposed exchange.

Because the Fact Sheet will be photocopied, it is important this initial contact letter be typed or handwritten. Thus, it will not have the appearance of every other, easy-to-toss-out form letter.

Dear Mr. and Mrs. ———:

We saw your listing in the Vacation Exchange Club's current directory and note your interest in exchanging somewhere along Florida's west coast. Our condo is situated on Sanibel Island, two miles (by causeway) from Fort Myers. Your home there in Vancouver, B.C., sounds just perfect for my wife, Alice, and me. So perhaps you and we might well be able to arrange a home exchange for two or three weeks next spring—say, May or June.

The enclosed Fact Sheet and photos will give you information about our condo, its location, and ourselves. We should add that in recent years we have had six exchanges—four here in the States, two in Europe. We neither smoke nor drink, and we generally exchange cars; we offer a 1990 four-door Honda Accord.

After looking over the enclosed, we hope you will be interested in spending some time at our Sanibel Island condo next spring—perhaps the first three weeks in June, though we are quite flexible as to dates.

Assuming you think all of this adds up to the possibility of an exchange between us, please send us complete information about your home and the area in which you are located . . . and feel free to contact us about our condo, this part of Florida, and any other questions you might have.

Very cordially,

Follow Up

The initial contact letter was well received by the potential exchangers in Vancouver. Indeed, within a week they answered that letter. With it they enclosed information about their home and themselves (both retired), photos, their willingness to include their car in the exchange, and a date was suggested and various questions were asked.

So here is a suggested follow-up letter . . .

Dear Mr. and Mrs. ———:

Thanks for getting back to us so promptly on this possibility of our working up a home exchange next spring.

We appreciate your giving us so much information about your home. The photos are great. While we do have a few more questions, at this point we feel there's a likelihood we might well be able to exchange with you folks next spring. *Finally*, we may get to Canada! But first—your questions:

1. Your suggested dates sound just fine to us: the three weeks beginning May 23.
2. Our Honda has an automatic transmission.
3. It is possible to rent bikes on Sanibel Island, and the condo complex has a covered rack for storing locked bikes.
4. There are two supermarkets on Sanibel Island. One is a mile from our condo, the other about two miles.
5. May–June is off season at Sanibel Island—no traffic problems. Shopping is easy; there's no need for reservations at restaurants or tennis courts or at golf courses—a big plus for tennis players and golfers!
6. Our May–June weather is ideal—daytime temps. 75/80 degrees, low humidity (not like August!), and lots of sun, a gentle breeze, and an occasional late-afternoon shower. Pool temperature: 80 degrees; Gulf temps: 78/82 degrees.
7. On the matter of cleaning, if you wish to have the condo cleaned weekly (or at the exchange mid-point), maid service is available; our exchangers pay for this cleaning service. On the day you depart, we arrange for the condo to be cleaned—our expense.

Now, we have a few further thoughts and questions . . .

As it happens, our guest room and guest bath are separated from the rest of the condo—almost like a little apartment. We would very much like to meet you folks and show you the ropes, so to speak, at our place and introduce you to our neighbors and our condo community. It would be great if you could plan to arrive at Sanibel Island a day or so before we leave for your place. Would this be possible?

Other questions . . .

1. As we would be making quite a few phone calls back to the States, how do you prefer to handle long distance calls?
2. Is it possible to take one- or two-day excursions in the waters north of Vancouver?
3. Would it be okay with you if at the last moment our son- and daughter-in-law should decide to be with us during the last week of our stay at your home?

I'm sure we'll have other thoughts and questions in the weeks just ahead, but I'm anxious to get this letter off to you without delay.

Very cordially,

There may well be three or four exchanges of correspondence—and perhaps a phone call or two—leading up to the eventual consummation of a home exchange correspondence. Chapters 6 and 7 present at length many of the exchange-related details that should, or must, be addressed by all parties to a vacation home exchange. It is covering, and agreeing upon, all the aspects of the exchange before the dates of the exchange that make for the most successful home exchange.

It's a Deal

With all questions, and other exchange matters taken into consideration, there comes that point in each exchange correspondence that a deal is made, or not made. If both parties to the correspondence agree that all systems are "go" for the exchange, then one or the other should confirm this fact in writing—in a letter such as the following.

Dear Harriet:

It was good talking with you over the phone the other day, because that gave us both an opportunity to discuss the home and car insurance matters—this after talking with our respective insurance agents; to answer our pool-cleaning query; and to deal with various minor aspects of our exchange arrangement.

So now . . . we agree with you: It's a deal! When we started corresponding with you several months ago, there seemed to be *so many* exchange arrangements to be made that Harry and I wondered if we'd ever get everything squared away. I guess part of our apprehension was because this is our first home exchange experience.

Even though our exchange date is three months away, I'm very glad we started our exchange arrangements *early*. It would be awful to leave all of that stuff to the last minute!

Probably in the weeks ahead you and we will have a few arrangement afterthoughts. We can clear up these matters in due course. Also, later we can make house-key and final arrival arrangements. You know my brother and sister-in-law will be meeting your flight and then bringing you to our house here—also getting you fixed up with our car—and introducing you to several nearby neighbors.

The other day a friend of mine asked: "Aren't you folks nervous about having some total strangers living in your home?" We said that we have no concern whatsoever about you folks occupying our home. After getting to know you through all of our letters back and forth—and the telephone calls—really we consider it a privilege hosting you here.

Harry and I send our special greetings and best wishes.

Very cordially,

Hospitality Exchange

In chapter 5 reference is made to "hospitality" exchanging, and pages 133 through 135 point out many of the advantages of this type of exchanging, which is certainly becoming an important part of the overall exchange scene. This suggested letter is for the use of persons interested in arranging for a hospitality exchange.

Dear Dr. and Mrs. ———:

I have just noticed your hospitality exchange listing in the recently received Intervac Directory. Now this is interesting, because for some months my daughter has been urging me to get back into exchanging . . . and to try a hospitality exchange—"get back into," that is, because my husband and I totally enjoyed a dozen or more regular home exchanges over a ten-year period up until his passing.

A widow now for the past year and a half, I'm beginning to get out and around more. I would just love to have a hospitality exchange there in London sometime in the next four to six months.

I am in my early sixties and maintain my own home here in San Francisco. I consider myself to be fairly independent—but not sufficiently so to want to do a "solo" regular home exchange with a family—that is, for them to be occupying my home while I would be alone at theirs.

My kids seem to come often for dinner, so I guess they like my cooking. Aside from an unhappy shoulder (due to a fall last year), I'm said to be in good health. My diet includes just about anything (and usually *too much* of everything!). I like the theater and concerts—not big on ballet, though—reading, playing bridge, watching TV game shows, sightseeing (and there's *so much* to see in London and San Francisco!). I stopped smoking decades ago but have no objection to those who still do. I'm not averse to a glass of wine with dinner . . . but can do very nicely without it. Here's a recent photo—my two daughters, their husbands, and assorted grandchildren. I promise not to bring the grandchildren with me!

I've lived in San Francisco, high on this hill, for the last twenty-three years. The house is really too large for me at this point—four bedrooms, three baths, and *lots* of space. I have my own car. Love to drive. And would be happy to tour-conduct you folks anywhere west of the Mississippi! (On second thought, let's just stick to California.) Well, enough about *me*.

If you would like to spend a couple of weeks in San Francisco sometime in the months just ahead, I'd love to hear all about you and your home in Chelsea, my favorite part of London. Do you have any pets? We had dogs for years, but I'm now down to one (very lovable) cat!

I'm looking forward to hearing from you at your convenience.

With best wishes,

Accumulating Credit in Home Exchanging

As has been emphasized in various of the preceding chapters, the *scheduling*—selection of mutually acceptable exchange dates—is more often than not the most difficult part of making home exchange arrangements, especially in the cases of simultaneous exchanges.

Exchangers with second homes have a decided advantage here, because they can agree to exchanging on *different* dates. The key to this type of exchanging is the "banking" of exchange arrangements by one of the exchangers. For instance, Exchanger A spends two weeks at the mountain home of Exchanger B in the spring. Thus B has "banked" (or is holding a credit for) two weeks at one of A's two homes—say, two weeks in the fall. A suggested letter which might be appropriate to one of these banking exchange situations follows.

Dear Mrs. ———:

With so many letters, and so much home exchange-related information going between us in recent months, I really feel almost like we know each other—a longtime friendship!

And so I'm particularly sorry to report that our son's June marriage rules out our living at your home later that month. This certainly is sad, because we know you are anxious to take your vacation during this same time frame. But perhaps all is not lost. In my initial letter, we included complete information about, and a photo of, our home at Long Beach Island, New Jersey. This is a great place—a natural for a restful vacation in June. So . . . instead of your coming to our main home here, why don't you arrange to spend those same two weeks at our home on the shore?

And how about us? Well, at some later date we can spend a couple of weeks at either one of your homes—coordinating, of course, our schedule with yours. At this point we don't have any particular dates in mind, but we might think about early spring or fall of next year.

In home exchange parlance, I think they call this "banking" a two-week exchange. In other words, because you will have been at our second home this coming June—and we will not be at your place at that point—you will simply "owe" us two weeks at one of your homes. You and we know there are some disadvantages of owning two homes, but there is at least one advantage—the possibility of using one's second home to "untangle" home exchange scheduling!

We hope you'll like this counter suggestion and look forward to hearing from you soon.

Very cordially,

Agreement

Generally speaking, home exchangers do not enter into formal home exchange "contracts." They consider the contents of their exchanges of correspondence cover all of the more important aspects of the exchange arrangements.

Nevertheless, as indicated in chapter 7, some exchangers are accustomed to drawing up an informal "letter of agreement" related to the exchange. The following suggested agreement includes many of the elements that experienced agreement-making exchangers feel are important in a document of this nature.

The elements of these agreements vary from one exchange situation to the next, but this suggested agreement might be considered as basic and should be modified to meet the requirements of each given home exchange arrangement.

HOME EXCHANGE AGREEMENT

It is the intention of the undersigned persons to engage in a "home exchange" arrangement. That is, we will occupy each others' homes simultaneously during a predetermined time frame.

Basically, we agree with the generally accepted and long-standing principle of home exchanging: we will treat our home exchange partner's home in the same way we will expect him to treat ours. Specifically . . .

1. We will provide each other with detailed information about our homes, including instructions for those appliances we will be using.
2. We will provide each other with names of, and telephone numbers for, plumbers, electricians, and others to be contacted in emergency situations.
3. We will provide each other with names of, and information about, the closest neighbors.
4. We will clean the home regularly and comply with the arrangements regarding departure cleaning.
5. We will lock the home and put security systems (if any) in place when we are away for short (or longer) periods of time.
6. We will provide each other with information as to such overnight periods when we may be away from the home and with information about such overnight guests as we may have.
7. We will adhere to such arrangements as are made regarding the use of the telephone and the handling of long distance telephone charges.
8. We will provide each other with ample closet and drawer space for clothes and other personal items.
9. We will respect the privacy of each others' closets, drawers, desks, files, and so on. And we will not snoop!
10. We will not use golf clubs, bicycles, wine cellars, deep freezing units, and/or other items not considered to be a part of the exchange.
11. We will replace such staple food items as coffee, sugar, condiments, and so on—as we use during the exchange.
12. We will endeavor to take special care of our partner's glassware, china, utensils, and other household items; should any of these be broken during our stay, we will replace them in kind or in money.
13. While we understand the host partners will be responsible for normal, basic repairs to the home and its appliances, we will reimburse them in full for such damage as we may do to the home and/or its contents.

Agreed		Agreed	
Name	Date	Name	Date

Cancellation

"They pulled the rug right out from under us—the bums! We were excited about this exchange and were beginning to get the kids' stuff packed—only ten days to go. The telephone rang—something about a family problem—and our vacation went up in smoke. No more home exchanges for *this* family!"

Chapter 22 confronts this "vacation cancellation" dilemma and suggests a parade of emergency steps that might be taken—ways in which this vacation, or *a* vacation, might just be put back on track.

Perhaps the following suggested letter would be of some help to an exchanger who has to be the bearer of exchange-cancellation news.

Dear Erik:

It's with great sadness I must tell you Mary Jo and I have decided to sell our home here and move to New York City, where I've just accepted a top position in my field—advertising.

This has been a time of real agonizing—uprooting the children from their schools here; selling this family home; renting an apartment in New York City until we decide where we'll wish to live permanently; leaving older relatives, and so on.

And, of course, (an especially sad part for us) this means we'll not be able to carry through with our long-planned home exchange with you and your family.

You folks, and we, have spent so much time and effort in working out every last detail of our exchange—with you folks coming here to the Washington area and us going to your home in Oslo—that we are *especially* sorry to be giving you this news now.

You have gone more than half way putting together our proposed exchange . . . and will be disappointed to get this word from us—"disappointed," a masterpiece of understatement!

In the past few days, Mary Jo has been in touch with no less than six good friends and three relatives, all who live here in this general area. With certainty we can say that we've got you covered: you and your family will be able to stay in the home of one of these friends of ours during the same August weeks you'd planned on being here. Fortunately, masses of people around here hurry off to vacations during the month of August.

Time is a little short, so we'll have to select the home in which you'll be staying. I will share with your new "host" our correspondence file, and then he'll be in touch with you, probably first by telephone.

And your responsibility to him? Nothing. You see, we will arrange with your host family to occupy *our* rented New York apartment next spring while we'll be in Barbados for a month.

And our trip to your home in Oslo? Well, that will have to be put on hold for a while, though we *hope* to be there sometime late next year. We'll keep in touch with you on this. If you are to be away on vacation next year, perhaps we could occupy your home at that time, or maybe at some other time convenient to your vacation schedule. At this point, frankly I am not as worried about our coming *there* as I am about your having a most enjoyable exchange experience here in Washington.

Finally, we're sorry to have had to back out of our arrangement, but, Erik, you have my word that you will be every bit as happy in the home we select for you as you would have been here in our home. This we can assure you.

Even though you won't be staying at our place, of course, we'll be keeping in touch; soon after your arrival in the States, we'll be giving you a ring. I'm sure we'll be able to get down to Washington to meet you folks during your stay.

Mary Jo and I send our greetings to you and Ingrid.

Very cordially,

Departure

During the actual exchange period, the partners to the exchange often wonder how things are going back home. Are our exchange friends enjoying their vacation? Have they had problems with our appliances? Or the car? Any disasters with the burglar alarm? These and other matters pertinent to the exchange can be dealt with in the departure letter, generally left in the home at the time of departure.

Dear Harry and Alice:

Aside from the fact that the weather was not too cooperative, we had one great time at your condo! We don't *believe* we've been here three weeks. It's seemed more like ten days!

The information you left us, Alice, was *most* helpful, especially when we couldn't figure out how to work that fancy clothes dryer you've got.

In our previous three home exchanges, it seems we always had a minor problem or two—with the car, the plumbing, or something. Not here, no problems. In fact, we didn't even break one single dish!

Your shopping suggestions were great. We did most of our food shopping at Bailey's. And we sure worked over your restaurant list. On our 24th wedding anniversary we splurged and went to the Nutmeg House . . . and we also did Chadwick's, The Timbers, and even Bangkok House.

We're so glad you suggested Naples Dinner Theater. We took friends and had a super-great evening—eating everything in sight and enjoying *Born Yesterday*.

The museums, the art gallery, the shell shops . . . we did them all. But best of all is this lovely condo of yours.

Now we just hope you enjoyed our place half as much as we enjoyed yours!

With best wishes,

P.S. In the refrigerator are a few Welcome Home goodies.

Bill Barbour, a former CEO of a book publishing company, and Mary Barbour, a former administrator of educational programs for disadvantaged childern, have traveled throughout the world on vacation home exchanges that have taken them as far west as Hong Kong and as far east as Switzerland.

Readers desiring to know more about vacation home exchanging may write the authors as follows:

Bill and Mary Barbour
Vacation Home Exchange
Services International, Inc.
16956-4 South McGregor Boulevard
Fort Myers, Florida 33908 U.S.A.